The Politics of Performa

D0480670

The Politics of Performance addresses fundamental questions about the social and political purposes of performance through an investigation into post-war alternative and community theatre. It proposes a theory of performance as ideological transaction, cultural intervention and community action, which is used to illuminate the potential social and political effects of radical performance practice. It raises issues about the nature of alternative theatre as a movement and the aesthetics of its styles of production, especially in relation to progressive counter-cultural formations. It analyses in detail the work of key practitioners in socially engaged theatre during four decades, setting each in the context of social, political and cultural history and focusing particularly on how they used that context to enhance the potential efficacy of their productions. The book is thus a detailed analysis of oppositional theatre as radical cultural practice in its various efforts to subvert the status quo. Its purpose is to raise the profile of these approaches to performance by proposing, and demonstrating, how they may have had a significant impact on social and political history.

The Politics of Performance will be essential reading for all students and teachers of performance, as well as professional theatre workers, and cultural studies specialists.

Baz Kershaw has had considerable experience of alternative and community theatre, both as a writer and director. He co-authored *Engineers of the Imagination* (1983), and has written for *Theatre Quarterly, Dartington Theatre Papers, Performance,* and other journals. He is currently Lecturer in Theatre Studies at Lancaster University.

The Politics of Performance

Radical theatre as cultural intervention

Baz Kershaw

London and New York

First published 1992
by Routledge
11 New Fetter Lane, London EC4P 4EE

Simultaneously published in the USA and Canada
by Routledge
29 West 35th Street, New York, NY 10001

Reprinted 1994, 1999, 2001

Routledge is an imprint of the Taylor & Francis Group

Typeset in 10 on 12 point Baskerville by
Witwell Ltd, Southport
Printed in Great Britain by
TJ International Ltd, Padstow Cornwall

British Library Cataloguing in Publication Data
Kershaw, Baz
   The politics of performance: radical theatre as cultural
intervention.
   I. Title
   792.01

Library of Congress Cataloging in Publication Data
Kershaw, Baz
   The politics of performance: radical theatre as cultural
intervention / Baz Kershaw.
      p. cm.
   Includes bibliographical references and index.
   1. Little theater movement–Great Britain. 2. Experimental
theater–Great Britain–History–20th century. 3. Theater–
Political aspects– Great Britain. 4. Theater and society–Great
Britain. I. Title.
   PN2595.3.K47   1992
   792'.022–dc20   91-39875

ISBN 0–415–05762–0   ISBN 0–415–05763–9 (pbk)

For Gill

Contents

Acknowledgements   ix
Introduction: In quest of performance efficacy   1

**Part I Theory and issues: alternative and community
theatre as radical cultural intervention**   13

1 Performance, community, culture   15

2 Reception, scale, terminologies   41

3 Carnival, agit prop, celebratory protest   67

Part II A history of alternative and community theatre   93

4 Experimentation in the 1960s
   *The community dramas of John Arden
   and Margaretta D'Arcy*   95

5 Consolidation in the 1970s
   *The popular political theatre of John McGrath
   and 7:84 Theatre Company*   132

6 Reorientation in the 1980s
   *The community plays of Ann Jellicoe
   and the Colway Theatre Trust*   168

7 Fragmentation in the 1990s?
   *The celebratory performance of John Fox
   and Welfare State International*   206

   Conclusions: On the brink of performance efficacy   243

Glossary   257
Bibliography   259
Index   266

Acknowledgements

Many fellow professional theatre workers, academics and students have contributed to this study, but I am particularly indebted to the following: the directors, actors, writers, technicians and administrators of all the community theatre companies I have worked with or visited, for giving unstintingly of their talent, time and knowledge; my colleagues and students in the Department of Theatre Studies at the University of Lancaster, for their unswerving support and lively interrogations (and especially Karen Clarke, for always smoothing the way); John Arden, Margaretta D'Arcy, Roland Muldoon, John McGrath, Ann Jellicoe, Albert Hunt and John Fox, for generously commenting on sections of the text; Professor Peter Thomson, for astute guidance in a research minefield; Chris McCullough and Professor Ted Braun, for succinct and singularly apt advice; my editors at Routledge, Helena Reckitt and Talia Rodgers, for making publication feel like fun; Dr Gillian Hadley, for incisive commentaries on wayward ideas, and incalculable sustenance; and Eleanor and Logan for my daily slice of carnival cake. The book would not exist in its present form without their various vital contributions, for which I am deeply grateful. Of course, any errors and all the opinions herein are my sole responsibility.

Parts of Chapter 7 have previously appeared in *Critical Survey*.

We need a type of theatre which not only releases the feelings, insights and impulses possible within the particular historical field of human relations in which the action takes place, but employs and encourages those thoughts and feelings which help transform the field itself.

Bertolt Brecht

Don't start from the good old things but the bad new ones.

Bertolt Brecht

Introduction
In quest of performance efficacy

Performance efficacy

This book investigates the potential efficacy of theatrical performance. It is about the ways in which, in a particular historical period, theatre practitioners have tried to change not just the future action of their audiences, but also the structure of the audience's community and the nature of the audience's culture. Paradoxically, the main lever for such changes has been the immediate and ephemeral *effects* of performance – laughter, tears, applause and other active audience responses. More fundamentally, the leverage has been applied to shift the culture of communities in particular directions because that might bring about more widespread and lasting modifications in culture and society as a whole. At the heart of this text, then, is the possibility that the immediate and local effects of particular performances might – individually and collectively – contribute to changes of this kind; that the micro-level of individual shows and the macro-level of the socio-political order might somehow productively interact. Hence, by efficacy I mean the potential that theatre may have to make the immediate effects of performance influence, however minutely, the general historical evolution of wider social and political realities.

Any attempt to *prove* that this kind of performance efficacy is possible, let alone probable, is plagued by analytical difficulties and dangers. However, these pale into insignificance when placed against those sometimes confronted by practitioners who make this kind of theatre. When performers aim to be politically efficacious the outcome can be, literally, arresting. Take, for example, the case of the Russian clown Vladimir Leonidowitch Durov in 1907:

Durov placed a German officer's cap, or 'helm' as he called it, in the circus ring and his trained pig ran to retrieve it. Using ventriloquism Durov made the pig appear to be saying 'Ich will helm,' meaning 'I want the helmet.' But the phrase could also be translated 'I am Wilhelm,' thereby equating Germany's Emperor, Wilhelm II, with a trained pig. 'The audience understood the pun at once and applauded it. The German police understood it too,' according to Russian critic Emanuel Dvinsky's account . . . Durov was arrested. The pig escaped without prosecution.

(Schechter 1985: 2)

We might compare this with the riot which greeted the fourth night of Sean O'Casey's *The Plough and the Stars* at Dublin's Abbey Theatre some nineteen years later, when a flying shoe hit one of the hapless players. The impact of the riot, if not the shoe, resonated through Irish political history for many years (Lowery 1984: 107). Ample anecdotal evidence of extreme theatrical effects is available (Brandreth 1986; Hay 1987), but generally such stories restrict themselves to the impact *in* the theatrical environment, to the obviously observable results. Historians and critics have habitually fought shy of committing themselves to unambiguous claims about the possibility of a more extensive socio-political efficacy of performance.

Yet surely such efficacy is the fundamental purpose of performance? There is a sense in which even shows that aim solely to promote ephemeral entertainment have long-term designs on their audiences. By encouraging a taste for escapism they may push social and political questions to the background of experience. Performances with a more overtly 'serious' purpose – shows which engage with current moral issues, for instance – are hoping more obviously to alter, or confirm, their audiences' ideas and attitudes, and through that to affect their future actions. However, once the audience has dispersed and re-entered the realm of socio-political action, how are we to measure accurately any influence that the performance may have on their behaviour? It follows that the crucial problems facing useful discussion of performance efficacy emanate not from the nature of theatre-in-itself but from theatre's relationship with the wider social order, in all its discursive and institutional complexity.

However, when the issue of efficacy is framed in this way we immediately run into difficulties which seem insuperable. How *can* we assess accurately the relationship between theatrical effect and subsequent audience behaviour? The commonest critical response has been to abandon the question, and to concentrate on less intractable problems of performance analysis. Ironically, this tendency has been reinforced by empirical work in the field, where the most common approaches to the issue – audience questionnaires and so on – seem always to produce inconclusive or superficial results (Bennett 1990: 92–8). But what if we reframe the question? What if we pay more attention to the *conditions* of performance that are *most likely* to produce an efficacious result? And what if we broaden the canvas for analysis beyond the individual show or production (but still including it) in order to consider theatrical movements in relation to local and national cultural change? If we consider the *potential* of performance (both in its specific sense as 'individual show' and in its general sense as 'a collection of practices') to achieve efficacy in a particular historical context, perhaps we can then squash the bugbear of empirical conclusiveness and construct an approach to analysis which will be more theoretically and indeed factually convincing.

An historical starting point

Between 1975 and 1980 I worked as a director with Medium Fair Theatre Company, a small rural community theatre group based in Devon. The company described itself as a 'cultural catalyst': its shows, and those of many other community theatre companies, were predicated on the possible *usefulness* of theatre to particular communities. By tailor-making performances for known audiences these companies hoped to change those audiences in some way, however marginally. Not only that: if a number of audiences in similar types of community, in a specific sub-region, could be changed by such a show, there might be a wider effect. Such a show might contribute to some kind of progressive social, even political, development.

As a number of companies in different parts of the country had been pursuing a similar ambition to Medium Fair's, it seemed sensible, in the early 1980s, to undertake a comparative analysis of their different practices. If those rural community theatre companies had overlapping aims, we could be talking about a movement; and maybe potentially the cumulative effects of that movement might be cited as a significant part of, or even an influence on, the general cultural and socio-political development of British society in the period.

Such hopes and ambitions were a fairly common affliction in the 1970s. And even in the early 1980s, when I spent the good part of a year visiting, and seeing shows by, every rural community theatre company in England (and a couple in Wales), idealism was still on the agenda. But by then the idealism was usually inflected by the need simply to survive in a worsening socio-economic environment. My visits did reveal a coherent, but very thinly spread, *theatrical* movement; the 'rural community theatre movement'. But I was surprised by the ideological range, the political spectrum, represented in the shows that I saw. Some seemed simply to be reinforcing the status quo through traditional forms of entertainment – music hall, for instance. Others were mounting a radical critique of particular social and political policies. Nevertheless, all the companies identified themselves as part of a wider movement: the British 'alternative theatre movement' (Kershaw 1983a).

Now the ideological variations between these companies raised a key historical issue *vis-à-vis* the 'alternative theatre movement'. Had there always been such a heterogeneity of policy, or had the movement ever been more ideologically coherent? Moreover, if there had been an ideological coherence, what was its nature and extent? For it could well be the case that the more extensive such coherence the greater the potential efficacy of the movement, and perhaps even individual practices within it. If I could demonstrate the ways in which the potential efficacy of particular shows related to the possible general efficacy of the movement, this might produce a convincing case for the impact of alternative theatre on British social and political history.

Very few studies of this kind have been undertaken for any theatrical movement, and certainly the job has not been done for British alternative theatre. So in part this book is the start of an attempt to fill a vacuum in post-war theatrical history. Raymond Williams gives a succinct general description of one of the tasks I set myself:

> there is normally a very wide gap between, on the one hand, general history and the associated general history of particular

arts, and, on the other hand, individual studies. It is, then, by learning to analyse the nature and the diversity of cultural formations – in close association . . . with the analysis of cultural forms – that we can move towards a more adequate understanding of the direct social processes of cultural production.

(Williams, 1981: 86)

Thus the 'formation' under scrutiny here is the British alternative theatre movement, and the 'form' that is the focus of this book's individual studies is community-oriented theatre, in the shape of key practices undertaken mostly in rural areas.

The examples of performance discussed in detail in this book aimed to combine entertainment with – well, if not instruction (*pace* Brecht) then debate, discussion, socio-political proposals and recommendations. They represent a theatre of social engagement, a theatre primarily committed to bringing about actual change in specific communities. The companies making this theatre aimed to combine art and action, aesthetics and pragmatics. Often they were dealing with material – stories, documentary information, images and so on – inscribed with questions of fundamental importance to their audiences. Always their starting point was the nature of their audience *and its community*. The aesthetics of their performances were shaped by the culture of their audience's community. Hence these practices can be categorised as 'community theatre', and this book could be classed as a study of that slippery genre. However, my choice of shows for detailed analysis was guided by a more fundamental impulse than curiosity about aesthetics.

The focus on potential efficacy suggests an investigation of the *specific functions* of theatre for carefully defined audiences, and that carries several major implications for the analysis of these practices. Principally, in order to assess their impact it becomes essential to study their context. If we wish to understand their potential meanings in that context (or any other) we will need to investigate how specific audiences might 'read' their performances. It follows that we must move beyond formalist analysis – which treats theatre as if it were independent of its social and political environment – and consider performance as a cultural construct and as a means of cultural production. It also follows that particular performances, as far as possible, have to be seen in their full cultural milieu: in relation to the aesthetic movements of which they are a part; in relation to the institutional structures of the arts; in relation to the cultural formations which they inhabit. Moreover, as culture is saturated with discourses of power, and as our chief examples of performance aimed to change the audiences' community and culture, we are dealing with a deeply political approach to theatre. This investigation, then, is fundamentally about the politics of performance.

Oppositional performance

British alternative theatre provides a particularly complex case for analysis from this perspective. As Raymond Williams is at pains to stress, *oppositional* cultural formations (particularly of a paranational kind) by necessity have an especially complicated relationship with their wider social context:

> they represent sharp and even violent breaks with received and traditional practice (a dissidence or revolt rather than a literal avant garde); and yet . . . they become (in ways separable from the facts of their dilution and commercial exploitation) the dominant culture of a succeeding . . . period.
>
> (Williams 1981: 85)

Clearly, Williams is alluding to shifts in the power relations of society, and just as clearly his analysis assumes the efficacy of cultural formations, such as the post-war counter-cultures of which alternative theatre was a part. Thus if his analysis is valid, it would follow that alternative theatre in some way may have influenced the dominant cultural values of Britain.

To some readers this implication will seem absurd – twenty years of political theatre (so one version of the argument goes) did nothing to stop Thatcher rising to power. Yet there is no doubt that alternative theatre enjoyed such far-reaching ambitions, that it hoped to effect a major change in British society. Given this, it is appropriate to treat seriously the possibility that alternative and community theatre may have managed to mount an effective opposition to the dominant culture, and may have modified its values, however slightly.

The practices of alternative theatre, viewed from this perspective, can best be considered as a form of *cultural intervention*. Three main factors support this view. Firstly, alternative theatre was a sub-set, as it were, of a much broader group of cultural activities which were all expressive of new ideologies, of new interpretations of existing social and political relations. In this perspective alternative theatre cannot be viewed as a predominantly aesthetic adventure equivalent to previous avant gardes, though it shares some of their characteristics. Rather, its social base was part of an entirely new twentieth-century cultural phenomenon – a series of counter-cultures, equivalent in their radical reappraisal of society to the nineteenth-century Romantics, and based (as romanticism was) in a new generational awareness. However, because of improved communication systems and increased international access to ideas and styles, the successive counter-cultures formed a mass movement which impinged on all aspects of Western society as a cultural alternative, or more accurately, a range of cultural alternatives. British alternative theatre was a relatively small segment of the new phenomenon, but in a number of ways it was central to the counter-cultures and to the methods they used in their attempts to subvert the status quo.

Secondly, for the most part alternative and community theatre had to create its own context. There were no ready-made venues or audiences to begin with, and there was only a very attenuated tradition of alternative practices upon which to draw. The creation of alternative theatre was not simply a matter of inserting a new style into existing buildings, or of enticing already formed audiences away from existing venues. The new practices had somehow to constitute themselves as an institutional force in relation to the established sectors of the British theatre industry. Thus from the small detail of how to convert an empty room into a performance space, to the grand endeavour of gradually setting up new national organisational infrastructures, the alternative theatre was engaged in an especially broad oppositional cultural experiment.

Thirdly, alternative theatre was expansionist. It sought to intervene in a widening range of communities and constituencies, to make a popular appeal to an ever-expanding audience. This populist impulse, when combined with the movement's oppositional ambitions, caused alternative theatre to develop exceptionally complex performative codes and strategies. Probably the most complicated practices evolved when alternative theatre mounted deliberate forays into alien territory, into contexts characterised by their likely resistance to oppositional ideologies. Hence, the detailed analysis of particular shows in this book concentrates on the potential of radical theatre in conservative contexts.

My investigation into performance efficacy thus focuses on an ideologically problematic series of practices. For to aim to be both oppositional *and* popular places performance on a knife edge between resistance to, and incorporation into, the status quo. On one side, there is the possibility (*pace* Williams) that, as part of the post-war counter-cultures, alternative theatre significantly contributed to progressive changes in the dominant culture, forcing adjustments in the general social and political order. On the other side, alternative theatre and the counter-cultures may have been simply absorbed into the dominant order through a process of repressive tolerance which effectively neutralised their oppositional ideologies and reinforced the status quo. The dialectic between successful opposition and debilitating incorporation will be a constant theme of my argument.

The structure of this text

This book is divided into two parts. Part I (Chapters 1-3) deals with questions and issues which are directly relevant to the whole range of radical theatre practices, and to British alternative and community theatre particularly. Chapter 1 explicates a theoretical framework for the subsequent arguments. It suggests, in the form of a speculative outline sketch, ways in which the conditions of performance (particularly in community and alternative theatre) may increase its potential cultural, social and political efficacy. Chapter 2 investigates the nature of alternative and community theatre through a study of its critical reception, its actual scale, and the terminologies that have been evolved to describe it. Chapter 3 considers the contribution of alternative theatre to the aesthetics of protest, focusing particularly on its use of agit prop and the carnivalesque. This third chapter also details the characteristics of early alternative theatre and provides an outline history of the movement/sector from 1960 to 1990.

Part II (Chapters 4-7) explores the relationships between individual community theatre performances, the evolution of the alternative theatre movement, and aspects of the wider cultural and socio-political history of post-war Britain. Each of these chapters focuses on especially representative and influential practices during three decades, concluding with an attempt to 'preview' the 1990s. The key practices are provided by John Arden and Margaretta D'Arcy (1960s), John McGrath and the 7:84 Theatre Company (Scotland) (1970s), Ann Jellicoe and the Colway Theatre Trust (1980s), and John Fox and Welfare State International (1990s). The development of alternative and community theatre as a whole is described mostly in terms of trends, as represented by the emergence of new types of approach to the production and distribution of performance. The wider cultural history focuses on the relationship of alternative theatre to other cultural institutions, particularly mainstream theatre and the state funding agencies, while the outline socio-political history tends to stress the structural tensions which affected the evolution of British culture generally during the period. Through juxtaposing these three types of material in each chapter I hope to suggest how the specific potential efficacy of performance and the general potential efficacy of the movement exerted complementary influences on the dominant order.

A thorough history of alternative and community theatre is beyond the scope of this book. In describing the main outlines of its development, inevitably I have left out a great deal of the historical detail that would render the result more conclusive. However, this is a necessary approach in the effort to show how changes in the structure of alternative theatre are the outcome of a dialectical engagement with cultural, social and political history. A full history of the whole movement and sector, meanwhile, is still waiting for the appearance of an appropriate historian.

This book can be read in a number of ways. The best perhaps is to treat it like a detective story, picking up clues in the investigation in sequence from beginning to end. However, other patterns of approach are available. For example, Part I can be treated like a lucky dip, with sections being pulled out individually for inspection and interrogation. Or the different strands of Part II can be read as parallel historical narratives. However, the overall argument explores a number of key theoretical concepts which are laid out in Chapter 1. I have included a glossary of the main terms for readers who wish to enter the text from different directions.

Inevitably this investigation depends partly upon a categorisation of alternative theatre practices which derives from existing critical and historical texts. I am especially wary of these categorisations because often they have been used (most commonly by mainstream critics and historians) to marginalise alternative theatre, through the construction of an orthodoxy which suggests that its abiding principal quality was aesthetic and ideological fragmentation. There is a hidden irony in this version of events, because aesthetic variety *was* ubiquitous in alternative theatre, but such formal and organisational innovation was mainly a tactic to keep one step ahead of ideological incorporation. Underlying the chameleon variety on the creative surface was a substantial body moving in a (mostly) radical direction. My stress on alternative and community theatre as a mode of cultural production aims to reassert its underlying ideological coherence as a cultural movement.

A cultural project

Essentially the alternative and community theatre movement was a relatively small part of massive, successive ideological formations which sought to change British society. Theatre companies engaged with the project of these formations in a wide variety of ways: by working with communities within the project; by working in communities that were opposed to the project; through alignment with political movements that shared some of the project's aims; through strategies which focused on local community development; through the democratisation of culture (taking the best of theatre to the culturally oppressed); and through cultural democracy (creating theatre with the oppressed). These various approaches all relate ultimately to the great socio-political forces which shaped post-war British society.

It is also important to note that British alternative theatre was only one part of a paranational theatrical movement, and that its approaches were developed in concert with projects in many other countries. In the United States groups such as the Bread and Puppet Theatre, the San Francisco Mime Troupe, and el Teatro Campesino were in the vanguard. Theatre Passe Muraille in Canada; Sistren Theatre in Jamaica; Doppio Teatro in Australia: these are just a few among many which are now spread across most countries of the world. Eugène van Erven, Ross Kidd and John McGrath, among others, have expanded on this point (van Erven 1989; Kidd 1982; McGrath 1990). And McGrath has recently essayed a useful summary of the aims which bind alternative and community theatre together across national boundaries:

> Firstly it can contribute to a definition, a revaluation of the cultural identity of a people or a section of society, can add to the richness and diversity of that identity. Secondly, it can assert, draw attention to, give voice to threatened communities, can, by allowing them to speak, help them to survive. Thirdly, it can mount an attack on the standardisation of culture and consciousness which is a function of late industrial/early technological 'consumerist' societies everywhere. Fourthly, it can be and often is linked to a wider political struggle for the right of a people or a section of a society to control its own destiny, to 'self-determination'. Fifthly, it can make a challenge to the values imposed on it from a dominant group – it can help to stop ruling class, or ruling race, or male, or multi-national capitalist values being 'universalised' as common sense, or self-evident truth: as such, it presents a challenge also to the state's cultural engineers, in Ministries of Culture, Arts Councils, universities, schools and the media.
>
> (McGrath 1990: 142)

I hope that this book will contribute to that necessary challenge.

Part I

Theory and issues

Alternative and community theatre as radical cultural intervention

Chapter 1

Performance, community, culture

I think the fringe has failed. Its failure was that of the whole dream of the 'alternative culture' – the notion that within society as it exists you can grow another way of life . . . What happens is that the 'alternative society' becomes hermetically sealed, and surrounded. A ghetto-like mentality develops. It is surrounded, and, in the end, strangled to death.

(Brenton 1981: 91–2)

if we think in terms of an expressive, rather than political revolution, then it is clear that the fringe, and the rest of the counter-culture, has not failed. It never had a coherent programme or a single identity, which is why single issues – feminism, ecology, community art – have become individual themes, rather than part of some overall strategy for change. But that does not detract from their significance.

(Hewison 1986: 225)

The roots of a theory

Whatever judgement is passed on the social and political effects of British alternative and community theatre, it must be informed by the fact that the movement was integral to a massive cultural experiment. From this perspective the leading edge of the movement was not stylistic or organisational innovation (though both these were fundamental to its growth); rather, its impact resulted from a cultural ambition which was both extensive and profound. It was extensive because it aimed to alter radically the whole structure of British theatre. It was profound because it planned to effect a fundamental modification in the cultural life of the nation. Hence, the nature of its success or failure is not a parochial issue of interest only to students of theatre. In attempting to forge new tools for cultural production, alternative theatre ultimately hoped, in concert with other oppositional institutions and formations, to re-fashion society.

The chief purpose of this chapter is to construct a theory which will facilitate our investigations into alternative theatre's potential for efficacy, both at the micro-level of individual performance events and at the macro-level of the movement as a whole. This requires that we address a number of basic questions about the relationships between performers and audiences, between performance and its immediate context, and between performances and their location in cultural formations. The answers will show how the nature of performance enables the members of an audience to arrive at collective 'readings' of performance 'texts', and how such reception by different audiences may impact upon the structure of the wider socio-political order. The focus will be on oppositional performances because the issue of efficacy is highlighted by such practices, but the argument should be relevant to all kinds of theatre.

My central assumption is that performance can be most usefully described as an *ideological transaction* between a company of performers and the community of their audience. Ideology is the source of the collective ability of performers and audience to make more or less common sense of the signs used in performance, the means by which the aims and intentions of theatre companies connect with the responses and interpretations of their audiences. Thus, ideology provides the framework within which companies encode and audiences decode the signifiers of performance. I view performance as a transaction because, evidently, communication in performance is not simply uni-directional, from actors to audience. The totally passive audience is a figment of the imagination, a practical impossibility; and, as any actor will tell you, the reactions of audiences influence the nature of a performance. It is not simply that the audience affects emotional tone or stylistic nuance: the spectator is engaged fundamentally in the active construction of meaning as a performance event proceeds. In this sense performance is 'about' the transaction of meaning, a continuous negotiation between stage and auditorium to establish the significance of the signs and conventions through which they interact.

In order to stress the function of theatre as a public arena for the collective exploration of ideological meaning, I will investigate it from three perspectives, drawn in relation to the concepts of *performance, community* and *culture.* I will argue that every aspect of a theatrical event may need to be scrutinised in order to determine the full range of potential ideological readings that it makes available to audiences in different contexts. The notion of 'performance' encompasses all elements of theatre, thus providing an essential starting point for theorising about theatre's ideological functions. Similarly, the concept of 'community' is indispensable in understanding how the constitutions of different audiences might affect the ideological impact of particular performances, and how that impact might transfer (or not) from one audience to another. Lastly, theatre is a form of cultural production, and so the idea of 'culture' is a crucial component in any account of how performance might contribute to the wider social and political history.

Viewed from these perspectives, British alternative and community theatre between 1960 and 1990 provides an exceptionally rich field of investigation, for three main reasons. Alternative theatre was created (initially, at least) outside established theatre buildings. Hence, every aspect of performance had to be constructed in contexts which were largely foreign to theatre, thus making it easier to perceive the ideological nature of particular projects. Next, the audiences for alternative theatre did not come ready-made. They, too, had to be constructed, to become part of the different constituencies which alternative theatre chose to address, thus providing another way of highlighting the ideological nature of the movement's overall project. Finally, alternative theatre grew out of and augmented the major oppositional cultural formations of the period. Particular performances were aligned with widespread subversive cultural, social and political activity, with the result that they were part of the most fundamental ideological dialectics of the past three decades.

This is particularly the case because, besides being generally oppositional, many individual companies and, to a large extent, the movement as a whole, sought to be popular. As well as celebrating subversive values, alternative theatre aimed to promulgate them to a widening span of social groupings. Hence, the movement continually searched out new contexts for performance in a dilating spectrum of communities. And often – particularly in the practices of community theatre – alternative groups aimed to promote radical socio-political ideologies in relatively conservative contexts. Thus, complex theatrical methods had to be devised in order to circumvent outright rejection. Inevitably, the whole panoply of performance came into play as part of the ideological negotiation, and all aspects of theatre were subject to cardinal experiment so that its appeal to the 'community' might effect cultural – and socio-political – change. In an important sense, then, we are dealing with a rare attempt to evolve an *oppositional popular culture*.

The nature and force of such a project prompt my fundamental interest in the potential efficacy of performance. So I am concerned now to see in what ways Brecht's dictum that 'it is not enough to understand the world, it is necessary to change it' might be exemplified in *both* its aspects by British community and alternative theatre, at both the micro- and macro-levels of performance. Thus, whilst it is obvious that alternative theatre did not bring about a political revolution, it is by no means certain that it failed to achieve other types of general effect. As Robert Hewison argues, the possibility that it did contribute significantly to the promotion of egalitarian, libertarian and emancipatory ideologies, and thus to some of the more progressive socio-political developments of the last three decades, cannot be justifiably dismissed.

Ideology and performance

Ideology has been described as a kind of cement which binds together the different components of the social order. It has also been likened to plaster, covering up the cracks and contradictions in society (K.T. Thompson 1986: 30). Whatever metaphor is preferred, though, the notion of shared beliefs is fundamental to most definitions of the concept. To put it at its simplest: ideology is any system of more or less coherent values which enables people to live together in groups, communities and societies. Thus, to the extent that performance deals in the values of its particular society, it is dealing with ideology. But in practice such dealing is far more complicated than this over-simple formulation suggests.

The concept of ideology has generated a minefield of inter-pretations regarding the ways it may relate to culture and society. The critical debates have been long and complex, as even the briefest glimpse of their major themes will show (J.B. Thompson 1990; Eagleton 1991). Marx used the term in a number of ways, but most influentially to refer to the ideas which express the interests of the dominant class of society. Durkheim broached the idea that for any society there may be a single social order which encompasses class differences, and thus a unitary ideology that can represent it. Recent Marxist theorists, following the lead of Althusser and Gramsci, gener-ally argue that there is such an order, that it is run by a ruling class, and that it is largely the function of cultural production to reinforce the structures of power by promulgating (in many diverse and complex ways) a dominant ideology which operates in the interests of such ruling classes. Subordinate social groups accept this ideology through a process of hegemony. This concept indicates the predominance of a form of consciousness (or set of beliefs) which serves the interests of an exclusive social group, the 'ruling class'. The majority in society, however, unconsciously collude in their own subordination because hegemony reinforces the dominant form of consciousness by making it seem 'natural' or 'common sense'. Thus, hegemony works to ensure that dominant ideologies remain generally unchallenged. The ruling groups maintain their power and their control over the social system because the majority accept their predominance as the norm (Althusser 1971; Gramsci 1971: 12–13).

In complete contrast to this position, the writings of structur-alist and post-structuralist theorists, such as Foucault, Derrida and Baudrillard, tend to resist the idea of ideology in a world in which, from their perspective, language has become dissociated from its object, the sign from what it signifies. For these thinkers, any notion of a stable system of meaning is anathema, and so ideological concepts, such as 'the self', imply a 'false trans-cendance' (Sturrock 1979: 15).

Between the post-structuralists and the neo-Marxists we can locate post-modernist theorists and cultural critics, such as Jencks and Collins. These argue for a pluralistic and de-centred competition of cultures and ideologies, within a society which has a multiplicity of orders in constant conflict with each other, thus precluding the possibility of a dominant ideology (Collins 1989; Jencks 1986). Again, the debates surrounding the idea of post-modernity – in what does it consist; in what ways does it affect society; etc. – have been complex and sometimes bitter. However, for the argument here I will adopt the version advanced by Fredric Jameson, who states:

> I believe that the emergence of postmodernism is closely related to the emergence of [the] moment of late, consumer or multinational capitalism. I believe also that its formal features in many ways express the logic of that particular social system.
>
> (Foster 1985: 125)

Jameson's argument raises the issue of whether or not a socially critical or effectively oppositional art can be created within the 'postmodern condition'. Viewed from this perspective, the question of the potential efficacy of performance – and the nature of alternative theatre history – takes on an increasingly acute and urgent resonance as post-modernism inflects ever-widening social and cultural discourses.

Hence, the neo-Marxist position, *vis-à-vis* ideology, in part informs my argument. The evidence for at least a set of dominant ideologies, if not a single ideology, is much too great to be ignored. For example, one does not need to be a feminist to see that most aspects of Western society are organised patriarchally, or a homosexual to see that heterosexuality provides the dominant values which regulate sexual relations. The question of whether or not such dominant ideologies add up to a singularity – a dominant ideology – is beyond the scope of this study, though I will use the phrase 'status quo' to suggest that those ideologies tend to be mutually reinforcing. However, it is obvious that British society, in common with other 'developed' societies, is far too complex to permit a monolithic hegemonic control of *every* aspect of its culture. Thus the conflictual version of ideology presented by the post-modernists will also in part inflect my argument, since the dominant ideologies of Western societies – and their ruling groups – are frequently challenged by alternatives. Within or alongside the dominant ideologies other, oppositional, ideologies may struggle for cultural space and may sometimes even modify the dominant ideologies to a significant degree.

Cultural institutions and products are clearly central to the maintenance of dominant ideologies, and are frequently the locus for ideological struggle in society. In particular, theatre and performance are major arenas for the reinforcement and/or the uncovering of hegemony. British alternative theatre generally pursued the latter course. Therefore, it is my contention that, as a result of its nature and scale, the movement offered a significant challenge to the status quo, and may even have contributed to the modification of dominant ideologies in the 1970s and 1980s. This general efficacy became possible because performance was especially well suited to the styles of celebratory protest and cultural interventionism favoured by the new oppositional cultural formations which emerged between 1965 and 1990. As the companies of the alternative theatre movement were usually aligned with these formations they had, in one way or another, ideological designs on their audiences. And whether they aimed to celebrate or to protest against the ideologies of their different audiences, their over-riding purpose was to achieve ideological efficacy.

Performance and efficacy

To have any hope of changing its audience a performance must somehow connect with that audience's ideology or ideologies. However, the longer-term effects – ideological or otherwise – that a performance actually might have on its audience, and their community or communities, are notoriously difficult to determine. This is ironic, given that we usually have little or no difficulty in observing, and even sometimes accurately describing, the immediate responses a performance provokes. It is doubly ironic in view of the well-documented power of performance to cause riots on occasion, and in view of the long history of censorship that theatre has suffered. If performance is powerless to affect the socio-political future, why then has it been taken so seriously by the successive powers that be? Despite this circumstantial evidence there has often been a widespread nervousness among theatre historians and critics about making claims for the efficacy of performance.

Nonetheless, the ghost of Aristotelian catharsis has haunted generations of writers on theatre. The most serious theorists of theatre, like addictive exorcists, have been drawn back continually to address the issue of the effects that performance might achieve. Recently, new arguments for performance efficacy have been evolved in the field of performance theory, the discipline born out of a fruitful coupling of anthropology and alternative theatre practices, initially in the work of the American director-academic Richard Schechner. Schechner aims to describe the structural and functional links between performance, community and culture in a variety of societies, and the admirable inclusiveness of this ambition leads to a fundamental tenet of performance theory: namely, that no item in the environment of performance can be discounted as irrelevant to its impact. Schechner thus defines performance as:

> The whole constellation of events . . . that take place in/ among performers and audience from the time the first spectator enters the field of performance – the precinct where the theatre takes place – to the time the last spectator leaves.
> (Schechner 1988: 39)

Obviously he wishes 'field' and 'precinct' to be indeterminate, so that performance may include events physically quite remote from the place in which performing itself happens. In Western theatrical terms, the *production* is simply the most concentrated part of the performance event. If we extend Schechner's logic, it follows that everything else which is done in preparation for, and in the aftermath of, the production is part of the performance and may affect its socio-political significance, and its potential efficacy, for the spectators.

Many theatre managers and entrepreneurs would find such claims unexceptional. In the hard-headed world of commercial theatre the full house, the open-ended run, and the cash till are measure enough of a show's social effects. Schechner would concur that theatre can be indisputably efficacious when viewed from this perspective:

> a Broadway musical is entertainment if one concentrates on what happenes onstage and in the house. But if the point of view expands – to include . . . the function of the roles in the careers of each performer, the money invested by backers, the arrival of the audience, their social status, how they paid for their tickets (as individuals, expense accounts, theatre parties, etc.) and how this indicates the use they are making of the

performance (as entertainment, to advance their careers, to support a charity, etc.) – then the Broadway musical is more than entertainment; it reveals many ritual elements.

(Schechner 1988: 75)

Schechner draws a line between entertainment and efficacy (and by excluding entertainment thus undermines the case that performance *per se* may achieve a lasting effect), but his points about the functional links between theatre economics and social structuring are vividly valid. During recent years arts bureaucrats world-wide have latched onto this 'justification' for the 'value' of culture (Pick 1988). New and refurbished theatre buildings invariably include a 'corporate entertainment suite', while the once-shunned street entertainer is now encouraged as an index of inner-city regeneration. Hence, arguments for the 'economic importance of the arts' assume the efficacy of theatre as an institution of cultural production. However, the influence of a cultural institution may operate independently of the particular aesthetic artefacts it produces or displays. This type of institutional efficacy does not necessarily reinforce the harder case for the efficacy of the artefact, the performance itself.

Nevertheless, the wider perspective of performance theory is particularly apposite for the analysis of alternative theatre, given that generally it constructs its own performance contexts. So we find a leading practitioner in the field, John McGrath, echoing Schechner when he writes:

There are elements in the language of the theatre beyond the text, even beyond the production, which are often more decisive, more central to one's experience of the event than the text or the production . . . notably the choice of venue, audience, performers, and the relationship between audience and performer . . .

(McGrath 1981b: 7)

Hence, in suggesting how community theatre performances may achieve ideological efficacy we will need to take into account all aspects of the event which bear on the ideological transaction between a theatre company and the community of the audience in any cultural context. How the audience gathers for a performance, and disperses when it is over, may be as important to its ideological reception of the show as, say, the style of performing itself.

In all forms of Western theatre the gathering phase is designed to produce a special attitude of reception, to encourage the audience to participate in the making of the performance in a particular frame of mind. In other words, the conventions of gathering for a performance are intended to effect a transition from one social role into another, namely, the role of audience member or spectator. A crucial element in the formation of the role is the 'horizon of expectation' which performative conventions create for the audience; that is to say, the framework within which a piece of theatre will be understood as one type of performance event rather than another (a pageant, a pantomime, a classical tragedy) (Bennett 1990). So the precise nature of the audience's role will vary. However, the anthropologist Victor Turner (who worked with Schechner) has pointed out that in some respects the role is always similar to that experienced by participants in ritual. It is a *liminal* role, in that it places the participant 'betwixt and between' more permanent social roles and modes of awareness. Its chief characteristic is that it allows the spectator to accept that the events of the production are *both real and not real*. Hence it is a *ludic* role (or frame of mind) in the sense that it enables the spectator to participate in playing around with the norms, customs, regulations, laws, which govern her life in society (Turner 1982: 11). Thus, the ludic role of spectator turns performance into a kind of ideological experiment in which the outcome has no *necessary* consequence for the audience. Paradoxically, this is the first condition needed for performance efficacy.

The nature of the audience and its responses has recently attracted the attention of critics such as Herbert Blau, Susan Bennett and Julian Hilton, who in part elaborate aspects of reception theory previously developed by Robert C. Holub, Hans Jauss, and others (Blau 1990; Bennett 1990; Hilton 1987). These writers tend to focus on the exceptional nature of the audience's role in theatre. For example, Julian Hilton argues that it produces what he calls 'performance consciousness', by which he means a collective imaginative capacity to engage in the construction of 'potential worlds' through the interaction of performer and spectator. He also notes that this interaction occurs on two levels simultaneously:

There is the on-stage conflict of forces which constitutes the plot of the drama, and there is the engagement with the audience in an imaginative act of constructing a possible world . . . Performers state by their actions that what they are performing is both real and not real, is in effect simply 'possible'. The audience . . . test the validity of the perceived meanings [of the performance] within the wider context of culture as a whole.

(Hilton 1987: 132–3)

Whilst I would argue that how the performers perform may often be less important than the conventions of gathering in creating 'performance consciousness', it seems to me that Hilton's account is at root an accurate one. Unfortunately, though, he spends little time discussing the ways in which the structural dualism of the performance experience might produce potential efficacy for its audience. In order to approach a fuller account, then, we need to theorise the relationship between the 'real' and 'not real' aspects of performance, for it is that relationship which determines the audience's reading of the significance of theatrical signs, and thus their potential effect on the future.

In *Theatricality* Elizabeth Burns provides a very useful proto-semiotic analysis of theatrical duality. Her account matches Schechner's and Hilton's in noting that performance takes place simultaneously on two levels. She describes these as 'interaction between performers and spectators and interaction between characters in the play' (Burns 1972: 31). Burns' model for analysis is the traditional mainstream one that sees theatre primarily in terms of character, dialogue, plot and so on. Nonetheless, her sociological perspective leads her to make a very useful distinction between two different types of convention which govern the audience's reading of performance. The first type she calls 'rhetorical conventions':

Between actors and spectators there is an implicit agreement that the actors will be allowed to conjure up a fictitious world . . . This agreement underwrites the devices of exposition that enable the audience to understand the play. These conventions . . . can be described as *rhetorical*. They are the means by which the audience is persuaded to accept characters and situations whose validity is ephemeral and bound to the theatre.

(Burns 1972: 31)

Clearly the notion of rhetorical conventions, or signs, is appli-
cable to all types of theatrical event. They produce the signals
that enable us to classify different shows as belonging to the same
genre or form, and to distinguish between different genres and
forms. Clearly, too, rhetorical conventions are not confined
solely to the performed show itself. They also structure the
gathering and dispersal phases of performance, though there
they tend to contribute less to the construction of genre or
form, and more to the particular type of spectator/audience role
that the event requires. Rhetorical conventions are thus crucial
to the ideological framing, via horizons of expectation, of
performing.

Burns calls the second type of convention 'authenticating
conventions', which:

> 'model' social conventions in use at a specific time and in a
> specific place and milieu. The modes of speech, demeanour
> and action that are explicit in the play . . . have to imply a
> connection to the world of human action of which the theatre
> is only a part. These conventions suggest a total and external
> code of values and norms of conduct from which the speech
> and action of the play is drawn. Their function is, therefore, to
> *authenticate* the play.
>
> (Burns 1972: 32)

Despite the rather limited mimetic model on which Burns'
description is based, the notion that there is a category of
theatrical sign directly engaged with the ideology of the 'real'
extra-theatrical world is crucial to an account of performance
efficacy. Authenticating conventions or signs are the key to the
audience's successful decoding of the event's significance to their
lives. They determine the audience's reading of performance by
establishing more or less transparent relationships between the
fictionality of performance, the 'possible worlds' created by
performance, and the 'real world' of the audience's socio-political experience outside theatre. In terms of my theoretical perspective, they enable an audience to perceive the specific ideological
meanings of the show in relatively explicit ways.

Now Burns' crucial distinction will allow us to extend our
analysis of the interaction of theatre-as-theatre and theatre-as-
social-event, between the 'not real' and 'real' dimensions of

performance. In particular the distinction will enable us to describe more accurately the kinds of *crisis* that performance may provoke for an audience, and to suggest how such crises are an essential element in the ideological efficacy of performance.

Examples of the immediate effects of crises provoked by authenticating conventions are easy to find – we need only look to the history of theatre riots. We have noted already how Sean O'Casey's *The Plough and the Stars* sparked off disorder at Dublin's Abbey Theatre in 1926. According to all the eyewitness accounts the trouble started during Act II, and centred mainly on O'Casey's linking of the nationalist cause to the low life of Dublin pubs and prostitution. The report in the Dublin *Evening Herald* matches others in pinpointing the 'desecration' of the Irish tricolour as a crucial trigger for the violence:

> There is an effort abroad to destroy nationalism and supplant it by internationalism, and the desecration of the National flag of a country. I should imagine the play would come under the Treason Act.
>
> (Lowery 1984: 42)

The example illustrates how ideology and the immediate effects of a performance may be intimately connected. That the event became especially memorable in Irish politics suggests that its impact stretched beyond the direct participants, and, at least on a symbolic level, may have achieved more than a modicum of influence in the subsequent history of Irish nationalism. If this is the case (and perhaps it is not such a big 'if' as might appear), then the connection between performative crisis and ideological efficacy would be established clearly.

The example of the Abbey riot also prompts two important qualifying points about crisis and efficacy. Firstly, the kind of crises provoked by the ideological significance of the authenticating conventions of a performance can as much reinforce dominant ideologies as support oppositional ones. Secondly, the longer-term effects of a crisis of authenticating conventions will depend centrally on their success in engaging with the fundamental values of the audience: both outrage and a sense of righteousness can last a long time when the most cherished symbols of belief are desecrated or celebrated (as was seen in the Salman Rushdie affair). Unfortunately, the riot in Dublin was efficacious for *both* sides of the dispute in ways that neither

O'Casey nor the Abbey Theatre desired. The riot caused
O'Casey to leave Ireland for good, and W. B. Yeats accused the
audience from the stage: 'You have disgraced yourselves again.
Is this to be an ever-recurring celebration of the arrival of Irish
genius? Once more you have rocked the cradle of genius.' He
was, of course, primarily referring to the rupturing of rhetorical
conventions.

Such ruptures usually signal a breakdown of the necessary
duality of conventions which allows performance to 'play' with
the audience's fundamaental beliefs, and to provoke a potential
crisis in those beliefs, *without* producing immediate rejection.
For it is the *ludic* nature of the audience's role that allows it to
engage with ideological difference, that allows rules to be
broken (via authenticating conventions) while rules are being
kept (via rhetorical conventions). This paradox links theatrical
performance to carnival and other forms of public celebration
which are designed to produce what Victor Turner has called
communitas: primarily 'a direct, immediate and total confrontation of human identities' (Turner 1982: 47).

As, according to Turner, *communitas* is the foundation of
community cohesiveness, then the paradox of rule-breaking-
within-rule-keeping is crucial to the efficacy of performance in
its contribution to the formation of (ideological) communities. It
is when this paradox is operating at its most acute – when a riot
of anger or ecstasy could break out, but does not – that
performance achieves its greatest potential for long-term efficacy.
For the 'possible worlds' encountered in the performance are
carried back by the audience into the 'real' socio-political world
in ways which may influence subsequent action. Thus, if a
modification of the audience's ideology (or ideologies) is induced
by crisis, whether as a confirmation or a radical alteration, then
the function of the rhetorical conventions of dispersal is to effect
a re-entry into society, usually in ways which do not lead to
immediate efforts to influence the existing socio-political order,
in whatever direction. In this respect, theatre which mounts a
radical attack on the status quo may prove deceptive. The slow-
burning fuse of efficacy may be invisible.

It should also be noted that audience members always have a
choice as to whether or not the performance may be efficacious
for them. For the ludic role of spectator permits the participant to
treat the performance as of no consequence to her or his life: it's

only a fiction, only a 'possible world', with no bearing on the real one. It also follows that if the spectator decides that the performance is of central significance to her or his ideology then such choice implies a commitment. It is this commitment that is the source of the efficacy of performance for the future, because a decision that affects a system of belief, an ideology, is more likely to result in changes to future action. It is in this respect that the collective impact of a performance is so important. For if a whole audience, or even a whole community, responds in this way to the symbolism of a 'possible world', then the potential of performance efficacy is multiplied by more than the audience number. To the extent that the audience is part of a community, then the networks of the community will change, however infinitesimally, in response to changes in the audience members. Thus the ideology of communities, and so their place in culture, may begin to have a bearing on the wider socio-political make-up of a nation or even a continent.

Community and performance

To pursue our quest of explaining how particular performances may achieve efficacy we need a concept which can mediate between the experiences of individual audiences and the structures that shape society as a whole. In other words, we need a concept which signifies concrete groupings of people and at the same time allows for the myriad ways in which many different social groupings may be organised. I shall argue that the idea of 'community' can supply this need, that it can be the conceptual lynch-pin which links the experience (and action) of individuals – including that of performance – to major historical changes in society. Raymond Williams reinforces this fundamental structural and ideological function of community when he writes of 'the importance of actual communities and forms of associa-tion as the necessary mediating element between individuals and large Society' (Williams 1965: 95). Hence, he conceives of community as the concrete medium of face-to-face interactions through which we transact ideological business with the wider social structure. That is to say, the networks of our mutual relations with others have inscribed in them values which may or may not be consonant with those inscribed in the larger social order. Community is thus a potential site of ideological opposition to the status quo, and a performance which engages with the ideological identity of a particular community may enlist powerful forces for change.

Obviously, the identity of any type of community can be maintained only by constant reinforcement of the values inscribed in its networks. But by what common process can communities as different, say, as pigeon-fanciers and feminists, villages and inner-city neighbourhoods, achieve their vastly differing identities? Anthony Cohen provides a stimulating and cogent thesis which addresses this question from a semiotic perspective. In *The Symbolic Construction of Community* (1985) Cohen argues that all communities identify themselves by creating boundaries between what is included and what is excluded as part of the community. These boundaries are established through the constant use of appropriate symbols by the networks of the community, including the notion of 'community' itself. All individuals in the community may not necessarily agree to exactly the same decoding of the symbols; in fact the internal ideological dynamic of communities often derives from differences of opinion in this respect. But, to establish the boundaries that provide the basis of a sense of community, any particular community's members must at least agree to use the same symbols. Obvious examples of such symbols are provided by, say, the CND peace sign or simply the name of a village or inner-city district. More complex examples are supplied by the word 'feminist' or by the topography of the local lovers' leap!

So the continual and collective making of meanings through the use of common symbols constructs the boundaries of particular communities and gives them their specific ideological complexion. As Cohen notes, this meaning-making activity:

> continually transforms the reality of difference into the appearance of similarity with such efficacy that people can still invest 'community' with ideological integrity. It unites them in their opposition, both to each other, and to those outside.
>
> (Cohen 1985: 31)

All communities are alike in this respect, though their 'integrity' may well be built on totally differing foundations. For instance, we can identify a distinction between communities of *location* and communities of *interest*. 'Communities of interest', as the phrase suggests, are formed through networks of association that are predominantly characterised by their commitment to a common interest. It follows that such communities may not necessarily be limited to a particular geographical area. It also follows that communities of interest tend to be ideologically explicit, so that even if the members of a particular community come from different geographical areas they can relatively easily recognise their common identity. 'Communities of location' are created through networks of relationships formed by face-to-face interaction within a geographically bounded area. Some communities of location are ideologically explicit – a religious order founded on a monastery, for instance – though it is much more common for their ideological values to be implied by the organisation and interaction of their networks. This is primarily because such communities usually include a variety of ideological interests within the one geographical area, and overt ideological disputes are generally avoided in the interests of the stability of the community itself.

Now, the differences between the two types of community are more a matter of tendency than absolute distinction: communities of location and interest are always intersecting, and individuals may thus be members of two or more communities simultaneously. Nonetheless, the idea of the ideological integrity of a community – whether it is constructed mainly by the location or the interests of its members – is crucial to an understanding of how performance might achieve efficacy.

Community and performance efficacy

At this juncture, the relationship between community and performance efficacy can be best demonstrated by a hypothetical example based on a community of location possessing a high level of explicit ideological integrity. Such communities will usually possess and use symbolism as a conscious part of their public domain. To identify key symbols for this type of community we need only look at any ceremonies or rituals which are regularly mounted. Take, for example, the town of Kilbroney in Northern Ireland. The town has a Protestant working-class population which lives mainly in segregated council housing estates. Each July the Twelfth, in common with many other towns and villages in the region, these people celebrate their

Protestantism through a day of parades, sermons, picnics, games and music: the Glorious Twelfth as it is called. Now, according to Sangestad Larsen, the symbols central to the Glorious Twelfth represent 'cleanliness, order, responsible management of property' and commitment to the 'true faith and the Crown' (Cohen 1985: 56). The symbols thus variously signify the beliefs and behaviour which structure the community (including the rules for separation from the Kilbroney Catholic working class), but the community's central symbol is the 'fresh-coloured Ulster flag'. Given this, we can envisage how a performance might use the Ulster flag (and associated symbols) to engage in a transaction with this particular community's ideology, in the hope of influencing its patterns of behaviour.

Our theoretical perspective demands that the flag must become part of an action that provokes a crisis which has inescapable significance for the audience, and this will involve the manipulation by the performance company of the relationships between the rhetorical conventions (or 'real' aspects) of performance and the authenticating conventions (or 'not real' representations) of the event. Now clearly the gathering of the Kilbroney Protestant community for a performance will be enhanced by a recognition of some of the meanings that are represented by the Glorious Twelfth. So any company mounting a performance for this audience would do well to ensure that, for instance, the performance space is neat, tidy and well organised and that the audience is admitted in an orderly and well-managed manner. In short, a company is likely to have more success in securing an effective transaction with the audience if the rhetorical conventions of performance are consonant with – confirm the boundaries of – the ideology of the community. In a sense, the company must reassure the community that it is able to represent its interests.

In contrast to this, and in order to approach efficacy, the performing itself must employ authenticating conventions/signs to discomfort or disturb the ideology of the community in ways that do not cause a riot or other kind of insuperable schism. To put this rather gnomically, the Ulster flag would somehow need to be damaged, but not destroyed (*pace* the tricolour in *The Plough and the Stars*). Moreover, in order to achieve inescapable significance for the audience, the closer the flag gets to being destroyed – the more fundamentally the community ideology is challenged – the greater the likelihood that the performance will become efficacious within the networks of the community. In other words, the ideological transaction of performance must deal with the fundamental constitution of the audience's community identity in order to approach efficacy. In so doing it may reinforce or modify that ideological identity, but in either case efficacy depends on the identity being challenged.

Now this example fundamentally reinforces a commonplace of dramatic and theatrical criticism; namely, that what may be challenging to one audience/community may be innocuous to another. To say this is simply to stress the *ideological relativity* of performance, to make the fairly obvious point that the same performance may meet with vastly different reactions in different ideological contexts: a show celebrating the IRA is one thing on the Falls Road, quite another thing in a British army camp. However, the point also underlines a crucial notion in the argument of this book: namely, that *the context of performance directly affects its perceived ideological meaning.* Consequently, in a competition to produce an especially dense formulation, we might cryptically claim that the ideological relativity of performance is a function of the potential variability of value systems inscribed in all aspects of its context. I will call this the *contextuality* of performance, by which I mean the propensity of performance to achieve different meanings/readings according to the context in which it occurs. The socio-cultural complexion of the audience, its sense of community (or lack of it) is the most crucial factor in evoking the contextuality of a text.

It should be clear that some texts are more susceptible to ideological relativity than others, and in this respect a major factor in a text's contextuality is what post-modernist critics have dubbed *inter-textuality.* As with the other concepts discussed here, different theoreticians offer varying definitions of inter-textuality. I take it to mean the ways in which a performance text gains meaning for an audience through its relationships to other texts, including the non-theatrical texts which communities produce, in the form of folklore, oral history, stories, legends and mythologies. However, inter-textuality is not simply a matter of direct allusion; the rhetorical conventions that establish a text as a member of a particular genre, say, are operating inter-textually. The same is true for the particular style created by authenticating conventions. So the construction of meaning inevitably involves inter-textuality, and the burgeoning of the mass media in the late twentieth century has made Western audiences especially skilled in inter-textual reading. We are skilful in establishing a productive relationship with texts that are allusive and multi-faceted, which break traditional rules of clarity and unity, which combine conventions from both 'high' and 'low' art forms. Thus, inter-textuality tends to make readers more active in the creation of meaning; it makes us into what John Fiske has called the 'producerly reader' (Fiske 1989: 122).

Fiske identifies the 'gaps, contradictions, and inadequacies' of popular cultural products as the source of their rich inter-textuality, and of course all texts share these characteristics to a greater or lesser degree. He quotes the pop star Madonna as a prime example of such a 'text'. The contradictions in the representations of Madonna's sexuality enable different readers to arrive at ideologically variable interpretations, in accordance with their judgements of representations of gender/sexuality by other texts. Hence:

> Madonna is circulated among some feminists as a reinscription of patriarchal values, among some men as an object of voyeuristic pleasure, and among many girl fans as an agent of empowerment and liberation. Madonna as a text . . . is incomplete until she is put into social circulation.
>
> (Fiske 1989: 124)

In a sense, inter-textuality is a foil to contextuality, in that it may feed contrasting ideologies within an audience from the same community. But also, an audience sharing the same ideological identity may utilise the inter-textuality of a performance in ways that produce collective readings. Hence, the ideological 'positioning' of the audience (or reader) in relation to the performance (or text) crucially influences both the range of what can be 'read' (via contextuality) and the types of 'reading' that may be available within the range (via inter-textuality). Contextuality/inter-textuality thus can provoke wide variations in readings of the same text.

The complexity that contextuality/inter-textuality engenders has driven some theoreticians of drama into a kind of critical reification which claims that only individual interpretations are ultimately possible. Hence, Martin Esslin writes that:

any attempt to predict what 'meaning' the performance as such contains, is bound to be doomed to failure, simply because that meaning must be different for each individual member of the audience.

(Esslin 1987: 21)

Of course, there is a sense in which this line of argument is entirely valid: the particular nuances of interpretation which individuals make are bound to vary to a greater or lesser degree. But the enlargement of differences of nuance to a principle of interpretation has profound ideological ramifications. In effect, Esslin is proposing an ideology of individualism which assumes that a society can function through discourses that do not produce common meanings. In my view the contradictory nature of this proposal renders it nonsensical, particularly in the context of the study of drama and theatre, as both quintessentially assume the possibility of a collective response based on the achievement of shared readings.

Such collective responses, shaped by the ideological identity of the audiences' communities, are the very foundation of performance efficacy. They are the first link in a chain that connects the individual experience of each audience member to the wider historical development of his or her society. A further crucial link is provided by the kinds of culture which establish common identities between different communities.

Culture and performance

The idea of community as a process of ideological meaning-making helps to explain how individual performances might achieve efficacy for their audiences. However, we need also to determine how different communities might be similarly changed by a single show, or a series of shows, even given the complex variability of readings resulting from contextuality and inter-textuality. We must acknowledge, too, that this problem – which encompasses the issue of how a theatrical movement may influence society – is bound to be exacerbated in contemporary societies which are subject to post-modernist pluralism. To express this, for the moment, in terms of a post-structuralist analysis: if signs are indeed in arbitrary relationship to what they signify, then (*pace* Esslin) all we can anticipate is a riot of individual readings whose disparate nature can only reinforce the pluralistic and fragmented society which produced them in the first place.

My purpose now is to defend the possibility of common collective readings of performance on an inter-community basis, to suggest how different performances for different communities might successfully produce consonant effects in relation to society as a whole. Such an account must use the difficult concept of 'culture', which, as Raymond Williams claims, is 'one of the two or three most complicated words in the English language' (Williams 1976: 76). Now the debates within cultural studies have produced an embarrassment of riches when it comes to definitions of 'culture', but Williams' arguments have been especially influential. Hence, I will adopt his notion of culture as a 'signifying system', by which he means the system of signs via which groups, organisations, institutions, and, of course, communities recognise and communicate with each other in the process of becoming a more or less influential formation within society. In other words, 'culture' is the medium which can unite a range of different groups and communities in a common project in order to make them into an ideological force operating for or against the status quo.

The British alternative and community theatre movement was a cultural formation in the sense adopted above. However, to establish the potential significance of the movement to British society as a whole we need to investigate its place in the cultural organisation of post-war Britain. That significance is partly a question of scale, and, as we shall see in the next chapter, it was by no means negligible in this respect; but even more important were the ways in which the movement was part of the great cultural shifts of the 1960s, 1970s and 1980s. For its cultural alliances clearly have a bearing on the possible extent of its ideological influence; its potential efficacy cannot be accurately assessed if it is isolated from the very forces that brought it about in the first place. Thus, it is crucial to my argument that British alternative theatre was, at least initially, part and parcel of the most extensive, and effective, oppositional cultural movement to emerge in Western countries in the post-war period: the international counter-culture of the late 1960s and early 1970s.

Much of the debate about the nature of the counter-culture (and later similar formations) has focused on its relationship to the class structure of society. For instance, consider the following seminal text written from this perspective:

> Middle class counter cultures are diffuse, less group-centred [than sub-cultures], more individualised . . . [They] precipitate . . . a diffuse counter cultural milieu . . . [They] are distinguished precisely by their attempts to explore 'alternative institutions' to the central institutions of the dominant culture: new patterns of living, of family life, of work or even 'un-careers'.
>
> (Bennett *et al.* 1981: 72)

However, it seems very unlikely that such a phenomenon could exist within the class constraints assumed by the analysis. Indeed, the authors' perception of the full impact of the late 1960s counter-culture suggests a much more extensive basis for the formation. They argue that the counter-culture:

> represented a rupture inside the dominant culture which then became linked to the crisis of hegemony, of civil society and ultimately of the state itself. It is in *this* sense that the middle-class counter cultures, beginning from a point *within* the dominant class culture, have become an emergent ruptural force for the whole society.
>
> (Bennett *et al.* 1981: 78)

Thus, 'class' is an inadequate concept for explaining exactly *how* the counter-culture might have achieved such extensive socially disruptive potential.

A number of cultural critics have argued that generational membership may provide a better explanation for the extensive influence of counter-cultures. That is to say, a full blown counter-culture is ultimately the product of a whole generation, in that all members of a particular generation may be decisively affected by their historical positioning. The theoretical foundation for such a view has been put forward by Karl Mannheim (Mannheim 1952). He argued that under conditions of particularly accelerated social change some generations evolve an awareness, and thus ways of living, which distinguish them sharply from previous generations. In effect, there is then a major rupture in the process of historical transmission. Not all members of the generation affected will respond to the rupture in the same way, but there will be a general tendency to raise fundamental questions about socio-political organisation, and to experiment with alternatives. Cultural critics who use Mannheim's analysis to explain the impact of the late 1960s counter-culture cite a wide range of social, economic and political facts to support the case. These include the breakdown of extended families owing to increased social mobility, the relative failure of education as a socialising influence, over-production and a surplus of commodities giving a false sense of affluence, and, above all, the hardening of the Cold War for the first generation that grew up under the shadow of the nuclear apocalypse.

Now this perspective has profound implications for our assessment of the socio-political status of the institutions of the counter-culture, including the alternative theatre movement. For a start, it moves those institutions from the margins of historical change to somewhere closer to the centre, for those institutions then represent a changed generational awareness both to the generation and to the rest of society. In addition, the institutions are a concrete embodiment and a widespread medium for the promulgation of alternative, and usually oppositional, ideologies. In addition, the generational locus provides a basis for the popularity of the institutions and their forms of production. Hence, the idea of the counter-culture thus conceived enables us to understand how the 'alternative' may become 'popular', how the socially marginal impulse of middle-class youth may become ideologically central to a whole society.

We can gain a measure of what this may mean historically by considering the nature of the cultural movements that in large part issued from the late 1960s counter-culture in the 1970s. Michael Brake gives the following succinct account:

> Ecology became a genuine political concern, leading to the development of pure-food shops, preventative medicine, organic farming and pollution campaigns against large corporations. The necessity to develop new, alternative legal, health and social services led to a new interest in community politics . . . Consciousness-raising 'rap groups' developed a recognition of oppressions outside traditional class lines, which became essential in the development of feminism and gay politics in their struggle against patriarchy and sexism.
>
> (Brake 1985: 95)

Thus, in this version the late 1960s counter-culture was a major stimulus to, and a partial source for, the ideological orientations of the great emancipatory and libertarian movements of the 1970s and 1980s. These included the gay rights and black consciousness movements, the women's and feminist movements, the community activist movement and the various movements that fought for the rights of people with disabilities, the elderly, the hospitalised and other types of socially disadvantaged group, and it may include even the campaign for a popular, grass-roots-based culture that was fought in the mid-1980s.

I am not suggesting, of course, that the late 1960s counter-culture *caused* these movements, for they have their sources in a widespread and continuing dissatisfaction with the inadequacies of late-capitalism in providing for the needs of minorities and marginalised groups. However, that initial counter-culture did provide a 'model' for oppositional action against hegemony, on a grand scale. Thus it is not unreasonable to view the subsequent movements as a series of counter-cultures. I suggest, then, that the late 1960s international counter-cultural formation provided the starting point for a long-term *cultural* revolution that was not dependent on class for its effectiveness, because it impinged on the awareness of a whole generation, and its successors, in more or less decisive ways. But how could a phenomenon that was so socially diffuse and historically distended possess anything like an identifiable ideology?

Theodore Roszak, who coined the phrase, identified the late 1960s counter-culture in ideological terms drawn from a number of theorists, such as Herbert Marcuse, Alan Watts and Paul Goodman. Roszak's study is in no way a systematic theoretical treatment of these writers' ideas, but his approach allows him a kind of conceptual audacity. In short, he identifies the ideological foundation of the counter-culture as an opposition to hegemony by a utopianist idealism which promoted an egalitarian ethic through the advocacy of participative democracy on a localised level (Roszak 1969: 200).

Now the profound simplicity of Roszak's interpretation indicates how this ideological root for the counter-culture provided the formation with three major advantages for its oppositional promulgation. Firstly, the ideology was amenable to adaptation and elaboration in a phenomenally wide variety of different cultural practices, from the politically engaged activism of anti-Vietnam rallies to the rural retreating of the commune movement. Secondly, it provided the counter-culture with the principle of non-bureaucratic institutional organisation. On this principle the movement formed itself into a multiple series of 'communities', able to operate independently, but also overlapping to form a network of more or less loose associations whose boundaries are defined in broadly similar ideological terms. Thirdly, the formulation was adaptable and was adopted by the subsequent cultural formations as a central element of their ideologies. Despite their sometimes profound differences, and the contradictions between them, they can be related to a singular ideological tendency which was in deep opposition to the status quo. So, at the very least, these movements were united by resistance to the dominant order; but also they maintained at least a modicum of ideological coherence through their commitment to egalitarianism and participatory democracy.

Thus, the idea of the counter-culture provides us with a key theoretical component for understanding how particular performances connected with general social change from the 1960s to the 1980s. For the British alternative theatre movement was only one, relatively small, part of the counter-cultural and emancipatory movements of the 1960s, 1970s and 1980s. As such it played, I think, a key role in promoting and popularising oppositional ideologies. And, as we shall see, its chief tactic was allied to the emergence of the aesthetics of anti-nuclear, anti-war and civil rights demonstrations in Britain and the USA. This is best described as a carnivalesque resistance to the oppressions of affluence, as promoted by the capitalist, technocratic and meritocratic status quo. We will be talking, then, about a new mode of *celebratory protest*, which challenged dominant ideologies through the production of alternative pleasures that were particularly attractive to the generations born in the 1940s and 1950s. And, inevitably, its audacity was greeted with an ambiguous embrace by the dominant socio-political order.

Chapter 2

Reception, scale, terminologies

All culture serves someone's interest.   (Tax 1972: 15)

What the . . . cultural historian studies are the social practices
and social relations which produce not only 'a culture' or 'an
ideology' but . . . those dynamic actual states and works
within which there are not only continuities and persistent
determinations but also tensions, conflicts, resolutions and
irresolutions, innovations and actual changes.

(Williams 1981: 29)

Of ideological struggle

British alternative and community theatre was a significant site
of cultural conflict in the 1970s and 1980s. The various interpretations and evaluations placed upon it by theatre historians and
critics reflect this conflictual function, and give a lively measure
of its ideological impact. There is little unanimity of response; in
fact, so various are their reactions that at times it seems they are
describing totally different domains of cultural production. We
should not be surprised by this. Alternative and, especially,
oppositional cultural practices issue a challenge to both
audiences and critics, and the more fundamental the challenge
the more potential it has to produce a riven reception. Ironically,
we may take the mixed press for alternative theatre as a measure
of its general success in raising essential social and political
issues, in uncovering the hegemony, in questioning the status
quo; because, of course, critical and historical discourses are as
much a part of the grand ideological struggles of history as the
practices they analyse and describe.

In this chapter I shall be concerned firstly with the general critical reception of alternative/community theatre by writers who occupy a range of ideological standpoints. Next I will present a brief statistical analysis of the scale of alternative theatre, which assesses its size in relation to the other main sectors of the British theatre industry. Then I will make a detailed investigation of the terminology which has been evolved to describe the movement as a whole and its various sub-sections. In particular, I will focus on the idea of community theatre as a type of work which was on the cultural cutting edge of the movement. I deal with these topics at this point because, of course, this text is just as much a part of the ideological struggle over the status of its subject as the texts it discusses; and readers have a right to know where it intends to locate itself in the swirl of debate that alternative theatre has generated.

The critical reception

Mainstream theatre critics and historians generally have failed to recognise the nature and extent of the socio-cultural impact of alternative and community theatre. Their descriptions are invariably inflected in fairly obvious ways by an ideological animosity which seeks to contain or diminish the achievements of the movement. Thus John Elsom writes:

> At best, the fringe was a piece-meal theatre, seizing many different ideas and discarding them, almost too soon after trying them out . . . By 1974 . . . the British fringe seemed to settle down to a useful but scarcely *avant-garde* rut, of cheerful small shows, transient companies of different hues, and new plays of varying merit.
>
> (Elsom 1979: 159–60)

And J. L. Styan:

> The British fringe is no doubt as evanescent as its makeshift stages, its uncertain finances and the fashionable banners it waves. Its concern has been to make an immediate appeal to the audience it finds. But in all this changeable activity the rebel playwright will become part of the established order . . . and we look for something of permanence to shoot up.
>
> (Styan 1981: 180)

The examples could be multiplied easily. What they usually signify is an incomprehension of the cultural significance of the movement. This is the result of an analytical perspective which insists on treating performance solely in terms of its *theatrical* significance. At best these critics misjudge the full ideological impact of alternative theatre; at worst they end up plainly patronising an expanding theatrical sector and its audiences, out of either ignorance or, occasionally, malice.

Assessments by observers with more understanding of the movement, however, show a remarkable variation. Writing in 1979 Catherine Itzin claimed:

> The statistics alone [for 1976] testify to the development of a new force to be reckoned with in British Theatre; an alternative which developed new audiences, a new aesthetic, a new kind and concept of theatre.
>
> (Itzin 1980b: xiv)

And a year later she made strong claims for:

> the fertility of this field of work and its significance to British Theatre as a whole. And the signs are that the work is continuing to develop, to take new directions in response to the times.
>
> (Itzin 1980a: 13)

But only four years later Steve Gooch was writing:

> As the sense of a 'movement' fragmented, so the inherent contradictions of the groups' situation re-asserted themselves more forcibly . . . Artistically, the political, fringe and community theatre, as a *field* of work, had not a lot to offer any more – except perhaps pain.
>
> (Gooch 1984: 57)

Three years on and Andrew Davies was just as pessimistic:

> seven or eight years ago I was not only convinced that there had been in Britain a fruitful tradition of alternative and experimental theatre (I still think that), but that it had a future too. Now I am much less sure of the latter proposition.
>
> (Davies 1987: 207)

Surprisingly, assessments of the movement's impact by key alternative theatre practitioners have also been remarkably varied. For example, Howard Brenton, who was involved in the early stages of the movement, when asked in 1974 if he thought the fringe had failed as 'an historical phenomenon', answered:

> the fringe was a historical thing [sic]. Where it went wrong was when the audiences became sophisticated . . . The fringe circuit audiences became spuriously sophisticated . . . and that was when it was time to get out – it was becoming 'arty'.
>
> (Brenton 1981: 92)

It may be, as Robert Hewison (1988: 225) suggests, that Brenton's reaction is shaded by the fact that he was beginning to gain some recognition in the theatrical mainstream. Ten years later, David Edgar, another playwright who had worked successfully in both mainstream and alternative theatre, offered a more moderate evaluation:

> the relative – and I must hammer the word 'relative' – failure of socialist theatre to create a new, mass working-class audience tended to mask the fact that a rather different audience *had* been built up, which was large enough to sustain the mushrooming number of touring groups and community theatres . . .
>
> (Edgar 1988: 164)

Another six years on and John McGrath, who had rejected a successful career in TV and the theatrical mainstream to work in alternative theatre, essayed a brief survey of alternative theatre groups in South America, Australia, Canada and other countries, and claimed, 'these companies are a new force in the Western world, giving voice to an international "alternative morality" ' (McGrath 1990: 141). Clearly, these claims are inflected by the relationships of the writers to the movement, as much as by the historical moment in which they were written. And just as clearly, the differences are not explained by widely varied ideological perspectives, for all three playwrights profess overt socialist or Marxist sympathies.

Two centrally linked issues are embedded in these differing interpretations. Firstly, in what ways was the movement peripheral, in what ways was it central, to British society as a whole? Secondly, if the movement indeed has a shaky future, is that because it has become even more culturally irrelevant or because, in a period of reactionary repression, it has continued to be a serious threat to the dominant ideologies? Initial answers can be proposed in the light of our investigations so far. For example, if we can call in some of the work of cultural theoreticians and historians as evidence, then alternative theatre's alliances with the successive counter-cultures ensured that it was dealing with many of the central ideological issues of the 1970s and 1980s. In addition, the attention lavished on the movement, even by unsympathetic critics and historians, suggests its impact may have been far more extensive than they allow. Given these considerations, alternative theatre might have mustered enough ideological muscle to shift the status quo in a progressive direction, if only by a liberalising inch or two. But we need further evidence to nudge us towards a more convincing account.

One problem hampering progress is that existing histories of the movement tend to offer partial reports and perspectives. Either they deal with a relatively narrow, though always important, range of practices, such as political or feminist theatre (Itzin 1980b; Wandor 1986). Or their historical or geographical span makes their accounts somewhat sketchy (Bradby/McCormick 1978; Davies 1987; van Erven 1989). Or their focus on playwrights tends to skew the picture away from actual production practices (Bull 1984; Chambers/Prior 1987). Or they are simply too idiosyncratic to be taken seriously (Elsom 1979; Hayman 1979). Most of these texts also are under-theorised, in ways that reduce the cultural significance of the movement, and this produces misjudgement about its potential efficacy. Steve Gooch provides the fullest attempt at a theory (Gooch 1984); but it is, significantly, a cultural critic, Robert Hewison, who offers the best (if incomplete) balance between history and theory (Hewison 1986). In many ways, though, the first two texts devoted solely to alternative theatre, Ansorge's *Disrupting the Spectacle* (1975) and Craig's *Dreams and Deconstructions* (1980), give the most accurate image of the range of practices in the movement through a judicious balance of historical fact *and* analysis. Despite their various limitations, all these texts are essential reading for anyone seriously interested in the field, and this study has derived stimulating ideas and useful material from all of them in varying degrees.

Inevitably, all these writers have engaged with problems of definition and, therefore, analytical method. The volatility of the movement and its astonishing, centrifugal growth has made this unavoidable. The development of a new cultural movement which is generally oppositional is bound to be erratic and more concerned with questions of survival than with careful self-assessment. In fact, internal disputes and the formation of factions are a condition of its growth, so self-reflective comprehensiveness is rarely on the agenda. This has led to an impression of fragmentation which has enabled unsympathetic critics to denigrate its achievements, and made it difficult for supportive observers to speak confidently about its actual scope. The proliferation of different approaches to production in the movement is at the root of this problem: amoeba-like, the variety of practices has spawned a confusion of categories and sub-categories, and even the generic tags attached to the movement have varied. To make progress in our attempt to determine its potential efficacy we must sort out the terminological jumble introduced by practitioners, critics and historians. But first a brief assessment of its scale as part of British theatre as a whole will help to place the terminological issues into perspective.

Some statistics

Statistical analysis of the arts in Britain was not considered a priority until the mid-1980s, when the pressures of neo-Conservative monetarism forced onto the funding agencies the issue of their contribution to the nation's economy. Detailed numerical information for the theatre industry in the 1970s is hard to come by, and this is particularly the case for alternative and community theatre. This situation improves throughout the 1980s, but figures for the alternative movement rarely appear as separate items: usually they have to be deduced from related statistics. Clearly, this reflects the status assigned to the movement, especially by the funding agencies, which are the main source of the relevant information; and, again, this is part of the ideological struggle that any oppositional movement faces.

Perceptions of alternative theatre's magnitude are heavily influenced by the terminology of *scale* which has been applied generally to the different sectors of British theatre. The terms 'small-scale' and 'middle-scale' were developed as the main planks of Arts Council policy for the movement in the late 1970s. The point of comparison was the size of a company's operation as judged by the number of seats in the venues that it typically toured. Obviously the categorisation was useful to the Arts Council and Regional Arts Associations in deciding on the level of funding for each company. But the constant use of the terms to refer also to an assumed *type* of work, e.g. 'small-scale touring', 'middle-scale touring', opened up a gap between the perceived status and the actual size of the movement considered as a *sector* of the British theatre industry, to the disadvantage of alternative theatre companies. Even if small-scale touring was added to middle-scale touring it could not possibly be as significant as the large-scale operation of the repertory and national theatres. Yet if we compare the different sectors of British theatre in terms of their productivity or percentage share of public subsidy, a totally different picture emerges. This statistical picture raises new questions about the relative popularity of the sectors, and has a direct bearing on how alternative theatre might relate to the great traditions of 'people's theatre' and 'popular theatre'.

We must acknowledge, though, that assessment of the scale of alternative theatre is fraught with difficulties. For example, the relative lack of direct statistics is partly a result of problems of definition. Hence, clear boundaries between it and the other sectors of the theatre industry are difficult to draw because so many categories of work have been established. In the 1970s the movement was awash with fluidity and fission. Groups transmuted from one constitution to another with remarkable frequency, often changing names in the process. Breakaway companies were formed out of disagreements, dissatisfaction, and the desire to cover new theatrical or social or political ground. Then towards the end of the decade, and on into the 1980s, a growing number of groups survived by mounting intermittent short-term projects, which might last anywhere between two and fifty-two weeks. Keeping an entirely accurate numerical check on these changes would be like trying to grasp the wind.

A further point is more fundamental to my overall argument: it is by no means always easy to distinguish between groups that were 'alternative' in the sense of being simply theatrically different from mainstream practices, and those that were 'alternative' because they pursued an ideologically oppositional policy. As a result, any statistics for alternative theatre may be useful mainly in showing the relative size of the different sectors of British theatre; but such comparisons should still be helpful to my argument, given that a high proportion of the sector always tended towards subversive ideologies. To generate useful figures we need a working definition of the most common type of company. The following analysis thus primarily focuses on:

> professional production companies of the smaller-scale – say, employing between 4 to 12 people – which toured performances mainly of drama nationally and/or regionally in Britain (excluding Northern Ireland) to adult or mixed audiences, mainly (but not exclusively) to venues which were not dedicated theatre spaces.

For the most part I have excluded the following types of organisation in compiling the figures: theatre-in-education teams, dance companies, performance art groups, children's theatre companies, puppet companies and producing venues. It should be acknowledged that this focus will produce relatively conservative statistics, especially *vis-à-vis* oppositional practices, as some – possibly, at times, many – of the excluded groups were by no means supportive of the status quo.

Even when we define the field so narrowly we are confronted, from the outset, with an accelerating growth. In 1980 Catherine Itzin claimed that:

> In 1968 there were half a dozen 'fringe' theatre groups: by 1978 there were well over a hundred 'alternative' theatre companies, plus another fifty or more young people's theatre companies. In 1968 there were 34 arts centres (with theatre facilities); by 1978 there were over 140, plus a good 200 small scale touring venues . . .
>
> (Itzin 1980a: xiv)

Earlier listings and directories enable us to trace that expansion (see Table 1). The big increase in 1976 reflects the publication of the first directories. All the same, it is clear that the early

Table 1 Alternative theatre growth, 1971–9

1971	1973	1975	1976	1977	1979
32	40	56	133	141	171

Sources: Time Out 1971; Hammond 1973; Chapman 1975; Itzin 1976; Lancaster 1977; Itzin 1979

blossoming of the movement generally followed a rising parabolic curve.

From 1980 the annual appearance of the *British Alternative Theatre Directory*, with a range of sub-sections, allows us to trace the evolution of the movement in some detail (see Table 2).

Table 2 Alternative theatre growth, 1980–90

	1980	1981	1982	1983/4	1984/5	1985/6	1988	1989	1990
Small-scale touring	89	122	163	191	203	220	194	195	187
Middle-scale touring	9	18	24	30	34	37	41	43	49
Community theatre	45	45	46	49	50	46	41	38	36
Totals	143	185	233	270	287	303	276	276	272

Sources: Itzin 1980a–1986; McGillivray 1988–91

By any measure the tables demonstrate an astonishing rate of growth overall, at least up to the mid-1980s. We must recognise that a proportion would not have been operating year-round, but this is compensated to some extent by the fact that the listings are not likely to be complete. We must also recognise that, increasingly, inclusion in the tables may signify 'alternative' only in the theatrical sense. For example, in the first half of the 1980s a small proportion of the middle-scale touring groups had just 'graduated' to occasional performances on the 'main' stages of the repertory theatres; and there had even been transfers into the West End. Nonetheless, the bulk of the ideologically oppositional companies belong to these categories; and community theatre features as a significantly large, and for the most part notably stable, proportion of those.

To flesh out this statistical skeleton it will be useful to make comparisons across the two decades covered by the tables. It happens that the best years for such a comparison are 1975/6 and 1983/4. (The two dates take us neatly from Callaghan's take-over of the Labour government to Thatcher's return to a second term of Tory rule!) The information available for these years enables us to make the most accurate assessments of the relative size of the four main sectors of the industry, namely, the national

drama companies (the National Theatre and the Royal Shakespeare Company), the repertory theatres, the alternative theatres
(together these comprise the subsidised sectors of British theatre),
and the West End theatres.

The most accurate figures relate to levels of grant aid to the
three subsidised sectors (see Table 3). In under ten years, the

Table 3 Sector comparison: subsidy/productions, 1976/7

	Alternative	Repertory	Nationals
No. of companies subsidised	110	60	2
Total subsidy (£)	1,413,086	7,507,124	3,784,773
% total subsidy	11	59	30
No. of productions	318	744	
% total no. of productions	30	70	

Sources: Itzin 1976; Chapman 1975; Cork 1986; Myerscough 1986

alternative theatre movement had grown from almost nothing to
a position of contributing almost a third of the product of
subsidised theatre, for just over a tenth of the total subsidy.
Obviously, the means of production in alternative theatre were
remarkably cost-effective.

Any calculation of the number of performances by alternative
groups in this period is bound to be speculative, for the venue
situation meant that the lengths of runs varied a good deal from
company to company. However, if we assume an average of
twenty performances per show, and three shows per annum per
company (the mid-decade directories indicate this is reasonable),
we can arrive at another useful comparison (Table 4). It would

Table 4 Sector comparison: number of performances, 1975/6

	Alternative	Repertory	Nationals
No. of performances	6,360	15,438	
% of total	29	71	

Source: Cork 1986

appear that alternative theatre may well have been managing to forge a significant audience of its own at this stage. As a cultural force, and possibly as a socio-political irritant to the status quo, the movement may have been on the verge of becoming a significant part of British theatre.

Eight years later, in 1983/4, the *British Alternative Theatre Directory* lists 270 companies in the categories we are using, and of these some 140 were receiving significant Arts Council of Great Britain/Regional Arts Association or local authority funding. This is the figure I have used in calculations for that year (see Table 5). The results are likely to be very conservative.

Table 5 Sector comparison: subsidy/productions, 1983/4

	Alternative	Repertory	Nationals
No. of companies subsidised	140	54	2
Total subsidy (£)	6,731,432	13,942,000	12,409,000
% total subsidy	20.3	42.1	37.4
No. of productions	560	588	
% total no. of productions	48.7	51.2	

Sources: ACGB, *39th Annual Report and Accounts: 1983/84*; Cork 1986; Myerscough 1986

Comparison with Table 3 demonstrates that the alternative theatre movement had almost doubled its share of the subsidy cake by 1984, whereas the slice claimed by the two nationals grew by just under a quarter, while the repertory companies' share shrank by something under a third. Even more astonishing is the fact that the gap between the sectors, in terms of numbers of productions, had almost closed.

Perhaps more surprisingly, the strengthened position of alternative theatre in the national picture is not significantly diminished even when West End productions are taken into account (see Table 6). In these figures the cost-effectiveness of alternative theatre is again underlined by its high percentage share of the total number of performances. Its relatively low percentage share of attendances is a reflection of the smallness of its typical venues. It is significant, though, that alternative theatre is likely to have attracted almost as many customers as the

Table 6 Sector comparison: performances/attendances, 1983/4

	Alternative	Repertory	Nationals	West End
Companies	140	54	2	48
Productions	560	588		169
Performances	18,480	14,750	2,738	15,141
% total performances	36.2	28.9	5.3	29.6
Attendances	1.8m	4.7m	1.9m	9.5m
% total attendances	10.4	26.2	10.5	52.9

Sources: Cork 1986; Myerscough 1986

two national theatres. However, these attendance figures may be especially conservative. John Myerscough reports that:

> The National Association of Arts Centres estimates that 19200 drama and dance performances (attracting an audience of 3.4 million) took place in upwards of 250 arts centres in 1983/84.
> (Myerscough 1986: 95)

Virtually all these estimated performances would have been provided by alternative theatre groups; and if this estimate is accepted then the sector got much closer to equalling the attraction of the repertory theatres. In any case it is plain that from any perspective alternative theatre had by 1983/4 become at least a fourth important force in the British theatre system. From a small group of informally organised companies in the early 1970s it had transformed itself into a significant new sector of the British theatre industry. By any account it had grown to a magnitude that was almost bound to have an effect on the culture of the nation.

Terminology: the generic categories

The rapid growth of alternative theatre was certain to produce confusions in the terminology used to describe it. For example, four main generic terms have been variously used to characterise the new phenomenon: 'experimental', 'underground', 'fringe' and 'alternative'. Despite the many variations, there are enough underlying similarities of usage to make a few generalisations possible.

'Experimental' is used mostly by historians and critics who wish to stress the aesthetics of theatre. These writers also tend to treat theatre as if its different styles can be categorised on a grand continuum or scale, ranging from the traditional to the experimental. The usage also usually implies the existence of *historical continuity* – even if it is a history of modernist disruptions and breaks – as in this extract from a key text on the internationalism of the twentieth-century theatrical avant garde:

> The important thing is that historical antecedents for the contemporary experimental theatre can be found, and it is interesting to see where and to discover that not too much is ever too new.
>
> (Croyden 1974: ix)

This approach also often downplays or ignores the context of performance as a source of its meaning: sign systems, conventions are often assumed to have a solely theatrical genesis. 'Experimental' was a term frequently used in the 1960s to denote the early beginnings of the alternative theatre, before its practices were manifestly allied to the new cultural movements.

The other main term of the late 1960s and early 1970s was 'underground'. In complete contrast to 'experimental', 'underground' was used to signify the counter-cultural origins and ideological affiliations of the new theatre. The term first appeared in the mid-1960s, when it was applied to the oppositional youth sub-cultures of the hippies and earlier 'hip' groups, such as the American beats (Melly 1971: 118). It draws an hubristic analogy between those movements and the French Resistance of the Second World War. A more precise denotation emerged when it was linked to the growing wave of publications generated by youth culture: the underground press (Neville 1971: 120). Robert Hewison confirms this linking of oppositional ideologies and the new newspapers and magazines when he writes, of 1966:

> A new radicalism was in the air: the launching of Britain's first underground newspaper (International Times) marks the point at which the counter-culture acquired a recognisable voice.
>
> (Hewison 1986: 94)

Later in the 1960s the term was extended to apply to the first alternative theatre groups. *Time Out* (initially another underground publication) in 1969 issued a 'Guide to Underground Theatre', reflecting a common usage in the counter-culture itself. The term obviously indicates the culturally combative nature of these early theatre groups, not mainly in relation to theatre or its history, but in relation to the dominant socio-political structure. It also denotes that each group is part of a wider cultural movement, and suggests discontinuity in relation to theatre history. 'Underground' is now used most commonly in theatre criticism as a historical term referring to the early phase (1965–70) in the development of alternative theatre.

In contrast, there has been a continuous historical battle for precedence between 'fringe' and 'alternative'. The length of this conflict – over two decades and still continuing – is indicative of the ideological commitment that writers have invested in the debate. Theatre historians customarily point out that the term 'fringe' derives from the Edinburgh Festival of the mid-1960s, when small theatre groups performed outside or on the 'fringes' of the official Festival. By the early 1970s (partly owing to the success of the Edinburgh fringe) it had supplanted 'underground' as the most favoured term to describe the alternative theatre. However, writers are often careful to stress its lack of precision. In publishing the first 'Potted History of the Fringe' the editors stressed 'its amorphous nature and unconstrained fluidity' (Hammond 1973: 37). A year later, in the first book devoted to the new phenomenon – sub-titled 'Five Years of Experimental and Fringe Theatre' – Peter Ansorge calls it 'that ambiguous realm of "stagecraft" ' (Ansorge 1975: Preface).

Despite – or perhaps because of – its imprecision, 'fringe' became the term most favoured by mainstream theatre historians in the 1970s, who frequently noted that it covers politically radical practices. Hence, it receives the back-handed accolade of a whole page in *The Revels History of Drama in English*, where Hugh Hunt manages a nice balance between the three key terms under discussion, before rising to a quaintly expressed conclusion:

Today the fringe has emerged from the underground to become a valuable alternative to the established theatre . . . while it would be a mistake to overrate the importance of some

of its manifestations, the 'alternative' theatre can play a vital
and demanding role in the maintaining of live theatre . . . and
a young public nourished on the 'telly', 'blue movies', 'pop
stars' and 'pot', will never again return to the formalities and
conventions of Irving's Lyceum.

(Hunt *et al.* 1978: 156)

This is typical of mainstream critics' usage, in that it plays down
the obvious centrist assumptions of the term by stressing how the
'fringe' is a positive extension or expansion of the theatre
industry as a whole. It is a tactic frequently employed in a bid to
assert ideological neutrality, but, as Robert Hewison points out,
'fringe' inevitably 'suggests a marginalisation' (Hewison, 1986:
185). And it has frequently been used – even by critics sympathetic to the movement – in ways which reduce the cultural and
social significance of the work it describes.

It will be obvious, then, why historians who are in ideological
sympathy with the general oppositional thrust of the movement
should prefer the term 'alternative'. Catherine Itzin was in the
historical forefront in this respect when she edited the first
Alternative Theatre Handbook, in 1975–6, and in a suitably
combative tone announced:

the people who do the kinds of 'theatre' work described . . . in
this book, have . . . rejected conventional or mainstream or
establishment theatre in favour of what some would hardly
regard as theatre at all, but which could appropriately be
called 'alternative theatre'.

(Itzin 1976: 1)

She goes on to stress the socio-political relevance of the *movement* as a whole, pointing out that it incorporates a wide range of
approaches, some of them ostensibly apolitical. Other sympathetic writers, such as Clive Barker, were using the word to replace
'fringe' in the mid-1970s, so that by 1979 it was commonly
employed by authors who wished to stress the oppositional
(social, political and aesthetic) and therefore cultural importance
of the sector. Hence, Sandy Craig, echoing Brecht:

Alternative theatre almost alone in the past decade has
identified itself with the tradition of the oppressed which
teaches us that the state of emergency in which we live is not
the exception but the rule.

(Craig 1980: 9)

Possibly the term had its heyday in the first few years of the 1980s. More recently even sympathetic writers have used it in a cautionary manner. Andrew Davies is typical when he notes that 'the tradition of alternative theatre has never been able to overcome certain major drawbacks' (Davies 1987: 208). But this reflects the changing ideological context as much as the imprecise nature of the term. That there is by now a *tradition* of oppositional theatre, however attenuated it may currently appear, seems to me just reason for adopting the term to characterise both the movement and the emerging sector.

Obviously, the ways in which these four terms are used by critics and historians provide a kind of shorthand key to their ideological positions. For instance, on the one hand there is the subtle oppositional insinuation of the Marxist playwright and alternative theatre director Steve Gooch's chapter heading: 'The Fringe – Samizdat of the West' (Gooch 1984: 33). ('Samizdat' was the circulation of unofficial literature in the Soviet Union.) On the other hand, John Elsom provides a fudgy apogee of usage with another chapter heading: 'Fringe Alternatives' (Elsom 1979: 141). In this context perhaps it is not irrelevant to note that Elsom stood for parliament in the 1983 general election – as a liberal.

Terminology: the sub-categories

Alternative theatre has generated a riot of sub-categories in its short history. This, of course, reflects the healthy cultural and theatrical experimentation of the movement. But it has also projected an image of fragmentation, produced confusion about the movement's identity, and made it difficult for historians to locate it in relation to earlier theatre traditions.

This is a point made by John Ashford, the founding theatre editor of *Time Out*, who in the early 1970s developed headings for the magazine's listings column which have influenced subsequent critics a good deal. Ashford identified five types of 'underground' theatre: (a) writer's theatre – in which texts (however produced) were central to the creative process; (b) experimental physical theatre – in which the score developed for the performers' bodies (and often voices) was central; (c) performance groups – 'the theatre end of performance art', in which (usually) non-narrative imagery was the main focus of staging style; (d) political theatre – groups which (usually) toured shows sympathetic to a broad range of left-wing political philosophies; and (e) community theatre – groups which catered 'for a special market' (Sutcliffe 1975: 12).

Peter Ansorge roughly follows these categories in *Disrupting the Spectacle*. Curiously, though, he combines 'community theatre' (Inter-Action) and 'performance groups' (Welfare State) in a single chapter. The subsequent directories add puppets, clowns, dance, mime, theatre-in-education, children's theatre, young people's theatre schemes, youth theatre, small-scale touring, middle-scale touring and producing venues. Sandy Craig's *Dreams and Deconstructions* adds women's/feminist, gay and 'ethnic' theatre to the agenda. Other prominent categories in the alternative theatre discourse (and the texts which discuss them most fully) include: black theatre (a less discriminatory version of 'ethnic') (Owusu 1986), theatre for disability (Johnson 1982), reminiscence theatre (Langley/Kershaw 1982), visual theatre (Goldberg [1979]1988), celebratory theatre (Coult/Kershaw [1983]1990), and community plays (Jellicoe 1987).

The range of the categories reflects the concern of the alternative theatre movement with *all* aspects of performance, reinforcing the case that performance theory is the most appropriate approach for the analysis of practices in the movement. The categories themselves describe different *aspects* of the whole process of performance, so evidently the same companies could be included in more than one category. But confusion then inevitably arises in making analytical comparisons between groups placed in different categories because the focus of attention is (a) steered towards different elements of performance and (b) based upon different assumptions about the relative important of those elements. So, far from clarifying analysis the terminology confuses it. The ideological nature of the discourse is wonderfully obvious – but how can it be rendered less confusing?

The sub-categories fall roughly into four types. First, those describing particular *techniques* or *processes*: puppet, mime and dance companies. 'Writers' theatre' could perhaps be classified with these, though it might be more justifiably grouped with the second type. That is to say, terminology which refers to an aspect

of *style* or *aesthetics*. 'Writers' theatre' would then denote companies using texts as the basis of performance, on a parallel with
performance groups which use visual montage (visual theatre) or
physical score (physical theatre). The third type of category
stresses the kinds of *meanings*, or cultural significance, that
audiences might expect to discover in a group's performance or
constitution: political, women's/feminist, gay and black theatre
are obvious examples. 'Celebratory' theatre is less precise, but
equivalent in intention. Inevitably groups in this category-type
were also concerned about the nature of their audience, and so
the category shades over into the next. Fourthly, there are the
categories which stress the *context*, or the nature of the audience,
for the particular practice: community theatre, theatre for disability, theatre-in-education, young people's theatre, children's
theatre. 'Reminiscence theatre' would probably fall into this
grouping as it is usually performed for elderly audiences, though
the term also obviously refers to a technique. If we bear this
typology in mind when considering individual companies from
different categories, then we may achieve greater clarity of
analysis.

The categories indicate obvious emphases in different
practices, and suggest various ideological orientations within the
movement, and these differences often gave rise to vigorous
debate. In practice, though, the issues of *context* affected the
whole of the movement for most of its history, because venues
had to be established for all categories of work. This meant that
even groups concerned mostly with stylistic innovation – with
techniques – were also experimenting with cultural development. The categories therefore initially represent a proliferation
of related practices, rather than a fragmentation of the movement; though as the movement expanded the diversification of
categories also suggests a certain loss of ideological coherence.
This was a product of both the growing size of the movement and
the ways in which it was responsive to, and influenced by, wider
socio-political history.

There is a fundamental paradox in this development, which I
will explore in detail later. The movement grew into a
significant sector of the British theatre industry in large part
because of its ambition to ensure an ideological impact on
British society. Yet its spectacular growth produced a burgeoning
of approaches that were not necessarily built on the same

ideological foundations. So it may well be that the growth of alternative theatre led to a reduction of its general socio-political efficacy. Perhaps this is the price to be paid by all oppositional *cultural* movements which successfully expand. Maybe this could be called the paradox of cultural expansionism.

The idea of community theatre

In some ways the expansionist project of alternative theatre can be identified most clearly in the practices of companies that defined their audiences in terms of 'community'. It was these companies which most vigorously sought out 'new' audiences and venues beyond the formations and institutions of the counter-cultures. And it is in their practices and policy state-ments that we can read the changing ideological nature of the movement generally. This is because the ideological negotiations that they undertook with their audiences were especially respon-sive to changes in the wider socio-political order. And that was the result of a ubiquitous stress on the *usefulness* of performance to the particular contexts which they chose or were invited to work in. It is for this reason that the later chapters of this book focus on performances which were designed to appeal to specific, defined communities.

I am referring to the self-styled 'community theatre compa-nies'. It should be noted, though, that the category of 'commun-ity theatre' has been used by critics and historians to encompass other groups, especially the women's, gay, black and political groups. However, the point at issue here is not which companies fit the category - that will always be open to debate - but what the category has been understood to mean in relation to the movement. For if, as I have argued, the idea of 'community' is central to understanding how a performance may achieve effi-cacy, the idea of 'community theatre' may be particularly useful in identifying the ways in which the alternative theatre move-ment as a whole sought to ensure an ever widening socio-political effect. This section thus offers a brief survey of the main ways in which community theatre has been characterised in the past fifteen years.

In 1983 a major international conference on 'Theatre and Communities' was held at Dartington College, in Devon. Thea-tre practitioners and academics from all over the world gathered

for a week-long examination of 'the contribution theatre practice
can make to the welfare of the community in which it occurs'
(Conference papers). The range of practices investigated was
astonishingly wide, so it is hardly surprising that the conclusions
offered in the plenary statement are so tentative:

> The theatre practitioners here seem to have in common a
> concern to facilitate a greater sense of relatedness among the
> people with whom they work, whether these people are
> present as audience or as participants.
>
> (Hulton 1985: 264)

In attempting to define what constitutes such 'relatedness', the
statement drew on the work of Victor Turner:

> Whenever people have the sense of being alive and wholly
> present to one another, we have the 'spirit of community' . . .
> Turner called this process . . . 'communitas'. Without 'com-
> munitas' the cycle of daily routines and repeated acts lacks
> authentic energy and people cease to be able to take care of the
> world because it is no longer their world.
>
> (Hulton 1985: 266)

Thus the practices of theatre in the community aim to empower
people through encouraging 'the continuous regeneration of the
spirit of community'. The statement lists twelve types of
approach to this aim by practitioners. But it is notably silent
about what such empowerment might be *for* in practice, or what
kind of 'community' the new inter-relatedness might produce.

The theme of 'new relationships', however, runs through most
of the literature on community theatre. For instance, the first
writer who dealt with the subject in any detail argued that
successful community theatre 'means [the company] identifying
with the people who live in a region, not in any simple audience
building sense, but with what most affects their lives' (Hunt
1975: 14). This was the conclusion that Albert Hunt came to after
studying four representative rural community theatre groups in
1974/5. Such 'identification' may have as its focus the provision
of theatre for people who find mainstream theatre inaccessible
for geographical or cultural reasons, but Hunt argues convincingly that more fundamental social and political purposes will
be found if companies concentrate on 'developing a genuinely
regional theatre based on people's needs' (Hunt 1975: 16). This

analysis projects us to the heart of the ideological nature of a theatre which aims to identify with the community, because performances which hope to address real needs must inevitably engage with questions of the community's values and beliefs. Community theatre grew rapidly throughout the 1970s, but the decade was almost ended before the first sustained analytical attempts were made to wrestle with its methods and their ideological implications. In 1978, 1979 and 1980 a trilogy of articles appeared in the journal *Theatre Quarterly*, each about an individual community theatre company. The articles were not planned as a trilogy – they were by different authors – but together they form a dialogue on the issues and problems facing groups which aimed to make theatre useful to different types of community.

The first one is about Medium Fair Theatre Company, founded in 1973 as the community theatre company for East Devon. In it I argued that the job of community theatre is to create a dialectic between the present state and future possibilities of particular communities, moderated by a knowledge of, and an identification with, those communities (Kershaw 1978). By challenging communities in a sympathetic way about their future, then such theatre may contribute to community development. This is a fairly anarcho-liberal version of empowerment (one that now seems to me to be too vague), which avoids specific identification of the 'enemies' that empowerment is aimed against, though the implication is that *any* agency which undermines self-determination and autonomy at least has to be interrogated about its ideological intentions.

In the second article, which is about TOOT (The Other Oxfordshire Theatre), Julian Hilton argues that community theatre should aim primarily to become an expression of the community for which it works (Hilton 1979). He links theatre with ritual and identifies two main types of event for community theatre: rites of intensification, in which the existing identity of the community is heightened and confirmed; and rites of passage, in which the aim is to produce a more 'mature community' by forging new combinations from community objectives and interests that are already present. The link with ritual signals this as a fairly conservative view of empowerment, so that the theatre company becomes principally an agency helping to fulfil the existing needs of the community.

The third article deals in part with Covent Garden Community Theatre, which was set up specifically to augment the campaign against the redevelopment of the inner-London area around the old market. Tony Howard reports that the aim of this community theatre was 'to be a mouthpiece, dramatising local issues' in the fight for self-determination (Howard 1980). This was a theatre of self-help and direct action against known groups of adversaries, in which the interests of the community were defined in opposition to other interested parties, such as the Greater London Council, the development companies, the planners. Empowerment in this version of community theatre was more a matter of providing extra muscle for the fist-fights of community politics. This approach was aligned with the more overtly radical practices of the explicitly political theatre companies, though the political focus was gained through the identification of the company with the immediate socio-political objectives of the community, rather than with the ideologies of party politics.

Taken together, the articles highlight the ideological delicacy of community theatre work, which issues from the negotiations of identity between the different companies and communities. Whether the aim is for performance to be instrumental in community development, or to be an expression of the community, or to reinforce the community in particular campaigns, the underlying impulse is to enable the satisfaction of community needs through attempts at increased empowerment. However, there is always the potentially dangerous assumption that, whatever the socio-political or cultural needs of the community, the company can in some way increase its power. The patronising implication then is that the community *needs* the company. It is clear, too, that the identification of needs is fraught with difficulties: the satisfaction of some needs, for example, may benefit one part of the comunity to the disadvantage of another – and a theatre company may well be unaware of this danger at the moment the needs are identified.

The central tactic employed by community theatre groups to build an identity with particular communities, while attempting to ensure that (a) they are not misreading the community's needs, and (b) they are actually wanted by the community, is *participation*. Indeed, by the late 1970s participation had become so central to community theatre practices that Naseem Khan, in the first generally available article on what she rather clumsily called 'The Public-going Theatre', claimed that it was *the* defining characteristic of the approach. Khan, though, wisely points out that participation can take two general forms: 'one in which the artist participates more fully in his/her local community; the other in which the community participates more fully in the creation of art' (Craig 1980: 68). Khan thus brings to greater prominence a theme which ran though the earlier trilogy, where distinctions increasingly were being made between theatre which was created *for* communities and theatre which was created *with* communities.

The distinction in part derived from the successful growth of the British community arts movement in the second half of the 1970s, a point which was reinforced and qualified by a 1980 conference on 'The Scope of Community Theatre and Dance'. This gathering brought together all the touring theatre and dance groups in the South West of England in order to explore the links between their practices. As the Conference report put it:

> There is no hard and fast distinction between the community artist and performer, but there is a kind of sliding scale against which different types of relationship with the community can be measured: from the community artist who is resident in a community and who encourages people to pursue artistic activities, to the community performer who visits a number of different communities and communicates with audiences using skills they do not possess.
>
> (South West Arts 1980: 17)

And the transactional nature of that last 'with' is reinforced by the Conference's conclusions on policy-making:

> Feed-back from communities should be developed by discussions with audiences, audience surveys, and through observers in communities advising on company policy. A central question that groups should always bear in mind: should a company alter its policy to fit a community or should it find an audience in the community which is willing to accept its own particular style of work?
>
> (South West Arts 1980: 19)

The stress on the *difference* of the community performer thus underlines how continuous negotiation of an ideological kind is

at the heart of community theatre. It is clear, too, that the chief
site of negotiation is the performance itself, whether it acts, as it
were, as a summation of the other types of negotiation ('feed-
back'), or as the forum for introducing new material into the
company–community relationship.

The point is reinforced as a major conclusion to the first book
on community theatre, Steve Gooch's *All Together Now* (1984).
Gooch sensibly avoids any attempt to define community theatre,
preferring instead to survey its main features. He follows previous texts in stressing the desire for identification between
company and community, and underlines the importance to
success in this respect of what he calls a 'conversation between
equals' (Gooch 1984: 79). This leads him to underscore the
importance of direct contact between performers and audience in
community theatre, and he suggests that the community
performer is more accurately described as playing 'amongst' the
audience, rather than 'to' it. At this point in his theorising Gooch
comes close to Eugenio Barba's idea of theatre as 'barter': a
performative 'exchange as the only possibility of finding
equality' (Barba 1979: 103). There is a clear connection here, too,
to Turner's notion of *communitas*. Gooch also discusses the
tension between the frequent use of historical popular theatre
forms and the (sometimes) radical aims of community theatre
companies, aims which he points out are frequently underlined
by the groups' constitution as collectives.

The ideological nature of the community theatre project (and
thus of alternative theatre as a whole) he sees as rooted in the late
1960s 'alternative society', and this causes it to be fundamentally
different from mainstream theatre in its aesthetic approach:

> Rather than draw the audience *into* a private vision of the
> world which creates its own 'reality' (a kind of totalitarianism
> in itself), the general approach taken by community theatre is
> to take *out* an interpretation of a broader social reality, often
> collectively arrived at, the final test of which occurs on 'the
> floor', that midway zone where the interests of actors and
> audience are addressed equally.
>
> (Gooch 1984: 83)

The metaphor of 'taking out' here refers not just to touring, but
to a style of production which always acknowledges the presence
of the audience, even when direct address is not used, in order to

articulate a 'common predicament'. He characterises that audience in broad terms as the 'non-theatre-going audience', but also makes the distinction between communities of interest and location. Generally it is clear that he has a socio-economically disadvantaged and a politically and culturally disenfranchised constituency in mind. Gooch is concerned to stress that the 'common predicament' in part is created by the history promulgated by the dominant culture, which has 'suppressed' socialist and feminist histories. The re-discovery of these histories in the 1970s contributed to the survival of a sense of a theatrical 'movement' as community and alternative theatre entered its second generation.

However, Gooch's overall assessment of the achievements of the movement by the early 1980s is decidedly pessimistic:

> it was the very 'corporate' nature of the Establishment's ideological control over the nation's cultural resources . . . which forced people to break away and 'do their own thing' in the sixties, and it is the failure of those initiatives to achieve a sufficiently powerful foothold in the cultural fabric of the country which has kept them peripheral.
>
> (Gooch 1984: 33–4)

As I have already noted, the different ways in which this may or may not be true is a central theme of this book. For example, even if alternative theatre has been peripheral to British culture as a whole (a claim I would dispute), it does not follow that community theatre failed to be centrally important to the various constituencies it worked for and with.

However, more recent writings on community (and alternative) theatre have echoed Gooch's point. In 1985 Carol Pinder ventured to discuss 'The Decline of Community Theatre?', and she suggests her title's questionmark is unnecessary (Pinder 1985). Similarly, Andrew Davies surveys a number of key community theatre companies before concluding that 'alternative theatre has produced few good works of its own; and the future looks increasingly bleak' (Davies 1987: 189). Unfortunately, such judgements are almost inevitable when the practices of community theatre are evaluated out of context, using criteria derived from mainstream theatre. The production of theatre for and with specific communities fundamentally modifies its potential functions: it may become a voice for the community or a weapon in a community's ideological armoury, in ways that rarely, if ever, occur in mainstream theatre. Thus the processes discussed above – identification, addressing needs, participation, and so on – may increase the potential efficacy of community theatre by enabling the community to see the usefulness of performance to its interests.

Similar considerations, viewed through the long perspective of European radical theatre traditions, led Bradby and McCormick to claim that:

> The linked concepts of drama as a weapon and drama as the voice of a particular community have had a powerful impact in Europe.
>
> (Bradby/McCormick 1978: 159)

As we have seen, subsequent analyses have unravelled some of the relationships between drama as a weapon and drama as a voice in community theatre. The notion that by identifying with the community a theatre company might in some way enhance the community's identity is surely a prerequisite to the voicing of common or related interests. And if those interests are in any way in conflict – either within the community, or in the community's relationship to society, or in the relationship between community and company – then performance can become a weapon. But whichever way the weapon cuts (and it can be dangerously double-edged), the intention of community theatre is to strengthen the self-determination of the community, to contribute to the empowerment of the community, and through that to augment the ideological survival of the community within – or against – the dominant socio-political order. As a consequence community theatre is particularly subject to contextuality, and this causes it often to develop especially subtle ideological negotiations with its audiences. Within the lengthening history of alternative theatre this was community theatre's particular contribution.

Chapter 3

Carnival, agit prop, celebratory protest

A polythene sheet was unrolled over the whole audience. I
came on stage, called a name, a series of objects was carried up
. . . – a chemistry set, a tree of test tubes, a huge Victorian vase
– as my calling got more frantic the drummer built up a
frenzied, delicate percussive pattern on the collected objects
. . . An audience plant fled shrieking . . . Long and Darling
sold newspapers smeared with strawberry jam.

(Nuttall 1979: 23)

Roland Muldoon . . . is the original socialist comedian. Yet
in his wild appearance, his manic energy, in the twisted,
stumbling, bubbling rush of his street patterns, and in the
daring leaps of an imagination which is both fantastical and
politically rigorously logical, he is in the mainstream of the
Music Hall and northern Variety tradition . . . He is the
Left's court-jester . . . loosening the straps on the puritanical
straight-jacket which the Left is so prone to impose on its
members.

(Craig 1980: 47)

Contradictory seeds?

This is 1965/6, and these are the apparently contradictory seeds
of British alternative theatre. The People Show was purveying its
surreal visions in a public hall in Notting Hill (at that time a
'trendy' part of London); whilst CAST (Cartoon Archetypal
Slogan Theatre) was pursuing political satire in the back rooms
of pubs in Camden Town (a working-class district with a high
proportion of immigrants). Ideologically, the two groups were

chalk and cheese, and stylistically they became the Scylla and Charybdis of many subsequent alternative theatre companies. Yet also they represent the ends of a single spectrum which spans the variety of the later alternative theatre movement, and which unites them despite their differences.

The key characteristics of that spectrum connect alternative theatre to the long historical traditions of popular and people's theatre in Europe and elsewhere, and raise fundamental theoretical issues about the interaction of aesthetics and politics. One strand of relevant debate centres on the idea of carnival and the carnivalesque, the symbolic overthrow of the hierarchic sociopolitical order in a wild frenzy of excessive anti-structural celebration. The People Show can be aligned most obviously with this discursive domain. A second strand focuses on agit prop and the use of satire as a weapon against the powers that be, in an effort to agitate the body politic by injecting unwelcome and disruptive propaganda into its main ideological arteries. CAST, in large part, occupied this particular aesthetic territory.

Some commentators on alternative theatre, such as David Edgar and John Bull, have characterised the difference represented by CAST and the People Show as a split, which throughout the 1970s and much of the 1980s divided the alternative theatre movement to its own disadvantage. Thus the political wing of the movement failed to learn from the imaginative aesthetics of the performance art groups, while the latter was weakened by ignoring the ideological commitment of the former. However, this argument seems to me to be flawed, because British alternative and community theatre is especially interesting for the ways in which it often ignored the traditional critical categories, and made massive innovative efforts to mix celebration and social criticism, to combine carnival and satire. Hence, most of the movement was engaged in the typical counter-cultural thrust of celebratory protest, and as a result it sometimes managed to create new kinds of carnivalesque agit prop.

This chapter investigates the relationships between these ideas and the grand endeavour of alternative theatre to become a major cultural force in Britain. Its central focus is the evolution of performance as cultural intervention between 1960 and 1990. It was alternative theatre's overall drive to intervene in an expanding range of venues and communities that aligned much of its practice with the putative aims of agit prop, even when the formal characteristics of agit prop were not much in evidence. Similarly, alternative theatre's alignment with the various counter-cultures ensured that carnival-like celebration of oppositional values and ideologies was often part of its project in practice.

The aesthetic strategies resulting from combinations of carnival and agit prop were most commonly used by alternative theatre in a continuous effort to resist incorporation into the status quo. However, there was often a dialectical relationship between iconoclasm and conformity, aesthetic freedom and social constraint, which was caused by its expansionist and populist ambitions. The ensuing ideological tensions can be traced in the shifting relationships between rhetorical and authenticating conventions in performance, as much in the action of individual shows as in the stylistic trends of the movement as a whole.

To illustrate this I will next take a closer look at the People Show and CAST, especially at how they were representative of much that was to follow. This will raise interesting issues about the nature of carnival and agit prop. I will also investigate how their differences have led to the construction of an alternative theatre history which distorts its actual evolution. The chapter continues with another version of that history, outlining general trends in the movement's use of conventions in the context of the successive oppositional cultural formations that emerged in British society between 1960 and 1990. My first concern will be to explicate the tensions within, and the apparent contradictions between, the lively variety of practices. Subsequently, the main focus will be upon their underlying unity of purpose as part of the main progressive cultural movements in British society.

The carnival of performance art

Robert Hewison suggests that the People Show was a kind of half-way house between the New York happenings of the early 1960s and the British performance art movement of the 1970s (Hewison 1986: 192). The idea nicely captures the group's seminal role in the evolution of British alternative theatre, as it links together its curious blend of aesthetic iconoclasm and organisational longevity. Jeff Nuttall, who was a kind of founder for the group, describes his colleagues as an 'improbable collection of wayward oddballs' (Nuttall 1979: 46). The People Show

has successfully maintained this characteristic through numer-
ous changes of personnel, the production (by the early 1990s) of
almost 100 shows, and despite the receipt of fairly substantial
Arts Council funding since 1973.

In explaining the group's stature in the alternative theatre
movement historians invariably cite its extraordinary style. For
instance, the Dadaists provide a reference point for John Elsom,
who was impressed by the 'shock running together of unlikely
images' (Elsom 1979: 155). Peter Ansorge stresses the ways in
which the group 're-defined the nature of the theatrical environment' and quotes a curiously inflected example from the Royal
Court's 'Come Together' festival of 'fringe' theatre in 1969.
People Show performers politely invited members of the public
into a nearby telephone booth, 'to see some dirty photos'. Once
inside, 'two sugar lumps were produced coloured with red ink,
or, alternatively, a bra stuffed with baked beans' (Ansorge 1975:
39). The calculated jokey effrontery of this event obviously
depended on the collusion of a willing 'audience', a characteristic
that gained the group a cult following in the second half of the
1960s. From its early shows in the basement of Better Books (in
Tottenham Court Road), to its more developed experiments at
the legendary Drury Lane Arts Lab, the People Show specialised
in improvising absurd imagery and environmental interventions
designed to disrupt the perceptual responses of the audience.
This was the aesthetic, and carnivalesque, equivalent of being
'freaked out' on psychedelic substances.

However, the People Show's anarchic celebration of creativity
through improvisation in performance also expressed a nihilism
which despaired of rational discourse and sometimes appeared to
glamorise the sado-masochistic. In *Bomb Culture* Jeff Nuttall
perceptively pinpoints the tendency:

> Frequently a savagery that began as satire, depicting, say, a
> politician engaged in some fantastic foulness, changed mid-
> way to sadistic participation on the part of the artist, as he
> expressed himself in the mood of the piece. This was always
> happening to Lenny Bruce.
>
> (Ansorge 1975: 53)

This shift in the focus of the action, from the metaphorical to the
real, from distanced satire to participatory excess, was
fundamental to the People Show's aesthetic, and it links the

satirical elements of the group's shows to the carnivalesque. In terms of the theory explored in Chapter 1, such shifts conflate rhetorical and authenticating conventions and confuse the role of the spectator, in an effort to shock audiences into a new kind of 'expanded', liberated consciousness. But often the aesthetic tactic created its own insidious oppressions. The very iconoclasm that represented a radically unfettered creativity was sometimes dangerously reliant on a formalist aesthetic that consisted of a curious reconstruction of an art-for-art's-sake ideology: self-referential, ego-bound, reactionary. This paradoxical dialectic, between an obviously oppositional radicalism and a decisive conservative containment, sometimes enfolded in a single moment of performance, is a characteristic of what might be called the decontextualised carnivalesque, the carnival which has no roots in the developed organisational structures of an oppositional community.

Carnival and contextuality

Despite alternative theatre's obvious affinity with the practice of carnival it was not until the late 1980s that its leading theoreticians developed an interest in the idea of the carnivalesque. This may be because these writers were approaching the issue from the political left, which in Britain has a long tradition of puritanical disdain for even the most moderate pleasures of the body. Nonetheless, in 1990 John McGrath argued that:

> The idea of 'carnival', as expressed by Bakhtin . . . remains very attractive in the twentieth century. His idea of carnival expressing the 'whole' human being . . . obscene as well as divine, is something that has meaning when set against the narrowness of the concept of humanity in mass telly-culture. And it is to this general area of celebratory, public, all-inclusive theatre that we should turn.
>
> (McGrath 1990: 153–4)

And only two years earlier David Edgar had extolled the virtues of carnival in a similar vein:

> it is this capacity to express the opposite in the same plane that is, for me, the most exciting aspect of carnival as Bakhtin defines it. Certainly, that idea is central to the project of

developing a theatre that can explore and inhabit the contradictions of our time without either denying their existence
or pouring detached scorn on all sides from a great height.

(Edgar 1988: 242-3)

It is a curious anomaly that the idea arrived in the public domain
of critical discourse on alternative theatre so long after the
carnivalesque was put into practice by such groups as the People
Show. Part of the reason for this was Edgar's influential reading
of the history of alternative theatre as consisting of two 'wings' –
of performance art and of agit prop; a reading which, as we shall
see, obfuscated the underlying identity conferred on seemingly
disparate theatre groups by their broad affiliation to the successive counter-cultures.

Yet there are notable parallels between the chief characteristics
of the 1960s counter-culture and the nature of carnival. For
instance, Bakhtin writes that:

> Carnival celebrated temporary liberation from the prevailing
> truth of the established order: it marked the suspension of all
> hierarchical rank, privileges, norms and prohibitions.
>
> (Bakhtin 1968: 10)

And the ideological nature of carnival as conceived by Bakhtin is
uncannily reminiscent of Theodore Roszak's counter-cultural
formulations:

> For a short time life came out of its usual, legalised and
> consecrated furrows and entered into the space of utopian
> freedom. The very brevity of this freedom increased its
> fantastical nature and utopian radicalism.
>
> (Bakhtin 1968: 89)

There are still further parallels, some of which are suggested by
John Fiske's useful treatment of Bakhtin's ideas (Fiske 1989). For
instance, carnival undermines the distinction between observer
and participant; it takes place outside existing social and cultural
institutions, occupying real space–time in streets and open
spaces; it is pluralistic, able to absorb contradictory practices
within a single expressive domain; it delights in the body and in
all the pleasures of the body, sexual, gustatory, scopophilic; it is
accessible and it is excessive, enjoying spectacle and grotesque

exaggerations of the norm. Above all, carnival inverts the everyday, workaday world of rules, regulations and laws, challenging
the hierarchies of normality in a counterhegemonic, satirical and
sartorial parody of power. And, like the counter-culture, carnival
appears to be totally anti-structural, opposed to all order,
anarchic and liberating in its wilful refusal of systematic gov-
ernance.

This last characteristic has caused some critics to condemn
carnival for providing a fantasy escape for the oppressed, thus
dissipating the potential for real revolution. For example, Terry
Eagleton has argued that carnival is 'a *licensed* affair in every
sense, a permissible rupture of hegemony, a contained popular
blow-off as disturbing and relatively ineffectual as a revolutionary work of art' (Eagleton 1981: 148). In this version of carnival
the anti-hegemonic upending of norms acts as a safety valve for
the ultimately regulated relief of oppositional pressure. Moreover, the prevailing order is strengthened, for at the end of the
carnivalesque day the revellers return to a living whose rules are
set by the dominant ideologies, with energies dissipated and their
sense of the liberality of the regime re-animated. The temporary
transgression of a hierarchical normality is a strategy for
reinforcing it in the long run.

A number of objections can be raised against this interpretation of carnival. Stallybrass and White, for example, have
argued that 'given the presence of sharpened political antago-
nism, it may often act as a catalyst and site of actual and symbolic
struggle' (Stallybrass/White 1986: 14). And in the first issue of the
radical British news-sheet *Wedge* (which was certainly available
to alternative theatre practitioners) Stamm underlined the function of carnival in continuously restoring the sense of a vital
collectivity which is more than simply symbolically opposed to
'class hierarchy, political manipulation, sexual repression,
dogmatism and paranoia' (Stamm, 1982). Thus, the roots of
carnival are to be found in the self-organisation of the community for the production of its own participatory pleasures, in
opposition to the hegemonic imposition of the pleasures of the
mass media and cultural industries. Inscribed in carnival's
disruptive anarchy is a submerged organisational structure.

This is a point powerfully argued by Victor Turner in his
analysis of the Rio *carnaval*, when he uses Caillois's classifica-
tion of games to underscore the variety of playful forms which

carnival frequently evolves. This variety ensures that carnival raises:

> everything human . . . to a higher power, the cognitive along with the emotional and volitional. For the spontaneity and freedom of *Carnaval* can *only* reach their uninhibited height . . . *if* there has been a full year of organising, plotting, and planning behind the scenes . . . one might regard the samba school [the basic organisational component of *carnaval*] . . . as a school in governance and administration wherein countless blacks learn the skills of politics at the grass-roots level.
>
> (Turner 1986: 130–1)

Such organisations may collude with the powers that be to ensure that carnival is simply a safety valve for dissatisfaction; but equally they may be the locus for a sustained opposition which defends the interests of the oppressed, the dispossessed and the disenfranchised. The organisational sub-strata of carnival can be the source of a resistant empowerment that, for the participants, is spectacularly confirmed by the 'popular blow-off' itself.

Turner's study pinpoints the importance of context to an assessment of the ideological meanings of particular carnivals. In similar vein Tony Bennett describes how the carnivalesque impulses of North of England wakes celebrations in the nineteenth century were first reproduced by capitalist entrepreneurs, then incorporated into the municipal planning, of 'pleasurable Blackpool' (Bennett *et al.* 1986). Bennett also provides a useful reminder that Bakhtin himself celebrated:

> not the carnival tradition as such but the direction in which that tradition was made to point, the specific ways in which its cultural and ideological meaning was inflected, in being articulated to the progressive currents of Renaissance humanism. It was the *fusion* of these two traditions and the new meanings which accrued to the carnivalesque as a consequence . . . that Bakhtin regarded as valuable.
>
> (Bennett *et al.* 1986: 147–8)

Thus, the specific ideological meaning of carnival derives from its contextuality, both at the concrete level of the local community and and at the more generalised level of socio-political history. If the carnivalesque is to contribute effectively to progressive change then it must be organisationally grounded in relation to wider cultural/philosophical movements. I would argue that in fact this happened in the successive counter-cultures in post-war Britain, particularly in their evolution of forms of celebratory protest, in such activities as, for example, anti-war marches, free rock-concerts, the Greenham Common fence decorations, Rock against Racism.

Alternative and community theatre was central to this evolution. From the start it was predicated on the potential power of the carnivalesque as an element of performance. This was most obviously the case for groups such as the People Show, Welfare State, Pip Simmons, and others for whom the breaking of established forms was a golden rule. But what of the more overtly political groups, such as CAST, Red Ladder and the later companies founded by socialist revolutionaries? Was there (more importantly, is there) such a creature as the Marxist carnivalesque?

The political carnivalesque

At first sight the first new political theatre company of the 1960s, CAST, seems more suitably located in the political left tradition of Unity, Theatre Workshop, and the Workers' Theatre Movement, than in the emergent formation of the counter-culture. Certainly this is where critical orthodoxy tends to place it. Sandy Craig, for example, argues that CAST 'owed little to underground experimentation apart from pace, the use of music and a general concentration on image as well as words' (Craig 1980: 32–3). The point seems to be reinforced by the fact that in 1965 the founders of CAST, Roland Muldoon and Claire Burnley, were working with the London Unity Theatre. Here we seem to have a watertight case of ideological *and* cultural continuity.

However, CAST was founded out of a classic dispute between the 'old' and the 'new' left, which arose when they were still members of London Unity. Muldoon describes it thus:

We weren't in the CP, but we were coming round to Marxism. We were young and we were part of an enormous resistance to established politics – CND, Ban-the-Bomb, anti-apartheid,

that sort of thing. We wanted to bring *this* into Unity. We
were expelled for our efforts.

(Itzin 1980b: 11)

The terms of the debate make it clear that this was more than a
dispute about political principles. The Campaign for Nuclear
Disarmament at this point was predominantly supported by
young people, so the argument was as much between generations
as between ideological camps. Moreover, the emergent counter-
culture was a generational phenomenon which overlapped
significantly with CND and other oppositional political movements. Muldoon and Burnley clearly were sympathetic to the
new formation – at least to its more militant aspects – and so the
differences between Unity and CAST were fundamentally
inflected by their cultural context.

The unhappy ejection from Unity had its benefits. Muldoon
and Burnley formed the company, and the company had to
identify new venues and audiences. Its overt ideological alliance
with the left inevitably stimulated a search for a working-class
constituency. CAST's realisation of what that might mean in
concrete terms, though, hints at a significant cultural disloca-
tion, a sense of not seeing the trees for the wood:

sitting in a hired pub-room in Camden Town . . . It slowly
began to dawn on us that the rooms where we held our
exploratory exercises were, on other nights, where our
potential audience sat.

(Itzin 1980b: 12)

The moment is a poignant and seminal one in the history of
alternative theatre. It is poignant because it demonstrates how
the tradition of the Workers' Theatre Movement, Unity touring,
Theatre Workshop, had somehow been lost to this new generation. It is seminal because it eventually led to hundreds of
experiments in taking theatre to, and making theatre with,
specifically identified communities. In this sense CAST was the
prototype political community theatre group.

The early work of CAST prefigured the style of a good deal of
subsequent alternative theatre as well. Roland Muldoon's energetic
and skilled performances were the foundation of the company's
impact. From 1965 and on into the 1970s the group devised a series
of shows which usually featured Muldoon as Muggins. *John D.*

Muggins Is Dead (1965-9), *The Trials of Horatio Muggins* (1967-73), *Muggins Awakening* (1968-72), and others established Muldoon as a clever performer and Muggins as an archetypal put-upon working-class clown, a kind of civilian Schweyk (but stupid) for the 1960s. However, CAST's performative conventions owed little to Brecht directly, and, surprisingly, not much more to the traditions of agit prop promulgated by the Blue Blouse and the Workers' Theatre Movement.

The rhetorical conventions that CAST adopted were clearly aimed at making political material fit for widespread consumption, particularly among the young, for they drew on popular performance traditions and contemporary media styles. Sandy Craig notes that, besides music hall and the Northern variety show, CAST drew heavily on imagery from television, cinema and radio (Craig 1980: 48), while Peter Ansorge describes the CAST style as surreal, anti-naturalistic, comic-strip, 'a kind of *engagé* Goon show' (Ansorge 1975: 57). Muldoon himself called CAST 'the first rock and roll theatre group' (Itzin 1980b: 14). And in line with this he characterised the company's preferred genre as 'agit pop' – a witty conjoining of traditional political and contemporary counter-cultural argot. The overall intention was obviously to escape the notion that ideologically committed theatre was inevitably humourless, to tout the typical counter-cultural message that politics could be fun.

CAST's authenticating conventions were based firmly in a class analysis of post-war Britain. Rejecting the two-dimensional figments of agit prop, Muldoon invented an alter-ego – Muggins – who could be inserted into any social context worthy of radical deconstruction. So Muggins was a totally new type of figure in post-war British theatre: a comic character who seemed to have a life independent of the plays he was in. Muldoon used mostly contemporary cultural reference points to cobble together a subordinate figure of fun who, in Ansorge's neat formulation, was forever 'slipping on ideological banana skins' (Ansorge 1975: 9). Sandy Craig supports this analysis. He sees Muggins as using Muggins to expose 'the left's doubts and weaknesses' (Craig 1980: 48). This aesthetic tactic cast Muldoon in the role of political ironist, carefully distancing himself (and CAST) from the character of Muggins and inserting satire in the gap. The satire poked fun at the ideologically unenlightened working class, but also at the po-faced puritanism of ideologically sound left-wingers, whatever their hue, from the palest of pinks to the most virulent vermilion.

So, whilst CAST approached its material from a Marxist perspective, the shows did not directly present a Marxist analysis in the didactic way that agit prop had. Rather, they projected a harsh satirical vision of British society from the point of view of an under-dog who was satirised along with all the rest. The ironic structure of CAST's performances, and the willingness to mount a critique of all ideological positions, was initially the outcome of what Muldoon engagingly called 'a gang ideology' (Itzin 1980b: 14). This was an angry group, a group bitter about the failure of the traditional left, who had much more in common with Lenny Bruce – whom Muldoon called 'the Shake-speare of entertainment' (CAST 1979: vi) – than with Arnold Wesker, say. And here, then, is the link with carnival; for Bruce was a carnivalesque comic, a performer addicted to the improvisatory release of eros, unafraid to break taboos in public, pursuing his project, as Charles Marowitz has it, 'to the furthest borders of rationalism and wing[ing] across . . . [to] a world no longer confined by logical positivism' (Marowitz et al. 1965: 253). In this sense, Muldoon was a Marxist Lenny Bruce, who used the satirical tool of Muggins to put an anarchically comic gloss on an ideological critique which encompassed both left- and right-wing perspectives. It is this 'Marxist carnivalesque' which most clearly connects CAST to the counter-culture and to other, non-political, alternative companies, including, of course, the People Show.

Agit prop, satire and irony

Agit prop received a particularly bad press from alternative theatre practitioners and critics in the 1980s. Eugène van Erven, for instance, claimed that in the 1970s many radical theatre groups 'dropped their agitprop label in order to pursue more enduring artistic forms' (van Erven 1989: 182). In much the same vein David Edgar has argued that agit prop 'can only present models of the world, and even then (frankly) not very sophisticated ones' (Edgar 1988: 234–5). He suggests elsewhere that this was because:

the form inevitably implied that the author had settled all the major questions of the story before the play had even begun. In that sense, agitprop caricature is a fundamentally elitist device, and its tendency towards a breathless, hectic hyper-energy results, it seems to me, from the awareness that the form denies the writer one of the most potent weapons in the dramatic armoury.

(Edgar 1988: 168)

The weapon he has in mind is *peripeteia*, a change of attitude in a character, or in the audience's attitude to a character.

The didacticism of agit prop may sometimes stem from ideological arrogance, but the accusation of elitism seems odd when applied to a form which was specifically designed to be accessible to the mass of working people. Perhaps, too, there is a simpler explanation for agit prop's ubiquitous speed and energy. Tom Thomas, who was a leading light in the 1930s British Workers' Theatre Movement, argued that:

Agit-Prop . . . has no stage, no curtains, no props . . . It is mobile – it can be taken to the people instead of waiting for them to come to you. And it is a theatre of attack . . . Individual items – songs, sketches, monologues can be improvised, can be shuffled and re-shuffled according to particular local needs.

(Samuel *et al.* 1985: 95)

Ewan MacColl provides an even more direct reason when he talks about finishing a sketch and moving on 'before the police arrived' (Goorney/MacColl 1986: xxiii). Agit prop's simple rhetorical conventions, such as caricature, energetic direct address, choral speaking, as Stourac and McCreery make clear (Stourac/McCreery 1986), are a necessary adaptation to the physical context for which the form was designed: the streets and squares of industrial towns and cities.

Similarly, agit prop's socio-cultural context required auth-enticating conventions that were ideologically unambiguous. This is hardly surprising given its origins in 1920s Russia and Germany, which Bradby and McCormick characterise as a period of:

extreme political conflict in which theatre could still be seen as one of the most effective instruments of propaganda, before it had been superseded by radio, film or television. Agit-prop theatre aimed not at unity, but at sharpening class differences in order to mobilise the working classes in what was presented as a struggle to the death with the bourgeoisie.

(Bradby/McCormick 1978: 21)

The promotion of class solidarity required a theatrical language that was quickly read in the urgency of the political moment, and which was deliberately simple. In this context the relationship between the sign and what it signified had to be unproblematic and transparent. If the form dealt only in answers, rather than questions, as Edgar suggests, then that was because the questions were all too patently inscribed in the situation of its intended audience.

Thus, a sympathetic reading of an agit prop performance derives from an acceptance that, for example, the satirical stereotype (the capitalist boss in top hat and tails) can be taken literally, as an appropriate or fair representation. It follows that agit prop can speak successfully, as it were, only to the converted, i.e. to the oppressed who think themselves oppressed. In a society where class divisions are relatively straightforward – Russia, Germany, Britain in the 1920s and 1930s – such a language may (and often did) make sense. But in Britain in the 1960s and 1970s, in conditions of cultural pluralism produced by political consensus, relative affluence and the ameliorating force of the mass media, the agit prop form becomes problematic. It becomes problematic partly because the chief oppositional formations – the counter-cultures – are not at all programmatic in their ideologies, making any kind of didacticism difficult. And it becomes doubly problematic because in a pluralistic society the 'enemy' to be attacked is not easy to identify.

A further level of difficulty arises because the oppositional formations of the 1960s and 1970s were not content simply to consolidate their identities: the project of the counter-cultures was essentially expansionist, and in alternative theatre this often discouraged the direct attacks favoured by agit prop – in the interests of speaking to the unconverted. In other words, the ideological urgency of opposition, particularly at the interface between counter and mainstream cultures addressed by most political and community theatre, had somehow to be tempered by tact and circumspection. As a result *irony* became important to alternative theatre, for, as Arthur Koestler argues:

Its aim is to defeat the opponent on his own ground by pretending to accept his premises, his values, his methods of reasoning, in order to expose their implicit absurdity. All animals are equal, but some are more equal than others.

(Koestler 1975: 73-4)

Of course, not all alternative theatre performances were ironic. Especially to begin with, the movement produced some shows which were every bit as aggressive, crudely stereotyped and ideologically simplistic as the most embarrassing examples of traditional agit prop. However, such shows were in the minority, and increasingly irony was employed to produce more complex ideological meanings.

Now, the ideological *raison d'être* of 1930s-style agit prop is completely undermined by irony and its attendant ambiguities. An ironic attitude to the sign is ruled out of this particualr theatrical court because irony always raises a query. It places an interpretive question mark against the stereotype, and thus against the idealism that constructs and wills the acceptance of the stereotypical sign as unproblematic. But the conjunction of direct attack and irony, especially in satire, exactly suited the needs of much of alternative theatre. In denigrating agit prop, contemporary critics seem to have overlooked this difference between alternative theatre's adaptations of agit prop and the original from which it derived.

Thus the socio-political conditions in late 1960s and 1970s Britain encouraged a new form of agit prop, one fundamentally inflected by irony. Moreover, the indirect attack of satirical irony was a principal route along which carnivalesque celebration and agit prop protest could meet. For carnival's delight in the excessive and the grotesque, its wild mimicry of the normal in order to reveal its basic absurdity, is at root a satiric impulse. Moreover, delight in absurdity and contradiction, especially in the exposure of contradictions in the dominant ideologies, may encompass a wide spectrum of oppositional stances. As Joel Schechter explains, Brecht's practice sometimes pushed the 'joke of contradiction' into the realm of carnivalesque humour (Schechter 1985: 38-9); while Foucault identifies Artaud alongside Nietzsche and Nerval as champions of the 'sovereign enterprise of unreason', which promises a radical freedom akin to that celebrated by carnival (Sturrock 1979: 97). In the 'society of the spectacle', Brecht and Artaud were combined on the site of celebratory protest in many of the practices of alternative theatre, encompassing approaches as contrasting as those of CAST and the People Show in a new aesthetic.

Carnival agit prop

Sandy Craig identifies the cohesiveness of alternative theatre as rooted in a predominant stylistic structure, which created 'a new relationship between stage and audience, a relation of engagement':

> alternative theatre, whether agit prop or performance art, is cartoon theatre in the sense that its narrative style is imbued with a visual consciousness . . . [which] emphasises action and the breaks, or commentary, between the action . . . This 'deconstructive' theatre is critical but life-enhancing.
>
> (Craig 1980: 28-9)

I would concur with this judgement, but I think it does not go far enough. The most innovative of alternative 'cartoon' theatre, whether of the CAST or People Show varieties, used satiric irony to construct a new genre: we might call it carnival agit prop. The genre was unusual in combining celebration and protest, and they were combined to different degrees according to the needs of the particular context for which a performance was designed. More often than not what was celebrated was an aspect of the audience or its community – ranging from the self-congratulatory cultishness of ardent counter-culturalists (fans of performance art) to the austere resilience of working-class strikers (glad for the distraction of agit prop). The protest, though, was always aimed at manifestations of the status quo, whether in its suppressions of drug-induced ecstasy, say, or in its oppressions of minority social groups. In short, the genre offered a movable aesthetic feast, hugely adaptable to the demands of the new methods of cultural production developed by alternative and community theatre.

We might envisage the genre in terms of a spectrum which stretches from carnival to traditional-style agit prop, from the anarchic celebration of total anti-structure (albeit dependent on an underlying organisation) to the energetic but tightly controlled communication of a clear, unambiguous message. Occasionally, alternative theatre groups worked, as it were, at the extreme ends of the spectrum:

carnival	agit prop
The People Show	CAST
early Welfare State	Red Ladder
John Bull Puncture	North West Spanner
Repair Kit	

More usually, most groups were somewhere in between. This was certainly the case for the community theatre companies, because they tended to be especially sensitive to the context in which they were working, and in Britain most communities, perhaps, are resistant both to outright carnival and to didactic directness!

Now I do not wish to push this schema too far - alternative theatre has been such a vigorous and variable creature that some of its behaviour is bound to beggar description - but the spectrum can be used, maybe, to throw light on the general relationships between context, text and ideology in alternative theatre performance. To begin with ideology - the spectrum can be extended as follows:

carnival	agit prop
implicit	explicit
ideological opposition	ideological opposition

In both cases, as we have seen, the two forms mount a more or less direct attack on the dominant ideologies, the status quo, which of course is why they were attractive to alternative theatre. So long as the forms were used in the context of the counter-cultures - the arts labs, at women's festivals, in centres run by black minority groups - then the full range of their techniques could be drawn on, from environmental staging to crude satiric caricature, in order to attack the opposition and celebrate being oppositional. In this situation all elements of the performance text, both rhetorical and authenticating conventions, were working to the same oppositional end.

However, when the counter-cultures made efforts to expand, and alternative theatre encountered contexts where support for

oppositional ideologies would not be automatic, the two forms
had to be combined in subtle ways. The relationships between
authenticating and rhetorical conventions were central to such
negotiations. For example, in contexts which were unquestionably conservative, oppositional messages had to be implicit:
hence, authenticating conventions might present a reassuring
'possible world' while rhetorical conventions drew on
carnivalesque techniques in order covertly to subvert the 'world'
represented. Or in a more liberal context the rhetorical conventions might promise reassurance – a good night out – while
authenticating conventions used satirical agit prop to question
the more reactionary elements in the context of performance. The
introduction of irony to the ideological transaction produces
even more flexibility in the use of conventions, for the audience
may have to suspend judgement about the exact ideological
purpose of the company, giving more space, as it were, for
negotiation.

Hence, the variable use of carnival and agit prop techniques
enabled alternative and community theatre to inflect theatrical
signs with ideological meanings that could be fine-tuned to the
particular context of performance. Where straightforward celebration of the audience's ideological identity was required,
carnival would be the basis of performance. Where a protest
about the oppressions suffered by the audience's community was
needed, satirical agit prop could be employed. As the two
approaches overlapped at the centre of the spectrum, they could
connect with other genres, such as realist, epic or documentary
theatre. But always performance involved differing balances of
celebration and protest in its efforts to render alternative
ideologies efficacious.

Issues in alternative theatre history

We can identify the emergent alternative theatre of the late 1960s
as a movement through its underlying commitment to a radical
egalitarianism, through its creation of carnival agit prop as a
new genre of performance, and through its widespread adoption
of 'cartoon' stylistics. However, from the very beginning these
commonalities encompassed a wide variety of specific practices.
Thus, not only can the People Show and CAST be taken to

represent the two ends of the aesthetic spectrum, but also the spectrum can be taken to represent most aspects of each company's operation, from their explicit ideological orientations to the details of their creative processes. So, one was politically engaged, the other attempted to transcend politics. One drew on popular performance traditions and the contemporary media for its style, the other aimed to make an entirely new aesthetic using the detritus of contemporary consumerism. One aimed to work as a unified ensemble, the other as a collection of distinct individuals. One went out looking for audiences in non-theatre venues, the other performed in studio spaces and expected the audience to come to it. One was organised as a co-operative, the other as a loose confederation. One aligned itself with existing political institutions (however tenuously), the other remained determinedly disaffiliated. One was concerned to increase the social and artistic accessibility of its performances, the other was happy to mystify through the making of performance out of relatively private codes. And so on. Clearly, the spectrum is very wide and distinctly almost contradictory when its ends are compared. Nevertheless, there was an underlying homogeneity to the forty or so new groups that were founded in the second half of the 1960s.

There have been few attempts at a comprehensive characterisation of alternative theatre's subsequent growth, and those that exist tend to focus more on the internal structure of the movement than on its relationships to the successive counter-cultural formations. This approach has down-played its underlying cohesiveness and highlighted its intrinsic variety, sometimes in terms of different 'camps'. For example, in 1978 David Edgar wrote:

As the 1970s progressed . . . the art groups themselves (like Welfare State, John Bull's Puncture Repair Kit, the People Show and others) developed their own performance circuits and their own devotees. Further, the agitprop groups . . . became progressively distanced from those who saw the business of play-making in a less measurably utilitarian light; and this split was stretched by the perception that . . . a number of radical writers began to see their work done on large, centrally heated stages.

(Edgar 1988: 163–4)

I am not contesting the accuracy of this assessment, so far as it goes. Presumably, Edgar is giving an account of those parts of alternative theatre with which he was most familiar; he does not mention, for instance, the many community theatre groups which occupied aesthetic territory between the performance art and agit prop companies. His assessment, though, has been taken up and elaborated in ways that further confuse the issue. John Bull, for example, writes that:

> The *avant-garde* occupied the territory of the counter-culture intent on by-passing the discourse of orthodox political debate, whilst the agit-prop groups remained essentially a part of activist class struggle, working usually, though not exclusively, under the umbrella of a particular left grouping. However, it would be misleading to suggest that, in practice, the division has been absolute. The relationship has been mutually symbiotic, the *avant-garde* being increasingly infused with a didactic seriousness as the seventies advanced, and the agit-prop groupings readily borrowing techniques from fringe and alternative theatre.
>
> (Bull 1984: 25)

What is misleading here is the claim that the agit prop groups somehow existed *outside* the counter-culture and so were not part of the fringe/alternative theatre. In fact, there was no contradiction, as I hope I have shown in relation to CAST, between membership of the counter-culture and class-based activism. On the contrary, such alliances were the source of new aesthetic forms and new approaches to cultural interventionism.

The interventionist ambition was also a stimulus to aesthetic variety, so that groups occupied increasingly small segments of the spectrum, thus making the movement seem kaleidoscopically confused. Hence, a detailed history of its internal structure, and its evolving trends, has yet to be written. The following chapters, in part, aim to begin the construction of such a history, especially for community theatre. However, it is important to my argument also to attempt a description of the overall evolution of alternative theatre in relation to the emergent counter-cultural formations in Britain between 1965 and 1990. For, of course, that cultural positioning was the source of much of the movement's general potential efficacy for British society as a whole.

An outline history of alternative theatre

We have seen that alternative theatre was engaged in a fundamentally expansionist ideological project, both in its development of an increasingly comprehensive set of ideologies which were variously opposed to the status quo, and in its desire to intervene in an ever-increasing range of social, political and cultural contexts. This growth makes descriptions of alternative theatre history in the context of oppositional cultural formations especially difficult, because it complicated the interaction between the two. In this field there are bound to be exceptions to any generalisations. However, this type of history should suggest how alternative theatre managed to preserve the sense of a movement, even as its approaches to making theatre became more aesthetically various and geographically dispersed. It should also assist the reader in placing the practices discussed later within the wider socio-political history. The following account suggests that changing uses of rhetorical and authenticating conventions reflect the movement's evolving interaction with successive cultural formations, and divides the history of alternative theatre into five main phases, each of some five to six years' duration.

The phases, to a large extent, were cumulative, in that earlier activities were continued in the later periods. The first phase covers the years from 1965 to 1970/1. Its chief characteristic was experimentation with all aspects of performance: it was a period of *initial experimentation*. The second phase covers the years 1970 to 1975/6, when there was a remarkable *proliferation* of approaches. The third phase was mainly one of growth and *consolidation* of already established practices, and corresponds to the period between 1975 and 1980/1. The fourth phase, covering the period from 1980 to 1985/6, saw a widespread *retrenchment and reorientation*. The fifth and final phase, 1985 to 1990, was one of *fragmentation*.

In the first phase (1965–1970/1) alternative theatre is primarily part of a sub-cultural formation and serves some of the functions of previous aesthetic avant gardes. The audiences for the earliest events of the movement tend to be drawn mainly from the youthful 'hippy' and 'flower power' sub-cultures, and the conventions of performance represent an explicit rejection of earlier theatrical traditions. Rhetorical conventions announce the 'alternative' nature of these performances to the wider society; authenticating conventions can be de-coded with total success only by members of the sub-cultures.

In the second phase (1970–1975/6) the sub-cultures have been absorbed into the counter-culture and alternative theatre is beginning to serve a growing variety of audiences drawn from different constituencies in the formation. This is particularly the case as the counter-culture expands in alliance with the nascent emancipatory movements of the 1970s. Audiences include people drawn from these movements, but often shows aim to attract a wider constituency. Hence, a greater variety of approaches emerges from the spectrum of practices. Rhetorical conventions are less concerned to signal the alternative nature of performances, more concerned with the type of audience role that performance aims to construct, and this makes them more accessible to people outside the counter-cultures. Authenticating conventions/signs become less exclusively coded than in the first phase: they are still rooted in the norms and beliefs of the counter-cultures, but as their ideologies have become more widespread their languages are more understandable to the wider population. There is little or no interaction with mainstream theatre.

The third phase (1975–1980/1) inaugurates a period of consolidation in which alternative theatre attempts to make increasing inroads into institutions and social groupings beyond its own cultural formation. Performances are mounted in a broadening variety of venues, and designed to appeal to constituencies of spectator ranging from the highly specialised (e.g. people with particular disabilities) to the broadly generalised (e.g. the 'family audience'). Rhetorical conventions aim to make access to performance as congenial as possible, to reassure the audience that the ideologies inscribed in the event will be non-threatening and user-friendly. Authenticating conventions/signs may sometimes directly challenge the spectators to make oppositional readings, in effect to be self-critical of their own ideological positions; more usually performances will mount an implicit criticism of the audience's position through an attractive celebration of alternative ideologies. There is still a clear distinction between alternative and mainstream theatre, but the margins are beginning to fray.

In the fourth phase (1980–1985/6) the relatively close links between the theatrical movement and the wider cultural formation(s) begin to disintegrate. In effect alternative theatre starts to become a series of specialist practices, each appealing to its own type of audience, each having more or less distinct ideological projects. Rhetorical conventions aim to consolidate the different identities of these contrasting constituencies, reinforcing their particular socio-economic interests. Authenticating conventions move in the same direction, developing a specialist language that is not easily accessible to groups outside the targeted audience. This phase witnesses the transition of alternative theatre from cultural movement to industrial sector, and as a consequence there is increased interaction with mainstream theatre.

In the fifth (and final?) phase (1985–1990/1) the cultural formations which were the basis of alternative theatre as a movement fragment into a series of interest groups, and the process of specialisation begun in the previous period is accelerated. This results in an industrial sector which is most notable for its pluralism, with some companies working for highly specified constituencies and others aiming to appeal to a range of 'markets', simultaneously or in sequence. Rhetorical conventions aim to reassure audiences, so experimentation in this area diminishes. Authenticating conventions follow suit, issuing fewer challenges to audiences, taking fewer risks with ideologically unpalatable material. The demarcation lines between the different theatrical sectors blur and finally begin to disappear; the oppositional thrust of the 'movement' is finally dissipated and dispersed.

Of course the model of a straightforward historical trajectory that informs this analysis is a grand simplification. In fact, alternative theatre in Britain can be characterised more accurately in terms of a changing relative balance between the main approaches sketched out above, than by any absolute shift from one type of general practice to another. For instance, it possessed a proselytising tendency from the start, but this was less marked in the late 1960s than in the late 1970s. And within the movement always there was a broad variety of different ideological groupings, from fundamentalist Marxist to the softest-edged liberalism. This was certainly the case for the community theatre companies, which were often pushing back the contextual borders. The more radical the ideology of these companies, the more pressure there was to evolve subversive strategies of performance that, on the surface, did not appear to promote conflict. It is such complexities which make accurate histories of alternative theatre so elusive.

The myth of '68

The problem of historical misprision arises partly because, as already noted, practitioners in the movement were not in a position to recognise the continuities and breaks between their own and earlier practices. As Steve Gooch points out:

> no real documentation of the Workers' Theatre Movement, of Unity Theatre, Joan Littlewood, Wesker's Centre 42 and other working-class or socialist initiatives existed . . . As a consequence people [in the alternative theatre movement] have had to learn by trial-and-error, making mistakes as they went along, instead of being able to refer to accounts of similar initiatives in previous decades where similar problems had been encountered and similar mistakes made.
>
> (Gooch 1984: 55)

We could also add to Gooch's list the less politically radical experiments of Eleanor Elder's Arts League of Friends and of Mary Kelly's village theatre movement in the 1930s; and in the 1940s the tours of Henzie Browne's Pilgrim Players and those of the Compass Players (Elder 1939; Kelly 1939; Browne/Browne 1945; Deller 1989). There is still much to be done by way of historical reconstruction.

This lack of documentation of earlier movements in part produced what I shall call the 'myth of '68'; that is to say, the idea that the alternative theatre movement was born out of the great social and political upheavals of 1968. Peter Ansorge prominently features this idea:

> It is impossible to deny, for instance, a link between the most publicised events of 1968 and the creation, in practical terms, of the new 'alternative' circuit of arts labs, cellar theatres and environmental venues . . . Unquestionably 1968 was the watershed.
>
> (Ansorge 1975: 56)

And Eugène van Erven concurs:

The generation of theatre practitioners that emerged under the rebellious spirit of '68 is responsible for creating decentralized, antiestablishment theatre for popular audiences throughout the Western world . . . I will focus my study on the decade immediately following the pseudorevolutionary events of 1967 and 1968 for it was then that the current wave of radical popular theatre received its vital impulse.

(van Erven 1989: 1–2)

Given the *événements* of 1968, the tendency to make that year the first one of an epoch is understandable, but lamentable. It is understandable because – especially for those who were there – the possibility of a political revolution growing out of the counter-culture seemed like a real one. It is lamentable because such mythologising often seems directed more towards raising the status of the storyteller than towards any attempt to achieve historical insight. If 1968 was a crucial year, and if you *were* there, then that gives your analysis a weight which makes it more difficult to shift. In short, it sometimes appears that the myth of '68 is part of the formation of a new theatrical and cultural elite.

Sandy Craig is more circumspect about the importance of 1968:

A myopic concentration on one year, 1968, distorts the emergence of alternative theatre by excluding a part of its history: the tradition of oppositional politics which extends from the 'old' new left through CND to the Vietnam solidarity campaign . . . [It also] ignores a number of previous projects which sought to re-define theatre. 1968 was in many respects, lift-off year for alternative theatre but, like all earthquakes, it was preceded by a number of warning tremors.

(Craig 1980: 18)

This seems to be a more fruitful approach to the issue. For surely it is the links to the wider cultural movements and the under-lying *continuity* with previous performance practices which suggest the fuller significance of alternative theatre? If we start our histories in 1968 we fall short of seeing how the movement engaged with the processes of social change – and ideological conflict – that, in Raymond Williams' phrase, form the long revolution of the post-war period in Britain (Williams 1965).

This is particularly the case for the practice of community theatre, which from the outset was on the expansionist cutting edge of alternative theatre. Thus I begin my detailed study of community theatre in the early 1960s, with the work of John Arden and Margaretta D'Arcy. For, whilst Arden and D'Arcy were not a part of the 1960s counter-culture, their community-based projects did have a direct effect on the younger generation which was committed to the new formation. From these early beginnings community theatre engaged with ideological problems of an especially acute kind, as it sought to balance the tightrope between populism and radicalism, incorporation and resistance during the subsequent three decades of British history.

Part II

A history of alternative and community theatre

Experimentation in the 1960s
The community dramas of John Arden and Margaretta D'Arcy

Conflict and contradiction in the 1960s

Conflict and contradiction were central to British cultural history in the 1960s. This is most aptly signalled, perhaps, by the extraordinary sub-cultural clashes between the Mods and Rockers that broke out at seaside resorts on the balmy Bank Holiday weekends of 1965 and 1966. Jeff Nuttall nicely captures the social significance of the running fights in his thumbnail sketch of the two formations:

> 'Mod' meant effeminate, stuck up, emulating the middle classes, aspiring to be competitive, snobbish, phony, 'Rocker' meant hopelessly naive, loutish, scruffy.
>
> (Nuttall 1969: 65)

The cultural bricolage of contrasting images obviously signifies traditional class alliances, but it also suggests major differences in attitude to the increasing affluence of the decade. The Rocker's gleaming bike probably cost more than dad had earned in a whole year in the 1950s. And the fact that the symbol of resistance itself was a celebration of a technology which depended on production-line slavery merely added contradictory spice to the Rocker's macho rejection of the emergent 'new order'. Similarly, the 'effeminacy' of the Mods was a parodic homage to the thrusting masculine world of big business. Sub-cultures, as Dick Hebdige demonstrates with great verve, are characteristically nothing if not contradictory (Hebdige 1979).

The internal contradictions in and between the two sub-cultures (and there are many more than I have indicated) are matched by further tensions with the 'parent' or dominant cultures. The contrast between the wild anarchy of the battles and the traditional image of the safe, peaceful, usually Victorian seaside resort was made much of in the press. The quaintly named 'generation gap' was simply the populist tag for a massive break in the orderly historical progress of the generations, which attracted more serious sociological discussion. The daily televising of scenes from the battles raised old questions about the influence of the media, with the added dimension of the 'breeding and feeding' debate – the presence of the camera creates the news it records. This heralded an early stage of the 'society of the spectacle' and politics as performance (Baxandall 1972).

The 'moral panic' which the TV images provoked in the parent culture, first identified by the sociologist Stan Cohen, was stingingly caught in the comment of one seaside magistrate:

> These long-haired, mentally unstable, petty little hoodlums, these sawdust Caesars, who can only find courage like rats, in hunting in packs.
>
> (Brake 1985: 64)

The obviousness of such distortions – in Michael Brake's odd phrase, the 'deviancy amplification' – is itself a spectacular signal that something more fundamental was at stake than a mildly disrupted weekend. The key to understanding this is Brake's contention that 'subcultures arise as attempts to resolve collectively experienced problems resulting from contradictions in the social structure' (Brake 1985: ix). A brief review of the more fundamental contradictions of the 1960s will begin to throw light on the part that British theatre played in the emergence of the new social order.

Firstly, at the start of the decade Alan Sillitoe had built a major work of fiction – *Saturday Night and Sunday Morning* (1960) – on the contradiction between increasing freedom to consume market goods and the mental and emotional slavery produced by production-line technology. The popularity of the book, and the subsequent film, show that Sillitoe had struck a particularly resounding socio-cultural chord. Secondly, the spread of physical and social mobility created an impression of decline in class differences which was flatly contradicted by even a passing contact with industrial relations. Arthur Marwick describes it in a timely metaphor as:

> the gathering cold war which affected British industrial relations, with a snobbish, often uninformed management entrenched on one side, with an immobile, unambitious, workforce, deeply attached to its long traditions, on the other.
> (Marwick 1982: 163)

Thirdly, the liberalisation of sexual attitudes, the increased availability of drugs (legal and otherwise), the partial domestic emancipation of women, the expansion of educational provision at all levels, and legal reforms such as the abolition of capital punishment (1965), the legalisation of abortion and of homosexuality between 'consenting adults' (1967), even the elimination of the Lord Chamberlain's powers to censor theatre (1968), and more, all contributed to the growth of the freedoms of the so-called 'permissive society'.

Simultaneously, however, an increase in crime, spectacularly underlined by events such as the Great Train Robbery of 1963 and the Moors Murders of 1965, led to greater demands for 'law and order' which made police powers, for the first time, a major issue in the 1966 general election. In addition, the extension of the powers of local government planners resulted in a massive increase in redevelopment and rehousing schemes which gave millions of Britons no voice in decisions about the reshaping of their social environment, and no choice about the kind of community they preferred to live in. In other words, a fundamental contradiction ran through many levels of the social order, between an individualist *laissez-faire* approach to issues of social morality and a highly structured collectivist approach to social organisation.

The nationalisation of culture

This was the central cultural aspect of the 'mixed economy': an uneasy alliance between the capitalist free market and a socialist welfare state. As the decade progressed, the state – in the form of either central or local government – grew to have increased influence in the area of cultural production. In the arts, the 1960s saw the true advent of subsidy as a mechanism for 'protecting' loss-making cultural organisations in the name of 'civic pride' or of 'free expression'. Whatever the rhetoric, the central factor remained an underlying trend towards the 'nationalisation of culture', or at least the culture of the high-art traditions: opera, symphony orchestras, art galleries, theatres. The government's grant to the Arts Council increased from £1.5 million in 1960/1 to £9.3 million in 1970/1 (Pick 1980: 15). Figures for local authority contributions are harder to estimate as arts budgets were usually included in subventions to libraries and museums, or even parks and cemeteries. But the pattern of civic spending can be best illustrated by noting that in the 1950s only one new theatre was built (the Belgrade, Coventry), whereas by 1970 twenty new theatres had been constructed, the majority of which were in the regions and their costs covered largely by local ratepayers (Rowell/Jackson 1984: 89). As the decade developed, this pattern placed radical theatre workers in increasingly difficult ideological straits.

Conditions in the mainstream theatres were not conducive to consistent radicalism, even of a relatively mild kind. As a result a few practitioners – most notably John Arden, Margaretta D'Arcy and Arnold Wesker – chose to experiment in non-traditional settings. Such 'structural' solutions were necessary because the mainstream institutions reinforced some of the central social and political contradictions of the decade. For example, the spread of theatre culture through the growth of the repertory movement contributed mostly to a strengthening of the privilege of the growing middle class: welfare-state democracy was reinforcing national inequalities. Such contradictions were endemic to all areas of the culture. As François Bédarida argues:

> During the 1960s, amid all the euphoria of growth, it began to seem that opulence had it limits and the logic of productivity its dangers . . . in the midst of abundance and state welfare, at least 5 million people, about 10 per cent of the population, lacked the means for a reasonable minimal standard of living . . . In another sphere it soon became evident that technological advance risked causing catastrophic damage to the environment.
>
> (Bédarida 1979: 257)

The first signs of popular resistance to this developing state – the dark limits to the 'cornucopia of capitalism', perhaps, in Bédar-ida's memorable phrase – emerged at the start of the decade in the moral opposition of CND to nuclear arms, in the birth of the New Left, in the resistance through rituals of parts of the youth sub-cultures, and in the theatrical experiments of the first community theatre practitioners. In the 1960s, with growing impetus, British society was a society in revolt, and the decade was increasingly notable for a revival of interest in ideology.

This is especially reflected in the growth of the international counter-culture, which established a major presence in Britain during the second half of the 1960s and set about challenging the status quo in multifarious ways. This challenge was fundamental. For, while sub-cultures may operate mainly at the level of style and have little or no effect on the dominant ideological formations, the counter-culture presented an explicit and generally coherent (though in some respects confused) oppositional ideology. The ideology stimulated a phenomenal blossoming of counter-cultural institutions – festivals, drop-in centres, free schools, communes, and so on – including alternative theatre.

The dominant social order attempted to accommodate and contain the expressive revolution of the counter-culture, as indicated by the phrase which was most widely used to describe its response to the challenge: 'the permissive society'. But the anarchically oppositional thrust of the new movement in all its manifestations often forced the oppressions of the status quo into high relief. Explicit ideological negotiations between extreme cultural positions were increasingly common in the media (Mick Jagger meets the Archbishop of Canterbury!). Thus, in this context the spread of alternative and community theatre is best seen as a new kind of cultural intervention, drawing ideological and stylistic sustenance from the internationalism of the counter-culture. As the decade drew to a close the new theatrical movement became increasingly important to the counter-culture's sense of cohesion and identity in Britain, and it began, too, to make tentative forays into alien territory, to a widening variety of communities. Not all of this work was overtly opposit-ional, of course. However, there can be no doubt that the alternative theatre movement as a whole had its roots in a fundamentally radical response to the hegemony of the Western status quo.

The emergence of alternative theatre

Images of impermanence and instability have frequently been attached, limpet-like, to the alternative theatre movement by mainstream critics. Yet a life-span survey of the groups that were set up in the 1960s reveals a substantial proportion with remarkable powers of survival. The People Show and CAST are still in operation as I write (in 1991), as are Welfare State, Action Space, Orchard Theatre and others founded around 1968. The same can be claimed for alternative venues opened in the late 1960s, including the Oval House (South London), the Combination (Brighton then Deptford), York Arts Centre and the Great Georges Project in Liverpool. Of course, none of these groups and venues continue in the same style in which they started, but they do represent a permanent core to a constellation of practices which has proved exceptionally tenacious, often despite – or because of? – serious opposition.

It is ironic, then, that the venue which has often been credited as the birthplace of alternative theatre was very short-lived. The American expatriate Jim Haynes opened the Drury Lane Arts Lab in 1968, and it has now achieved legendary status as a kind of creative crucible for its times. Something of an explanation for this can be found in Haynes' autobiography, which is lit throughout by an extraordinary open-mindedness:

> You went there [to the Arts Lab] and you didn't know what was going to happen to you or what you were going to do. You might meet someone, have dinner, have a cup of tea, go and see a film, a project. You could go to a concert, or see dancers. In the evening the theatre would go on from 5 or 6 o'clock to 1 or 2 in the morning and at weekends we were open all night long. I would go through the Lab warning that in one hour, thirty minutes, or right now, in the theatre so-and-so was going to perform or something and people would just drop in to see what was going on.
>
> (Haynes 1984: 153)

Haynes generated a remarkable sense of creative freedom in the dilapidated two-storey warehouse. There was an atmosphere which suggested that if an artist wanted to do anything enough, then almost anything was possible. This quality was deeply rooted in the expressiveness of the counter-culture, and this in turn gave the Arts Lab the status of a genuine *cultural* laboratory. It closed down in 1969, but in its brief life iᴄ fostered the founding of a number of influential alternative theatre groups, including Pip Simmons Theatre Company, Stephen Berkoff's London Theatre Group, and David Hare's Portable Theatre. But its more fundamental importance lies in the way it represented the real possibility of art as a socio-political force, by becoming a focus for the ideology of the counter-cultural formation and providing audiences which were exceptionally receptive to the new experimentalism. Thus the Arts Lab was a centre of cultural as well as aesthetic innovation.

By 1968 many of the main approaches on the alternative theatre spectrum had emerged as clear options for the new generation of theatre workers. On the overtly political side, CAST was joined by Albert Hunt's Bradford College of Art Group, by Ewan MacColl's annual Festival of Fools, by Bill Stickers Street Theatre, and by the Northend Troupe. On the carnivalesque side, the People Show was accompanied by the psychedelically inclined Exploding Galaxy, Mark Boyle's Sensual Laboratory, and the John Fox/Mike Westbrook Cosmic Circus. Others occupied the broad middle ground, variously mixing social comment with formalist experiment, as in the secular ceremonies of Welfare State, the vocal explorations of the Roy Hart Theatre, the near-psychotic improvisations of The Switch, or the body-based imagism of the Wherehouse Company. Community theatre ranged from the participatory ethic of Bill Marsden's Contemporary Theatre to the presentational street-populism of Inter-Action's Dogg's Troupe. (Theatre-in-education incorporated this range of approaches as well.) The movement was a rich foment of disparate ingredients, held together (just) by the capacious ideological pot (no pun intended) of the counter-culture.

The whole spectrum was enriched in 1969 and 1970 by the founding of at least a further twenty-nine new groups, all exploring tributaries opened up by the earlier companies. For example, Wherehouse La Mama, Freehold and Triple Action (all 1969), influenced by Grotowski and Chaikin, concentrated on the actors' physical expressivity and the collective devising of texts often based on religious or literary sources. These helped to establish the new studio circuit in arts labs, and in university union and college spaces. Some of the more overtly political groups, like AgitProp Street Players (later re-named Red Ladder), searched for the working classes in factories, pubs and socials; whereas Bruce Birchall's Cambridge-based PSST! (Please Stop Screaming Theatre!) aimed to work with campaign groups. Interplay, an offshoot of the community arts organisation Inter-Action, moved north to work with local communities of location in Leeds, thus initiating the start of a decentralising trend that was to continue throughout the following decade.

The new companies worked across a remarkable range of venues, but all of them outside existing mainstream theatre buildings. The fact that many of these venues were new spaces for performance meant that the rhetorical conventions governing their use could be inscribed with an alternative ideology. The venues were often difficult to find (there was little or no advertising). Differential seat prices were generally considered undesirable, and they were anyway usually impossible. Informality in dress and behaviour were, ironically, *de rigueur*. Hence, these early groups used this restructuring of the gathering and dispersal phases of performance, and the consequent blurring of the audience's horizon of expectation, to explore a hitherto inaccessible range of authenticating conventions that usually represented counter-cultural values.

The challenge to dominant methods of production led most of these groups to attempt to create anti-hierarchical and egalitarian working methods. At worst this led to the 'everyone must do everything' syndrome, in which the anti-structural tendencies of the counter-culture produced theatrical waste and inefficiency. But many groups still had 'directors' (though more often than not they adopted the role of reluctant leaders in public). More importantly, the relationship of such leaders to performers, technicians and administrators was determined more by ideological than by organisational imperatives. So the desire to develop collective and collaborative procedures was almost ubiquitous, and this was an index of the general commitment to counter-cultural ideas of participatory democracy.

This tendency raised the question of authorship to a high profile. Where written texts were used they were frequently the outcome of group work in rehearsal: whether focused on adaptation from existing material, or starting from scratch, collective devising was the preferred approach. The playwright, like the director, became a member of a team with equal responsibilities for the show's significance. And this was the organisational correlative of the de-centring of the written text as the chief source of communicative signs in production. Most critics from the mainstream read this as an abandonment of the word, as a retreat from the precision of verbal language into a vaguer physicality, and this is usually assigned to the influence of Artaud on the British experimentalists following Peter Brook's 'Theatre of Cruelty' season at the RSC in 1964, and by the visits to London of the Living Theatre, the Open Theatre, and the Bread and Puppet Theatre. However, this evolving aesthetic, and Artaud's contribution to it, are more fruitfully seen as promoting a notion of performance as text in which all codes are of potentially equal value. Many of the alternative theatre groups formed in this period were practising post-modernists in this sense, well before the dubious dawn of post-modernism proper.

By 1970 the key ideological, organisational and aesthetic features of the alternative and community theatre movement were relatively easy to detect. Whether organised for touring or resident projects, the groups worked outside the existing theatre system in venues where their counter-cultural messages would be welcomed. Relationships between performers and audiences, and between companies and communities, were characterised by a new directness. This aimed to both de-mystify the art form, especially to strip it of the mystique of professionalism, and to promote greater equality between the stage and the auditorium. (Even aggressive attacks on the audience can be read as a challenge to them to be as 'tough' as the performers.) Hence, audience and community participation became central to alternative theatre aesthetics, and it was encouraged in a wide variety of ways: for example, in the form of adaptations of interactive techniques drawn from popular historical genres such as pantomime and music hall; through techniques derived from the popular media of comic-strips, film animation, cinema and television which encouraged more active approaches to the reading of performance; through the adaptation of environmental forms such as fun-fairs and festivals to produce the sensory, wrap-around effects of psychedelic spectacles; through the physical participation of the audience in the action of the show, reminiscent of the techniques of 'primitive' rituals, psychodrama, and the new practices of educational drama.

All these approaches to participation were ultimately designed to enhance the status of the spectator, to place her in a more ideologically efficacious position *vis-à-vis* the show, project and company – in short, to empower her. These were the theatrical means for reproducing self-determination (which sometimes tipped over into self-indulgence), egalitarianism (which sometimes produced a holier-than-thou hierarchy), and participatory democracy (which was sometimes a cover for despotism). In this sense, then, the rhetorical conventions of performance were as important as the authenticating conventions in reinforcing and developing the ideologies of the counter-culture.

Such cultural expansionism was inevitably doomed to carry a load of hubris and failed endeavour. Hence, the effects of particular performances could be as uncomfortable as the venues which housed them. Perhaps the most common shortcoming was an obscurity produced by incoherent codes, though the general desire to produce something new and distinctive led to other types of excess. John Pick's accusation that the new movement mostly manifested 'youthful self-indulgence' can, to an extent, be upheld against individual companies at all points on the spectrum of practices (Pick 1989: 60). Unfortunately Pick fails to acknowledge that such excesses were the result of a new cultural zeal, a growing effort to construct alternative theatrical languages which would reinforce and extend the emergent counter-cultural formation. In fact, the excesses could be (and were) read as authenticating the formation through a deliberate celebration of wayward experimental extravagance, a mischievous generational poke at the po-faced propriety of mainstream theatre in particular, and 'straight' society in general.

By the start of the 1970s the scale and the extraordinary variety of alternative theatre had inched it onto the bottom of the national cultural agenda, so that even the first full-scale enquiry into British Theatre (commissioned by the Arts Council) could not afford to ignore it:

> Recently, a quite extraordinary proliferation of 'multi-media' groups has also occurred . . . Of the utmost variety and type, their appeal is mainly to one sector of the young: they express a very genuine dedication to their ideas, and, incidentally, a general distrust of the establishment. We believe . . . that it

would be desirable for more of this kind of work to be seen in the Provinces [*sic*] and not confined to London.

(Arts Council of Great Britain 1970: 61)

Such nice lines in urbane and centrist irony were bolstered by negligible financial commitments: at this point the Arts Council was contributing less than £60,000 per annum to alternative theatre (compared with £600,000 to the National Theatre and Royal Shakespeare Company). Yet despite the predictable response of the 'establishment', alternative theatre was flourishing as the new decade began.

Early community theatre

Given the burgeoning of the new movement, it is surprising to reflect that prior to 1965 the number of significant theatre projects outside the mainstream could be counted on one hand. One of the earliest was established by Peter Cheeseman at the Victoria Theatre in Stoke-on-Trent. In 1962, at the invitation of the local council, he converted an old cinema into a 347-seat theatre-in-the-round, and initiated a community-based policy which continues to this day. The central strand of the Victoria's work for the locality has been provided by the famous 'Stoke documentaries'. Based on local history, the theatre has produced almost one a year since 1964, making it 'one of the few reps in the country genuinely to have earned the title "community theatre" ' (Rowell/Jackson 1984: 157). Cheeseman's ideological orientation is no more than mildly radical, but his achievement at Stoke – on the fringes of the mainstream – shows how much local commitment has been lost to the rest of the repertory movement in the last three decades.

A much more serious historical disjunction flowed in the wake of another early 1960s project in cultural experimentation. Initially, Arnold Wesker's Centre 42 promised a new and major partnership between the arts and the trade union movement in Britain. To start with, the organisation took its name from a resolution (Number 42) passed at the annual Trades Union Congress in 1960:

Congress recognises the importance of the arts in the life of the community especially when many Unions are securing a shorter working week and greater leisure for their members.

(Itzin 1980b: 102)

Centre 42 was initially conceived as a producing company set up to promote a 'cultural revolution' (Wesker 1970). But its first initiative, in 1961 and 1962, was to mount a series of festivals in regional towns and cities, which combined poetry readings, folk music, art exhibitions, and theatre. Whilst the idea of a festival series was new, the only genuine cultural innovation was Charles Parker's multi-media documentaries, *The Maker and the Tool*. These were participatory productions about the main industry of each city, put together with the co-operation of the unions in those industries. The rest of the programme for the festivals, in the main, consisted of existing material, much of it emanating from London. Wesker and Centre 42 were accused of cultural imperialism, trying to force middle-class art on the masses, by both left- and right-wing critics. The attacks turned out to be fatal. The unions withdrew their support and, despite having such luminaries as Harold Wilson and Lord Goodman for friends, the organisation floundered (Coppetiers 1975). On the positive side, its legacy perhaps includes the successful 1970s British arts centre movement. On the negative side, its failure justified continued union indifference to cultural issues, a state of affairs that was only marginally eroded by the efforts of political alternative theatre groups in the 1970s and 1980s.

The third main cultural experiment of the early 1960s had a much lower public profile than Centre 42, even though it was mounted by a mainstream playwright who was nearly as well-known as Wesker. John Arden, together with his partner Margaretta D'Arcy, appears to have initiated the experiment almost by accident, and it differed from Centre 42 in other significant ways. It was local, non-professional, small-scale, low-cost, and took great care *not* to proclaim its acute radicalism. Its first manifestation was a nativity play in a tiny village in Somerset. It subsequently reappeared as a kind of counter-Centre 42 festival in a Yorkshire village, then as a play for children in Devon, before reaching its 1960s apotheosis in London, in one of the most extraordinary events of early counter-cultural and alternative/community theatre history.

The first community dramas

In 1963, well before the advent of the late 1960s international counter-culture, an eccentric advertisement appeared in the British theatre magazine *Encore*:

> John Arden has conceived the idea of establishing a free Public Entertainment in his house . . . No specific form of entertainment is envisaged but it is hoped that in the course of it the forces of Anarchy, Excitement and Expressive Energy latent in the most apparently sad person shall be given release.
> (Gray 1982: 23)

At the time John Arden and Margaretta D'Arcy were living in the village of Kirkbymoorside in Yorkshire. The curious strategy of advertising a local and rural event in a national avant garde theatre journal is nicely matched by the notion of public anarchy in a domestic setting. In the advertisement Arden mentions Arnold Wesker, drawing attention to the implicit contrast between the dotty idea of the home-spun entertainment and the grandiose plans of Centre 42. From the outset a tone of ironic good humour was set for the event itself.

Three years later, in 1966, Arden acknowledged that:

> The Kirkbymoorside venture *was* directly derived from Arnold Wesker's ideas – indeed in my advertisement in *Encore* . . . I acknowledged this. Perhaps it was rather facetious acknowledgement, but then the whole ad was facetious.
> (Trussler *et al.* 1967: 56)

Despite the facetiousness, Arden's up-front urbanity has a double function. Firstly, it signals a serious purpose: why else should he stick his neck out by advertising in a national magazine? Secondly, it warns against solemnity and pretentiousness. So if the aims of the experiment appeared faintly ludicrous, then at least its aesthetic would be good fun. This prototype community arts project, working well outside the traditional arts establishment, would be more like a party than a professional presentation. Kirkbymoorside was to have its own innovative slice of carnival cake.

This kind of tongue-in-cheek naivety, a straightforward type of

sophistication, had caused Arden problems in his earlier work for
mainstream theatres, particularly at the Royal Court. Audiences
were perplexed by the 'Brechtian' *Serjeant Musgrave's Dance* and
by the use of commedia dell'arte to investigate the social issue of
ageing in *The Happy Haven*. On the surface, the puzzled
reception was the result of Arden's unusual style, or rather, styles.
In the seminal article 'Telling a true tale' (1960; in Marowitz *et al.*
1965) he describes how his work derives from the British ballad
tradition and writers closely linked to it, such as Chaucer,
Skelton, Shakespeare, Dickens, Hardy, Joyce. Influences from
this Leavisite 'great tradition' are then married to techniques
drawn from 'low' popular performance traditions, such as
melodrama, pantomime, circus, music hall. The purpose of the
wedding is entirely serious: 'It seems to me that this tradition is
one that will always in the end reach the hearts of the people'
Arden claimed (Marowitz *et al.* 1965: 126). He obviously had
extensive populist ambitions. In addition, he often maintained
that the ultimate aim of his work was an ideological one: to
create 'social criticism'.

Arden's ideological standpoint in this period has been the
subject of a good deal of critical debate. Critics in the literary
tradition, such as John Russell Taylor, Ronald Hayman and J.
W. Lambert, generally have argued that Arden's 'critical detach-
ment' from his characters produces an amoral outcome in which
one political perspective is as valid as the next (Taylor 1978;
Hayman 1979). By way of acute contrast, Albert Hunt has
written:

> John Arden's political position has always, it seems to me,
> been completely clear. He is a revolutionary who instinctively
> and intellectually rejects authority.
>
> (Hunt 1974: 21)

The issue is significant for the way that the different critical
positions incorporate contrasting ideological attitudes to theatre
as cultural production. The dominant critical treatment of
Arden's work relies heavily on the tired old idea that art and
politics do not happily mix. For critics such as Russell Taylor
and Hayman, once the ideological message appears clear the
'poetry' automatically disappears. Arden, of course, took the
opposite view.

Arden's own assessment of his ideological position in this period, particularly in respect of his work outside the mainstream, was characteristically lucid:

> Any sort of community drama can present only work on a modest scale . . . for anything larger I have had to make use of the professional theatre with all its remoteness, its irrelevance, and its inability to attract a 'popular' audience. This is not a satisfactory situation, but it can't be cured by literature. Arnold Wesker has tried, Joan Littlewood is trying . . . Until the political problem is solved, I doubt if we shall make much progress with the artistic one. Who's for a revolution?
>
> (Trussler *et al.* 1967: 57)

For Arden, community-based drama is not simply an aesthetic alternative; it is a method for mounting an ideological project which is in clear opposition to the status quo.

In 1967 Arden acknowledged that Margaretta D'Arcy had taken the lead in his move towards community-based experiments. But it is also clear that Arden's own ideological outlook makes such a move perfectly logical, and that he was completely aware of the pragmatic limits of such projects. D'Arcy and Arden's early explorations of community theatre were 'modest' in the sense of being very localised and of having clearly limited political ambitions. However, in forging a new approach to performance as cultural production these projects had extensive implications for later practices, especially for the ways in which they might exploit new relationships between texts and contexts. This was achieved through the incorporation of two major qualities in their approach to the community. Firstly, whilst obviously having a clear ideological position themselves, Arden and D'Arcy always maintained a non-dogmatic political openness rooted in creative originality. To put this gnomically: they avoided propaganda, but they were not afraid of agitation, particularly when accompanied by a sense of anarchy and the carnivalesque. Secondly, they demonstrated an extraordinary commitment to the interests of local communities and to the potential creativity of the people in them.

My analysis of their achievement will concentrate on three projects which spanned the 1960s. The first was mounted in the village of Brent Knoll in Somerset, in 1960. *The Business of*

Good Government was probably the first ever attempt to make a
radical nativity play. The second was the domestic festival in
the small Yorkshire town of Kirkbymoorside in 1963. Arden's
playwriting contribution to the festival was *Ars Longa, Vita
Brevis*, a remarkable squib of a play. The third was an agit prop
piece, *Harold Muggins Is a Martyr*, staged in conjunction with
CAST at the London Unity Theatre in 1968. Four years later,
following a famous dispute with the Royal Shakespeare Company, Arden and D'Arcy announced that they had 'gone on
strike' against mainstream theatre in favour of alternatives. All
their subsequent projects have consistently pioneered radical
approaches to ways of working in, with and on behalf of
particular communities.

Most theatrical critics and historians have ignored the 1960s
projects (and many of the subsequent ones). They have promoted an orthodoxy which sees them as detracting from the
more important task of writing for mainstream theatre. For
instance, John Russell Taylor thought that Arden's growing
commitment to community-based drama and theatre was 'dis-
appointing to those who eagerly await his long delayed
breakthrough to wider acceptance in the everyday professional
theatre' (Taylor 1978: 104). The weight of that 'everyday' betrays
an astonishing cultural presumption. The dominant critical
orthodoxy is sometimes inflected with the nastily sexist and
racist suggestion that Arden was a weak man seduced and led
astray by the wild Irish woman. This is nonsense, for their
collaboration was clearly a matter of mutual interest; and the
benefit of this to the history of community and alternative
theatre is inescapable.

However, even historians of alternative theatre have usually
overlooked the importance of Arden and D'Arcy's community
dramas. For instance, Andrew Davies' *Other Theatres* (1987)
makes no mention of them at all. Only Albert Hunt, Frances
Gray and Simon Trussler have paid the projects anything like
the attention they deserve. These critics recognised that Arden
and D'Arcy were the first post-war professional theatre workers
of national standing to devise new approaches to locally based
community drama. More importantly, they have consistently
explored the promotion of radical ideologies in more or less
conservative cultural contexts. In the 1960s, virtually single-
handedly, they invented prototypes which later became the

common currency of the extensive community drama and arts movements of the 1970s and 1980s.

British society in the early 1960s

In the general election of 1959 the Conservative Party was returned to power for a second term of office, with Harold Macmillan – 'Super-Mac' as he was called by the media – as Prime Minister. But the new government soon ran into serious trouble. Poor economic planning produced a large balance of payments deficit and, despite the imposition of severe credit restrictions and inept attempts to control pay rises through wage freezes, the Tories were forced to adopt a policy of deflation. As unemployment rose to 800,000 by 1963, the only sensible way to end the so-called stop–go approach to the economy would have been to reduce military spending abroad.

The government had hoped to achieve this by increased reliance on independent nuclear weapons. But by 1960 plans to produce a British rocket – Blue Streak – were abandoned because of escalating costs, and in 1962 the Americans scrapped Skybolt, the air-to-ground missile that Britain had negotiated to buy as a replacement. The only alternative available was the American Polaris, so Macmillan struck a deal in which British warheads would be fitted to US missiles in newly built British nuclear submarines. But the political strings attached to the deal meant, in effect, that British nuclear policy was controlled by the Americans. In the wake of the Cuban missile crisis of 1962 – when President Kennedy ordered a blockade of Cuba to prevent Russia from building nuclear silos on the island, and the world teetered on the brink of nuclear catastrophe – it was hardly likely that the US would have settled for anything less. As the temperature of the Cold War steadily fell, Super-Mac lost some of his sheen.

Events on the domestic front had not helped the Tory image. The Liberals made significant gains in the popularity polls between 1959 and 1962, mainly as a result of the government's mismanagement of the economy and foreign policy, but also because Labour was divided over the issue of nuclear disarmament. The Campaign for Nuclear Disarmament was flourishing, with the Aldermaston to London marches increasing in size each year, while the emergence of the New Left signalled a shift from

Marxist economic determinism to a concern for a more humane, less 'alienated' social order among the new generation of educated radicals. The second half of the 1950s had witnessed a marked increase in general affluence, but this had not been matched by progress towards a fairer, less divisive society. Thus in the early 1960s, as François Bédarida argues, 'two value systems were confronting each other' (Bédarida 1979: 250). On the one hand, there was the traditional world of old class conventions, where everybody knew their place in a stable hierarchy of behaviour governed by a universally accepted morality: the tail end of Victorianism, as it were. One the other hand, there were the new imperatives of the capitalist 'affluent society', in which individualism blossomed, the post-war consensus collapsed, and voices rose in clamorous complaint against inequality, injustice and the pursuit of self-interest.

Two national scandals fuelled the conflicts and contradictions. In 1963 the Minister for War, John Profumo, lied to the House of Commons about his liaison with Christine Keeler, thus initiating an inquiry that uncovered a network shot through with 'a salacious mixture of sex and security' (Sked/Cook 1984: 185). This led to revelations about the activities of Peter Rachman, a slum landlord who unscrupulously exploited tenants living on or below the poverty line. 'Rachmanism', it became clear, was rife in the land. The Opposition, under the new leadership of Harold Wilson, made much of the contradictions. In Sked and Cook's words:

> it seemed as if the top of British society was wallowing in decadence while the poor were left to the mercy of assorted bullies and thugs.
>
> (Sked/Cook 1984: 187)

Macmillan's famous 1959 electioneering claim to the nation that it had 'never had it so good' rang increasingly hollow. The new prosperity produced by fourteen years of Tory rule was itself fuelling the flames of revolt. Young cultural activists, such as Arden, D'Arcy and Wesker, were inevitably drawn into the fray, even as they took up retreat in remote rural corners of old England.

Politics in church

The origin of Arden and D'Arcy's first experiment in radical community drama was quietly bizarre – in a typically English way. A casual conversation between Arden, D'Arcy and the vicar of Brent Knoll village resulted in the latter suggesting that they might care to make a play for the church. The conversation was so amicable that the project was taken up as a 'mutual idea'. The outcome was *The Business of Good Government,* a one-act version of the nativity story which was performed by the villagers in the church as part of the 1960 Christmas festivities. Hence, the meeting with the vicar was the first stage in an active, dialectical dealing with cultural (and thus socio-political) contradictions. Two professionals with experience in the leading avant garde theatres of Britain work in an obscure village church with amateur performers. A revolutionary playwright chooses to write within a (mostly) reactionary religious tradition. A couple of outsiders to the village become centrally engaged in an ideological re-focusing of the community's need for a Christmas celebration.

Arden and D'Arcy were living in Brent Knoll while Arden held a playwriting fellowship at Bristol University. The village nestles on the west side of the 300-foot high conical Knoll, which is a major landmark of the north Somerset flats. The church is partway up the slope, forming a classic architectural focus for the community. The Exeter–Bristol mainline railway runs nearby to the north and the A38 trunkroad just to the south, but in the early 1960s Brent Knoll was still a relatively isolated place. Agriculture on the surrounding flatlands and roadside services provided the main local employment, though some villagers commuted to Taunton, Bridgewater and Weston-super-Mare. Topography and economics fostered a community cohesiveness, in which moderate prosperity was the foundation for considerate conservatism.

As obvious outsiders, Arden and D'Arcy tactfully based their whole approach to the project of a village play on an ethic of responsiveness and accessibility. Hence, they were careful to include all the usual events of the nativity in the play – the visit to Herod of the three Wise Men, the Shepherds in the fields, the visit of the Angel, the arrival of Mary and Joseph at the Inn, the Nativity itself, and so on. The accessibility of the story was complemented by the production style, which operated on two levels simultaneously. Firstly, the celebratory nature of the whole event was emphasised through rhetorical conventions drawn from church ceremony. The play opens with a procession of the characters through the audience to the altar area. Throughout the show the Angel speaks from the church pulpit. The processional is repeated when the Shepherds and the three Wise Men approach the child Jesus. The performance concludes with the singing of the Corpus Christi carol and a final procession of the characters out of the church.

Secondly, Arden was keen that the production should avoid the slavish imitation of professional theatre that plagues most amateur performances. This was clearly part of the effort to forestall inauthenticity. In the process of finding appropriate conventions the key term became 'improvisation'.

> there are no fixed rules governing such improvisations and variations – Bertolt Brecht has said 'If it works, it works.' – the one essential condition is that the meaning of the play should never be obscured. The rest is a matter of taste and of adaptation to local circumstances.
>
> (Arden 1963: 5)

Hence the production's authenticating conventions were designed to encourage the audience to read the significance of the text without distraction. The style of writing combines mummers-play plainness, straightforward speech for local non-professional voices, with Brechtian scenic economy. The combination creates a feel of down-to-earth formality, and the 'ordinary' language spoken by mythical characters puts the action of the old story into a fresh perspective.

For any theatre to work in this type of context it has to forge most of its conventions from existing materials. So we find Arden and D'Arcy adapting to the circumstances of the community: to the physical shape of the fifteenth-century church, to the need to collage rather than design costumes, to a non-professional system of casting, to the 'naturalness' of the inexperienced actors. The basic genre is the familiar one of religious allegory, the list of characters is wholly in keeping with what the audience might expect, even the writing allows for the kind of declamatory direct address that is typical of the non-professional nativity style. All the theatrical signs are clearly intended to make the authenticating significance easily accessible. The central question then is: do these adaptations lead to a compromise of Arden and D'Arcy's radical ideological position?

Simon Trussler suggests that they did when he claims: 'the [community drama] experiments were designed rather to develop a disappearing sense of community than to put across a particular message' (Trussler 1969: 182). But this is greatly to simplify the subtle uses of the context of performance achieved by the production. Frances Gray is probably nearer the truth when she argues that the use of action derived from religious services, in, for instance, the opening procession, gave the audience:

> a sensation of being participants rather than observers; they join in an act of celebration and of worship. But the close, informal contact between actors and audience also makes it possible for them to be confronted by the action and made to question it.
>
> (Gray 1982: 37–8)

Albert Hunt concurs with this last point when he comments on the central actions of the play that: 'They show us *why* Herod acted as he did – but leave us to judge the actions' (Hunt 1974: 114). But how do Arden and D'Arcy attempt to ensure that the authenticating conventions of the show are efficacious in this critical sense? That is to say, that the questioning is radical and the judgement sound?

In his Preface to the published text Arden recommends that future productions should follow his lead in abandoning all the current trappings of the professional theatre – proscenium, hidden lighting, make-up, etc. – in favour of a 'realist' style. His intention is obviously to avoid disguising the reality of the performance context, *pace* Brecht. In the context of Brent Knoll church this effect would encourage an awareness of the *actual* community networks formed by the relationships between the performers and their friends and relatives in the audience. The technique aims to produce a sense of community, with its underlying ideology, and through that the audience is *implicated* in the action of the play. That is to say, the community is watching a part of itself enact the well-known story, so on the 'real' level of rhetorical conventions (as Frances Gray suggests) they are encouraged to identify with and support the potential meanings it constructs.

But Arden and D'Arcy do not simply provide Brent Knoll with

a localised version of the Christmas story, for they place as much emphasis on the politics surrounding the nativity as on the nativity itself. They use two framing devices to achieve this effect: firstly, they make much more of Herod's interest in the birth of Jesus than is usual in such plays; secondly, the Angel is assigned a flexible presence in which he/she may be 'not only a Divine Messenger, but also the Presenter of the Play, the Prompter, Herod's conscience, a kind of Devil, and a Palace Official' (Arden 1963: 10–11). These devices enable Arden and D'Arcy to throw new light on the old story, to show the familiar as strange, and to turn the story into a powerful comment on the current socio-political situation.

Thus the allegory focuses the political issues clearly and simply: Judaea is Britain and Herod is the British Prime Minister. To the West is Rome – the USA – to the East is Persia – the Soviet bloc. To preserve the (unstable) political pact with Rome/USA, Herod/PM must order the slaying of the innocents, the sacrifice of some of his own citizens. Herod's central speech ironically echoes Harold Macmillan's famous claim that 'You've never had it so good.' It is addressed directly to the audience:

> You are richer and happier than you have ever been! Your children are receiving opportunities for education and advancement that your own fathers could not have imagined in their wildest dreams. Dare you see this prosperity destroyed in one night? You answer me – no. You answer me – King Herod do what you believe to be necessary and we your faithful people will follow you as always in loyalty and trust! (*To the angel.*) You understand, I am putting a very particular mark against my name in the history books . . . It is fitting that the honour of one man should die for the good of the people.
>
> (Arden 1963: 49–50)

But the issue is not simply about the honour of the individual, as Herod himself makes clear. The order is patently given *on behalf of the community*. This is the central potential reading of the authenticating signs of the allegory as a political parable, the explicit ideology inscribed in the play. This reading is further reinforced by the rhetorical conventions of the production: for, to the extent that the networks of the community are reaffirmed by those conventions, then the actor playing Herod can be read as representative of the community. In judging Herod's decision the audience is encouraged to judge themselves: given similar issues would they decide for the state, or against it?

Thus the play raises fundamental ideological questions about democracy and state power, about responsibility and oppression, which clearly related to current national and international affairs: the Cold War, the management of the economy, the 'necessity' of unemployment, contradictions in the social order. The impact is reinforced by the portrayal of Herod. Far from being presented as the villain of the piece, Herod is a reasonable man, a political manager faced with a chronically difficult 'business' decision concerning the well-being, as he sees it, of the majority: the similarities to Super-Mac are by no means coincidental. The representation of Herod clearly is intended to provoke a crisis in the audience, and the crisis is about the nature of good government. Given the widespread concern in the early 1960s about Britain's declining status in world politics, such issues were almost certain to have much more than a local resonance. In effect, the crisis that the portrayal of Herod seems designed to produce underlines the connections between the local ideological identity and global politics.

Hence, *The Business of Good Government* dealt with major contemporary issues of political power, in an accessible, immediate and possibly inescapable way. The production was accessible because it used well-known rhetorical conventions to create a sense of celebration (this links it to the carnivalesque, perhaps; certainly it connects with Turner's notion of *communitas*). It was immediate because the authenticating conventions reproduced the political agitations of the times (without being propagandistic). It was inescapable, maybe, because it used the unique text–context dynamic to produce a subtle, but hard-hitting, crisis for the Brent Knoll audiences. This was the foundation of its potential efficacy.

Carnival in Kirkbymoorside

At root the Kirkbymoorside festival initiated by Arden and D'Arcy in 1963 was a gesture of resounding generosity. The basic idea was outrageously simple: they ran an 'open house' for a month, stimulating free public entertainment through an all-embracing invitation to all-comers to create enjoyment for anyone in the village.

The context made this approach even more extraordinary. Kirkbymoorside preferred to see itself as a small market town, though with only 2000 inhabitants it was probably closer to being a largish village. The town boasted two schools, a small library and five churches, but no cinema or theatre. The chief sources of local employment were a brick works, a small glider factory and agriculture, plus seasonal work in the holiday industry gained by commuting to Scarborough and York. However, in line with national trends, unemployment in the town rose steadily in the early 1960s; and its isolation dramatically increased when the local railway station was closed by the Beeching plan in 1962. This was a hard-working, no-nonsense kind of community, still remarkably religious for the period (the churches attracted good congregations), economically depressed, but by no means lacking in typical Yorkshire vigour. Hardly the place, though, for a full-scale carnival blow-out.

Of course, the audacity of the festival plan was calculated. Arden and D'Arcy had moved to Kirkbymoorside at the start of 1963, and Arden is himself a Barnsley-bred Yorkshireman. In 1966 he described the situation to Walter Wager:

> Our cottage was not in the town itself but half a mile away in a funny little collection of houses that ran alongside a disused railway and a disused gasworks . . . We discovered that our neighbors [sic] . . . were travelling gypsified tinkers . . . They have their class awareness but they accept me as being a licenced eccentric . . . these people regard me as being on their side.
>
> (Wager 1968: 252)

Also he recalls how he had overheard a local teacher wondering 'why . . . Arden chose to live with the scum of the earth and the beggars' (Wager 1967: 252). Thus, in geographical and cultural terms Arden and D'Arcy had placed themselves on the periphery of the town. As a result, their 'eccentric' social positioning in the town, and the 'anything goes' approach to the whole event, worked to offset any suggestion of mainstream cultural imperialism, à la Centre 42. This strategy seemed to succeed. By all accounts the festival managed to maintain a delicate balance between imported presentations and indigenous participation, between 'high' art forms and 'low' social events. There are even indications that the extremes were sometimes integrated.

Ian Watson, who helped to organise the festival, described the total outcome as follows:

> There were readings and performances of Machiavelli, Brecht, Arrabal, O'Casey, Jarry, Livings, Owen, Jellicoe. The Mikron theatre company stopped off on its way to the Edinburgh festival . . . Poets wandered in to give readings of their work . . . Chaplin, Fields and others shared the screen with the Kirkbymoorside films [made by the community] and other documentaries. Actors and local people improvised scenes around unusual newspaper stories . . . Local artists, singers, groups, dialect story- tellers, and performers of all kinds found audiences for what they had to offer.
>
> (Trussler 1969: 183)

The *Yorkshire Post*, a newspaper not famous for its indiscriminate enthusiasm, described the response of the local young people:

> Many of the local youths and children, regular visitors both . . . played darts, drank coffee, twisted in the garden (a sand pit), acted to each other and sometimes a larger audience on a rough outdoor stage.
>
> (*Yorkshire Post*, 20/8/1963)

Responses among the adults were mixed. They 'reacted . . . more with bewilderment than disapproval' according to the *Yorkshire Post*. But it would seem that overall the festival met a generally warm welcome from the town. At root this was likely, because the emphasis throughout was on off-beat creative celebration for all, with who knows what outcome.

In the late 1970s Arden characterised the ideology of the festival as 'based on broadly libertarian anarchistic artistic views . . . Its politics were implicit rather than overt, and very much of the unstructured sixties' (Itzin 1980b: 26). A kind of cultural anarchy, celebration, the spirit of Dionysus and the carnivalesque, a combination of gaiety and danger runs through all of Arden's work in this period. Thus the Kirkbymoorside project was radical in a broadly cultural sense - a cheerful disruption of routine, a light-hearted intervention into community networks - rather than in any specifically political way. It did, however,

produce one example of stunning ideological subversion in the
playlet *Ars Longa, Vita Brevis*. This vigorous squib has the
remarkable distinction of being staged within one year (1963/4)
by the Royal Shakespeare Company – as part of the Peter Brook/
Charles Marowitz 'Theatre of Cruelty' programme – and by the
Company of the Kirkbymoorside Girl Guides.

The idea for the play grew from improvisations that D'Arcy
had been doing with children in Kirkbymoorside and Dublin,
and the value of such work finds an amusing stress in Arden's
1966 comment on the text:

> When we . . . directed the play ourselves with the
> Kirkbymoorside Girl Guides we threw out all the dialogue,
> except the two bits of verse, and let them improvise their own
> words throughout. The result was, we thought, much more
> successful than any of the productions we have seen where my
> dialogue was adhered to.
>
> (Trussler *et al*. 1967: 53)

Obviously, improvisation gives the performing group a large
degree of control over the authenticating conventions of
performance. So the Girl Guides (or any other ideologically
close-knit group) could create conventions that they (and probably their audience) found amenable and accessible. A film shot
by David Naden during the festival shows the guides rehearsing:
the girls are relaxed and lively, their soft Yorkshire accents
making an inviting contrast to the harsh themes of the scenario
they are playing.

Arden's scenario dramatises the misplaced enthusiasm of authority for order at all costs. The main character, Mr Miltiades, is
an art teacher who turns his classes into military exercises.
Rather than sketch reality as they see it, his class is compelled to
draw geometric figures. The image of straight lines is throughout linked to the idea of military violence. Albert Hunt reports
on the scene in which the art class becomes a marching-ground
drill:

> In [the] production with Girl Guides . . . at Kirkbymoorside,
> the Headmaster shouted 'What do you think you're doing, Mr
> Miltiades?' 'Teaching them to draw straight lines.' came the
> reply.
>
> (Hunt 1974: 116)

It is ironic that the headmaster disapproves of Miltiades' style of teaching. Towards the end of the show, whilst out hunting, he knowingly shoots the art teacher, who is disguised as a tree as he takes part in a real Territorial Army exercise. This is presented as a positive release for Miltiades' wife, who has one of the 'bits of verse' that Arden insisted should not be replaced by improvisation:

> I shed a tear upon his bier
> Because to me he was ever dear.
> But I could not follow him in all his wishes
> I prefer the quick easy swimming of the fishes
> Which sport and play
> In green water all day
> And have not a straight line in the whole of their bodies.
>
> (Arden 1964: 30)

Anti-militarism is joined to feminism in ways that oddly prefigure the counter-cultures.

The spectacle of a quasi-military group of young Yorkshire women engaged in playing out an anti-authoritarian celebration of freedom and spontaneity is very satisfying. This is particularly the case as they used their own words to authenticate the dramatisation. So, although there are no explicit political references in the text, the context here gives the performance a clear and concrete subversive ideological significance, offering an implicit radical challenge to any militaristic and authoritarian tendencies within the community. Moreover, the rhetorical conventions of the performance made it easily accessible in the gathering phase, while the use of commedia-style half-masks and toy weapons gave the show a child-like quality, as if the girls were acting out a playground game. Francis Gray argues that productions of the play work well:

> because its spirit is childlike . . . it is about play. Play is a serious activity: children pretend to be other people, other things, but they do so by telling the truth as they see it.
>
> (Gray 1982: 127–8)

The innocent-but-knowing play is used to undermine and criticise the mis-use of power, an issue that was much in the news in the scandal-torn early 1960s (and, implicitly, had particular relevance to Beeching's closure of Kirkbymoorside station). But at the moment that the show mounts a radical critique of authority through its authenticating conventions, its rhetorical conventions are used to disarm criticism of its critique.

This indicates again Arden and D'Arcy's skill in making the context of performance central to the significance of the text and its reception. The performance certainly had the potential to question the proper uses of power at the local level of the community, as it used symbolism that was integral to most British communities – schools, teachers, the Territorial Army. But the allegorical form linked the local to the current national mis-uses of power, thus increasing its chances of achieving ideological efficacy. This may partly explain the success of the Girl Guide's version. Perhaps it gave them some satisfaction to know that Arden thought other productions were less successful, including, of course, the one by the Royal Shakespeare Company under the direction of Peter Brook.

The accessibility and directness of the Brent Knoll and Kirkbymoorside plays were unquestionably attractive to the audiences for which they were designed. In 1966 Arden could confidently claim that they 'are the two most popular plays I have written . . . or rather partly written' (Trussler et al. 1967: 57). This success no doubt encouraged him in the same year to accept an invitation from the Beaford Festival in North Devon to produce a further piece for a non-theatre venue: *The Royal Pardon*. And in 1968 Arden and D'Arcy embarked on a project which was to set an acute test of their growing reputation for mounting successful community-based theatre projects.

British society in the late 1960s

A lot happened in 1968 on the international scene: in America Martin Luther King and Robert Kennedy were assassinated, Richard Nixon was elected President, and major confrontations took place at the Democratic Convention in Chicago; in Greece the Fascist generals consolidated the power they had seized the year before; in Vietnam the Viet Cong launched the Tet Offensive (and there were massive anti-war demonstrations in many countries); in Czechoslovakia Russian tanks rolled down the streets fully armed; in Northern Ireland British troops arrived to 'keep the peace'; and of course in Paris the students took charge of the streets and major public buildings in *les événements de Mai*. The

Parisian uprising was reproduced, on varying scales, in Milan, Berlin, Warsaw, Belgrade, Mexico City and Tokyo; while in Britain there were occupations and sit-ins at Guildford, Hornsea, the LSE, and other colleges and universities. And, oh yes, the Royal Smut Hound (as Kenneth Tynan dubbed the Lord Chamberlain) was muzzled.

The spectacular signs of international instability and unrest had their counterparts in the British political system. In 1964 the tiny majority of Wilson's new Labour goverment initially ensured unity in the party and general support from the left. During the next two years, despite severe economic problems, the government introduced a series of reforms in social benefits, and in industrial and race relations, which were broadly egalitarian. However, an embarrassing failure to meet an election pledge to re-nationalise the steel industry, coupled with continued support of America's escalation of the Vietnam war, caused disquiet in Labour's more radical wing, though not in the electorate as a whole. Under Wilson's skilful guidance, and thanks to notably weak opposition from both Conservatives and Liberals, Labour continued to top the opinion polls, winning the 1966 election with a comfortable majority of ninety-six.

The next two years, though, witnessed growing contradictions in the government's policies. On the social front, a series of liberalising reforms were introduced, such as the lowering of the age of majority to 18, faster conversion of secondary education to comprehensive schooling and a major expansion of higher education (including the founding of the Open University), abolition of the death penalty, easing of the laws on homosexuality, divorce and abortion, and so on. But on the economic and industrial front Labour was forced to take decisions which were deeply unpopular with the unions, the militant left, and, increasingly, the general public. Gradually it became clear that Wilson's government had no overall strategy. The liberalism of its social policy was generally progressive; but its other policies, by and large, represented a failure to control the economy, an abandonment of socialist principles, and a growing intervention by the state into people's daily lives. The public became disillusioned with politics, while the left became bitter at the government's sell-out to international capitalism and its reluctance to condemn American foreign policy, especially the war in Vietnam. If the international situation was worsening, and if the domestic

scene was getting more desperate, then the British government seemed to be doing precious little to improve matters.
The seeds of revolt might have been sown by our neighbours, but
it seemed that our own guardians were assiduously watering
them.

Yet the political scene needs to be set against the changing
texture of daily life in order to put the widespread disillusion and
revolt into its proper perspective. For the state had not been
entirely unsuccessful in its efforts to improve the average person's
lot. The backdrop to the dissatisfaction was growing consumer
affluence. Arthur Marwick provides figures for the scale of this
growth in the 1960s:

> In 1956 only about 8 per cent of households had . . . refriger-
> ators; this rose to 33 per cent in 1962 and 69 per cent in 1971.
> Television sets had been a rarity in the early 1950s; but by 1961
> 75 per cent of families had one, and by 1971 91 per cent. By
> 1971, also, 64 per cent of families had a washing machine.
>
> (Marwick 1982: 121)

Similarly, the number of cars on British roads increased from 5.6
million in 1960 to 11.8 million in 1970. Such wealth made the
state's apparent poverty of principle all the more frustrating for
radicals, especially when public disillusion seemed to spring
from material greed. It wasn't that people did not have enough;
they wanted more. The desire for excess was reproduced in many
areas of British culture, as a moral *laissez-faire* sanctioned, for
example, experimentation with drugs and sexuality. And of
course cultural activists could not avoid the paradoxes and the
contradictions of the new freedom. In the theatre, as elsewhere,
old garments were being shed.

Disunity at Unity: *Harold Muggins Is a Martyr*

In 1968 Roland Muldoon and the other members of CAST met
John Arden and Margaretta D'Arcy at their house in Muswell
Hill, North London. Muldoon reports:

> He opened the door and there was no carpet on the floor and
> you had to draw up a house brick to sit down. It was quite
> surprising really, to see this great playwright living like that.

And Arden said he . . . was really into resistance and he said
'I'd like to write a play for you.'

(Itzin 1980b: 21)

The play that Arden and D'Arcy finally wrote with CAST was
Harold Muggins Is a Martyr, and it became the focus for a series
of almost epic encounters between three generations of political
radicals committed to subversive cultural action.

Muggins . . . opened at the London Unity Theatre on June 14,
1968, and was performed by actors from CAST and Unity Theatre.
Albert Hunt and John Fox (who was soon to found Welfare State)
were brought down from Bradford by Arden and D'Arcy to turn
the approach to the theatre into an 'environment'. As well as foyer
sideshows, the project finally included street performances, and
improvised shows by local children instigated by D'Arcy. Simon
Trussler sees it as an extension of Arden's community drama
projects. Catherine Itzin calls it 'one of the classic legendary events
in political theatre' (Itzin 1980b: 20). However it is described, the
occasion provided a kind of creative crucible, in which great
cultural and ideological questions were addressed in the most
concrete of terms, as an attempt was made to forge an efficacious
relationship between overtly radical performance and the local
community. Such ambitions, though, were bound to be shot
through with the contradictions of the late 1960s.

In 1967 CAST had been the first company to perform at the
newly refurbished Unity Theatre in Goldington Street, North
London, an area of old Victorian streets and 1930s council flats
which housed a mixed and mobile population of immigrant
(mostly Greek) and indigenous working-class people. Shortly
following the meeting at Arden and D'Arcy's house Unity was
again available. But the tight schedule of the new project forced
the ideological differences of the three parties involved – CAST,
Arden/D'Arcy, Unity Management – into high relief. Roland
Muldoon pinpoints them very succinctly:

> I thought we might be able to capture the original Unity spirit
> if we put on a successful production there . . . Arden brought
> John Fox from the Welfare State down to build funny things
> around the theatre, and we went in and put a red flag up. The
> Management Committee at Unity took a decision that it
> would offend the neighbourhood.

(Itzin 1980b: 344)

The dislocations are finely caught in that dismissive 'funny things'. Arden, who from the outset had wanted a community-based production, suggests yet more complexity when he claims that Unity 'did not want to be identified with the local working class lest it impede their vision of representing the whole of the Labour movement' (Itzin 1980b: 344). Perhaps it was inevitable that the 'old guard' at Unity would end up resentful when confronted by the confusions offered by the combination of CAST's Marxist internationalism and Arden/D'Arcy's socialist localism, especially as both were inflected by the anarchic expressivity of the counter-culture. On a more prosaic level, what was being attempted certainly did not fit neatly into any existing aesthetic categories.

The basic ideological purpose of *Muggins* . . . was clearly inscribed in both the rhetorical and authenticating conventions of the production itself, which was defiantly populist. The text drew unashamedly on the topical scandal of protection rackets – the gruesome Kray twins were an obvious reference point, as Simon Trussler's word-sketch makes clear:

> a rambling tale of a cafe proprietor caught between rival protection-racketeers, but himself prone to exploiting his handful of employees . . . Muggins, of course, embodied Average Man – not to mention Harold Wilson – exploited . . . by the corruptive and manipulative pressures of his society . . . [conveyed] by a coven of characters with comic-strip names.
>
> (Trussler 1969: 185)

The play combined Arden and D'Arcy's penchant for allegory and parable with CAST's keen eye for the topical target, as the parallels between Muggins and Wilson, Mr Big and America, the Cafe and Britain were gleefully drawn to emphasise the failure of Labour to produce anything more principled than a shady deal with capitalism. But the epic inclinations of Arden and the agit-prop iconoclasm of CAST also coalesced to make a show which was ostensibly didactic – attacking the capitalist exploiters on behalf of the oppressed working classes – but which also ironically refused to condemn totally its dubious protagonist, Muggins. Trussler suggests that this was why, on the first night, the audience and actors argued for ninety minutes after the end of the show – a sign of efficacy?

Trussler also describes how the environmental enhancement of the foyer succeeded for at least some of the King's Cross working classes:

> Half-term students from Bradford College of Art [with Albert Hunt and John Fox] . . . transformed the theatre approach and its facade into a sort of ultimate amusement arcade, to the delight of a largish proportion of the neighbourhood kids.
>
> (Trussler 1969: 185)

But efforts to involve the local community in more explicit ideological negotiations met with much less success:

> the closest contact the company made with the Saturday shopping crowds [was through] fairly primitive forms of street theatre [advertising] the forthcoming attraction.
>
> (Trussler 1969: 186)

In addition, the surface oddity of the event made it attractive to mainstream cultural formations: here was a unique example of a nationally known playwright mixing it with underground political rabble-rousers. The media treated the project as something of a political circus, giving it all the hype of national reviews, trend-setting audiences, a box-office sell-out, a *succès de scandale*. The core audience was an odd mixture of Unity Labour stalwarts, Royal Court theatre-buffs, and counter-cultural 'freaks' from the Arts Lab circuit. It is hardly surprising that the local people stayed away – and this had a profound effect on the ideological transaction of the show. This was a repeat of the sad scenario of Joan Littlewood and Theatre Workshop at Stratford East, with a singular difference. Mainstream theatre culture had only partly annexed the project, for it brought together a federation of new radical theatre workers and, according to Colin Chambers, 'provided a background to what became the major catalyst for the counter-culture in the next few years . . . the AgitProp information service' (Chambers 1989: 388). Such contradictions were typical of the period, and they often embraced more fundamental ideological rifts.

A paradoxical nudity

The abolition of the Lord Chamberlain's role as stage censor in 1968 produced a wave of nudity in the theatre, ranging from the exploitative *Oh Calcutta!* to the explosive *Paradise Now*. D'Arcy and Arden were keen to question the sexist exploitation of the fashion, and so they included a scene with a stripper in *Muggins* . . . Albert Hunt provides a cool description of the scene:

> One of the gangsters who is transforming Muggins' cafe introduces a stripper. With great excitement Muggins asks her to strip in front of him. She does so, beautifully but coldly, showing him, and the audience, an attractive body. But when she's completely naked, Muggins simply says, disappointed 'Is that all?'
>
> (Hunt 1974: 127)

The three main parties involved in the project had differing attitudes to this nudity, which are especially telling in the light they throw on culture as a site of ideological conflict, and performance as a discourse for ideological negotiation. Various kinds of authenticity can be read as being at stake in the moment of nudity.

The differences were extreme. According to Arden: 'Unity . . . put the clamps down on this scene. We successfully resisted: said "No nude, no play" ' (Itzin 1980b: 344). Muldoon's version runs as follows:

> Arden said, we'll have a naked woman and confront the audience with her. So I said, 'No shit man, we'll have a naked woman at the back with light bulbs going up and down on her tits, throw it away, you know.' As we believed it was a throwaway point that was being made. And he said, 'No, no, we'll make a big point of nudity.' So we said, 'But we come from a different generation than you, John.' And then the shit hit the fan. And he said 'You're more arrogant than Sir Laurence.'
>
> (Itzin 1980b: 22)

Arden and D'Arcy's aim was 'to analyse the sexual exploitation of women' (Trussler 1969: 186); and in order to prevent media distortions they asked critics not to mention the scene during the run of the play. So in the one image the three parties invest censorious outrage, anarchic playfulness and serious socio-political experimentation.

These differences link the whole project to long historical perspectives of cultural practice. We can detect in Unity's stance more than a hint of the type of left-wing puritanism which, for instance, led the Workers' Theatre Movement to reject the image of chorus girls as a potential weapon in the fight for a popular radical culture in the 1930s (Davies 1987: 105). That kind of separation of gender from ideological negotiation, of current pleasures (however contaminated) from long-term politics, was part of a process of internal repression and oppression in 'old guard' left-wing radicals. It was the type of attitude that the New Left had fought vigorously to eliminate.

Roland Muldoon's wish to 'throw away' the nudity clearly is intended to add disgust to shock, to challenge sexism through a transgression that invites the rejection of an object of desire. That this tactic rested on the construction of a deeply sexist sign – the degradation of the female body to sex-object – and thus produced an irreconcilable contradiction in the ideologies inscribed in the moment of nudity, is seen by Muldoon as exciting. Celebration of such contradictions was common in the cultural practices of the late 1960s counter-culture, when theatre workers were often prepared to take such ideological risks. But of course the danger created was always double-edged, as we saw in relation to the People Show. The subversive ideological outrage was itself dependent on exploitation and oppression.

D'Arcy and Arden's approach to the nudity was both more cautious and more daring, but it depended for its success on an especially tricky use of the ideological interaction of rhetorical and authenticating conventions. They were cautious because they did not want the nudity to reinforce sexism and patriarchy. They were daring in trying to use a sexist sign in order to nullify the salacious enjoyment that it was usually designed to promote. In directing the scene D'Arcy devised three tactics in the effort to neutralise exploitative readings. Firstly, she asked Tamara Hinchco, the actress who had agreed to do the scene, to perform the stripping 'coldly', without any indication of pleasure. The idea was to construct 'new' rhetorical conventions of 'cold stripping', in order to prompt anti-sexist readings of stage nudity. Whereas traditionally striptease reduces female sexuality to an *object* of desire, by breaking the usual rhetorical conventions of striptease the actress may make the audience aware of her own subjectivity. She may thus interrupt the gaze of the (particularly male) spectator with her own consciousness, reversing the usual power relations of voyeuristic striptease. Secondly, the striptease is performed for Muggins' 'benefit', so the spectator observes his observation of the event. Obviously, the logic of the scene requires Muggins to get salacious enjoyment from the striptease, but his lack of reaction aims to subvert the spectator's 'normal' reaction by undermining expectation. Thirdly, Arden and D'Arcy's request to the critics not to mention the nudity was intended to prevent anticipation of the stripping. Arden/D'Arcy were trying to use the conventions of the gathering phase to set in motion a process of ideological decontamination, so to speak, to reduce the scene's potential for readings that would produce erotic indulgence. Hence, all the rhetorical conventions of the stripping aimed to encourage the audience to deconstruct the implicit exploitative and oppressive ideologies written into the usual means whereby strip becomes a tease. By implication they were attempting to authenticate a non-sexist ideology.

Obviously, Arden and D'Arcy were walking on ideological hot coals. The upsurge of 'permissiveness' in the second half of the decade in part gave public licence to licentiousness. However skilled the actress, the gaze of the male spectator may continue in uninterrupted sexual rapture. However skilled the actor, Muggins' disappointment may appear unjustifiably dislocated from its object. However well the striptease scene was performed, it may not have transcended the fashion set by *Oh Calcutta!* and *Hair*. This trend encouraged the idea that the sexism of stage nudity could be ignored in the interests of free expression – one of the main contradictions of the early counter-culture.

If the various aspects of the project did not quite connect with each other, it was partly because of the unintended disjunction between the event and its community context. The full impact of its egalitarian satire, including the risky use of nudity, depended on the presence of an audience with at least a modicum of ideological integrity, such as the local community might provide. Given this, the carnivalesque transgression of its rhetorical conventions, and the socio-political agit prop satire of its authenticating conventions, might have worked to produce an effective celebratory protest.

But the underlying contradictions of the event prevented a coalescing of protest and celebration in a meeting between working-class and counter-cultural formations. Instead those contradictions simply animated the fractured ideology of a heterogeneous metropolitan gathering. If the show was ideologically efficacious, it was because it exacerbated the growing social conflicts of the times.

Yet despite these fundamental shortcomings, *Harold Muggins Is a Martyr* was a seminal and far-reaching project for the ways in which it created a dialogue between three different ideologies and their approaches to cultural production in the late 1960s. If Unity's approach harked back to the patriarchal and puritanical tendencies of the old-style left, and if CAST was immersed in the anarchistic and 'permissive' rebellion of the counter-cultural present, then Arden and D'Arcy were looking forward to the massive feminist and community activist movements of the 1970s and 1980s. That all this could be incorporated into a single project, and much of it into a single scene, gives a measure of the kinds of contradiction that were confronting British culture as the decade neared its end. In this socio-political context it is hardly surprising that many young (and not so young) theatre workers were beginning to re-think the established relationships between performance and community; that a new generation was beginning to search for forms of cultural production which would be increasingly efficacious in the great ideological shifts affecting British society at the start of the new decade.

Chapter 5

Consolidation in the 1970s
The popular political theatre of John McGrath and 7:84 Theatre Company

Crisis and confrontation in the 1970s

If the Mods and Rockers were crucial signs of the conflicts and contradictions of the 1960s then the punks serve a similar function for the crises and confrontations of the 1970s and early 1980s. The blatant effrontery of punk emerged on the streets at the end of the long hot summer of 1976, and its style reflected the ideological nightmares that were plaguing the rest of British society. The vision of youth gone completely off the rails was more excessive than that projected by any previous sub-culture, creating an aggressive visual and behavioural style that was riddled with deliberate contradictions. Self-mutilation (safety-pinned noses) jousted with self-exposure (torn t-shirts and string vests); sado-masochistic emblems (belts, buckles, chains) battled with tropical–exotic hair-styles and make-up (green mohicans, children's glitter-dust). Record sleeves looked like terrorist ransom notes, and the music was cacophonous, almost totally tuneless. The anarchic assemblage of conflicting ideological signs was perhaps most purely caught in the frequent juxtaposing of the CND peace sign with the Nazi swastika. Here was a widespread discourse representing socio-political anomie.

The sources of punk in the wider culture are complicated, though Dick Hebdige captures the accuracy of its reaction very neatly:

> the punks were not only directly *responding* to increasing joblessness, changing moral standards, the rediscovery of poverty, the depression, etc., they were *dramatising* what had come to be called 'Britain's decline' by constructing a

language which . . . appropriated the rhetoric of crisis.

(Hebdige 1979: 87)

Inevitably punk produced a widespread 'moral panic' in the parent society. Yet punk's aggression and violence were mostly only fashion-deep, and its anarchy and nihilism were tempered by more positive qualities. For example, it represented a healthy demystification of creative work in its production of both music and 'fanzines'. As with 1950s skiffle, anyone could form a punk band or produce a magazine. And by 1978 punk had aligned with the liberationist pop-music movement, Rock Against Racism. Yet the tensions of punk were symptomatic of deep problems that had been troubling the wider society, so that 'crisis' can justifiably stand as the cultural keynote of the decade.

In the 1970s the myths that Britain was a significant world leader and had a fundamental social stability gradually collapsed, as apparent affluence gave way to major economic traumas and widespread signs of dissatisfaction in the populace erupted into acute civil strife. There were bitter and politically disastrous national miners' strikes in 1972 and 1973, bringing four years of Conservative rule to an end in 1974. In 1973 the IRA began a major bombing campaign in Britain, killing many civilians. Unemployment began to rise in 1974, quickly passing the psychological watershed of 1 million in 1975. In 1976 there were spectacular signs of racial tension in riots at the Notting Hill Carnival. More large scale violence occurred between police and pickets at the Grunwick film-processing plant in 1977, where a broad left alliance fought for the trade union rights of a mainly Asian workforce. By then it was clear that the British manufacturing industry was in chronic decline, forcing Callaghan's Labour government to make massive, ideologically contradictory, cuts in public expenditure in 1978. A year later this led to a series of co-ordinated public sector one-day strikes which brought 1 million workers out in the 'Winter of Discontent'.

Thus the tradition of British tolerance gave way to confrontation and the final breakdown of the post-war consensus. The conditions of crisis produced major problems in all aspects of society, but perhaps nowhere more fundamentally than in the labour market and the wider economy. For instance, the rate of unemployment rose with astonishing rapidity to pass the 2 million mark at the end of the decade. We can read this as an index

of the breakdown of a collectivist approach to industrial management, or as the forced introduction of a structural mechanism for
depressing the value of wages. In either case the problem
represents a major new split in the social fabric of the nation – a
particularly ironic spectacle in a period of Labour government
(1974–9). The obvious ideological confusion that plagued
Wilson's, then Callaghan's, governments was merely the tip of
an unstable socio-economic iceberg. For the country's industrial
and economic problems were preventing its full participation in
the *laissez-faire* economy of the new international capitalist
markets. It was the promise of a breakthrough to further
affluence that swept Margaret Thatcher to power in 1979,
pledged to a policy that (in David Wood's trenchant phrase)
would produce a 'middle-class uprising' (Marwick 1982: 189).

Hence, the conditions of continual crisis and confrontation
created an unavoidable impression of social fragmentation and
loss of control. Given this, it is remarkable, as Arthur Marwick
points out, that 'participation, involvement, consumer protest
and action . . . were dominant motifs of the seventies' (Marwick
1982: 247). Marwick rather charmingly cites the rise of the
Campaign for Real Ale as useful evidence, though he could as
easily have noted the growth of the alternative theatre and
community arts movements. On a larger scale still, it is patent
that the almost continuous industrial strife was the product of
expanding participation at the grass roots. Similarly, organised
resistance to the racism of the National Front, and the
spectacular successes of the women's and gay liberation movements, were massive signs of participation and involvement in
new ideological formations. In short, the feminist, gay, anti-
racist, community activist and other libertarian movements of
the 1970s gave specific ideological focus to forms of local
participatory democracy. New types of community action and
new approaches to culture were forged during the decade,
confronting the status quo of the arts establishment, particularly,
with original styles of ideological resistance.

'Community' and 'culture' in the 1970s

The ideological confrontations of the 1970s can be traced in the
uses of two concepts that are central to my investigation:
'community' and 'culture'.

Halfway through the decade Raymond Williams noted that
' "community" never seems to be used unfavourably, and never
to be given a positive opposing term' (Williams 1976: 66). This
explains why by then it had been adopted by a wide range of
grass-roots cultural groups; and that can be read as a matrix for a
general dissatisfaction with the society of crisis. The term was
used extensively to cover buildings (community centres), services
(community medicine), movements (community arts), and art
forms (community theatre). Such usages always suggested a
nexus of localised, positive, cohesive and caring qualities; all as
an alternative to the angst and anomie produced by 'society'.
Towards the end of the decade, though, the oppositional conno-
tations of the word were given an ironic twist as it was increasingly adopted by state agencies. Local authority 'community
workers' traditionally had managed to balance the ideological
tightrope between the demands of the state and the street; but
there could be little doubt about the final allegiances of
'community policemen', or the intentions of 'community polic-
ing'.

In some respects 'culture' moved in the opposite direction, as
its older, restricted and hierarchical signification as 'the best
that civilisation has produced' was placed in conflict with a
broader meaning. Following the lead given by cultural critics
such as Richard Hoggart and Raymond Williams, and
reinforced by the growth of cultural studies in the Open
University and elsewhere, the term gradually gathered inflec-
tions from a more liberalised and radical discourse. In a parallel
development, the EC-funded Council of Europe stimulated a
radical rethink of the relationships between culture and society.
For instance, in 1976 the Council published J. A. Simpson's
Towards Cultural Democracy, and this was only one of a series
of influential texts issuing from the various international
symposia, conferences, studies and action-research projects
mounted across Europe by the Council (Simpson 1976).
Virtually all this work focused on the 'demystification of
culture' (Jor 1976); some of it concentrated on the uncovering of
the hegemonic functions of the high arts and the cultural
heritage (Faulds 1976); fundamentally it recommended a new
approach to the production of 'culture'.

The central drive of this new approach insisted that the
cultural policies of the state should be de-centrist and egalitarian,

and that resources for cultural production should be dispersed across a wide range of localised, grass-roots, creative initiatives. It argued for a plurality of cultures within each nation state (in this sense, if not in many more, it prefigures post-modernism), and for the rights of citizens to participate non-professionally in the production of their own art, as well as to be presented with artworks made by professionals. It was, of course, fundamentally anti-elitist. Underlying the whole argument was a keen aware-ness of the political and ideological nature of all cultural production and distribution.

The British Arts Council's response to such arguments was predictably guarded. The Council's 1977 Annual Report, for example, opined:

> By all means let us develop art at a less demanding, popular level; but to dismiss as elitist the subsidising of the great works of the past or the often 'difficult' works of contemporary artists, is to condemn the lock on the door of enlightenment because you have failed to give people the key that fits it.
>
> (Arts Council of Great Britain 1977: 8)

The Arts Council's position here represents a typically British strategy when faced with a major challenge and a potential crisis: the reiteration of traditional platitudes. But a singular result of the Council's policy in the worsening economic conditions of the 1970s was a widening of the gap between the haves and have-nots in the British theatre system. A brief look at the treatment of the National Theatre and the Royal Shakespeare Company during the decade will demonstrate the point.

The National Theatre's new complex of buildings on the South Bank of the Thames opened in 1976/7, and in the following year the Royal Shakespeare Company extended its London-based work by opening the Warehouse, a studio theatre close to the Aldwych Theatre, the company's main metropolitan venue. Thus by 1977/8 the two theatres were running seven different auditoria: three on the South Bank (Olivier, Lyttleton, Cottesloe), two in the West End (Aldwych and Warehouse), and two in Stratford-upon-Avon (Memorial Theatre and the Other Place). Three of these – the Cottesloe, the Warehouse and the Other Place – were the most privileged 'fringe' (occasionally perhaps 'alternative') venues in the land. These three acted as a kind of conduit through which the most effective theatrical innovations, and some of the most talented practitioners, of alternative theatre could be brought within the sphere of the main companies. This can be read as a form of cultural imperialism: the two nationals drawing on the successes of the alternative movement in order to consolidate their dominance of the British theatre system. One tragic event associated with this process was the suicide of Buzz Goodbody in 1975 (Chambers 1980); some related results are reflected in cold statistics.

In 1970/1 the two nationals were receiving 30% of the total Arts Council funding allocated to theatre, and by 1980/1 this had steadily risen to 43%. Equivalent figures for other building-based production companies – effectively the repertory theatres – were 62% (1970/1) and 41% (1980/1); and for touring companies and projects – most of which went to alternative theatre – the figures were 2% (1970/1) and 12% (1980/1) (Cork 1986). Thus, in broad terms the repertory theatres had lost out to the alternative theatre movement and the two nationals, but the latter had made a gain over both the other sectors. Moreover, the two nationals' gain of 3% over alternative theatre (13% against 10%) was paying all or a substantial part of the costs of the three new studio auditoria.

The economic irony of these figures is patent, and the ideological ramifications for the subsidised theatre industry are quite astonishing. The centrist and hierarchical policies of an undemocratic Arts Council were substantially reinforced on the national cultural agenda by the consolidation of the national companies, at the expense of the repertory theatres, *and* by a significant annexation of alternative theatre practices and personnel. It is not surprising that this caused great bitterness among radical practitioners in alternative theatre in the seventies, adding further fuel to the confrontational ethos of the decade.

Yet despite all this, alternative theatre flourished in the seventies. This is particularly the case for the first half of the decade, before Arts Council strategies for the containment of the movement were developed. The five years between 1970 and 1976, the second phase of this history, can justifiably be called a period of expansion and proliferation for alternative theatre. And even in the second half of the decade, when the movement came under increasing pressure from neo-conservatism, it managed to consolidate its position on the cultural agenda of the nation. Ideological and aesthetic experimentation, especially when they were on the side of self-determination and localised democracy, seemed to thrive in the general socio-political context of crisis and confrontation.

Alternative theatre in the 1970s

There was an astonishing proliferation of new alternative theatre groups in the first half of the 1970s, so that by mid-decade the number had almost quadrupled, to over 150. An impressive range of innovations in performance was introduced to audiences throughout the country by the decentralising impulse of the movement. Geographically, the spread reached from Land's End to John o' Groats, and there was an ideological variety to match. For example, the populist Footsbarn Theatre Company, founded in Cornwall in 1971, exemplified the counter-cultural ambition to unite anarchic expressivity with communal day-to-day survival:

> We are as alternative as you can get – no wages, live in a community, grow vegetables, chickens, etc. . . . The word 'alternative' alienates the people we play to . . . working people. These working people are not all trade unionists or furry freaks. A lot of them are conservatives, but what the hell.
> (Itzin 1976: 25)

Two years later, and 700 miles further north, John McGrath set up the Scottish 7:84 Theatre Company as a collective determined to promote Marxist analysis of local history through sub-regional tours of shows which celebrated Celtic resistance to centuries of repression and exploitation.

This first flood of companies also included other overtly political groups which toured nationally, such as Foco Novo, General Will and Joint Stock. The first few women's and gay groups were founded towards mid-decade, led by the Women's Theatre Company, the Women's Theatre Group and Gay Sweat-shop. The first black companies were set up, including Temba, the Black Theatre of Brixton and Tara Arts. And there was a notable boom in community theatre, with companies such as Interplay, EMMA, Medium Fair, Perspectives and Pentabus well established by mid-decade. New groups which concentrated on aesthetic experiment ranged from the sub-Grotowskian R.A.T. Theatre to the visually spectacular Lumiere and Son, and from the satirical neo-naturalistic Hull Truck to the storytelling minimalistic Shared Experience.

By mid-decade six main categories of work were clearly established, forming the foundations for the consolidation of alternative theatre in subsequent years. First, there were the community theatre companies, with policies which aimed to make theatre available to communities of location which might not otherwise encounter live performance. Second, there were the overtly political companies which were aligned with socialist or Marxist philosophies, and which usually defined their audiences as 'working class'. Third, there were the campaign companies, which were aligned with communities of interest engaged in major social and therefore quasi-political campaigns, such as the women's and gay liberation movements and the black consciousness movement. Fourth, there were the populist companies which described themselves as working in the tradition of popular theatre, attempting to appeal to as broad an audience as possible. Fifth, there were companies concerned primarily to extend the language of performance aesthetics, and they can be sub-grouped according to their interests in four main aspects of style, (a) the visual and/or physical, (b) the environmental, (c) the musical, (d) the improvisational. Sixth, there were companies devoted to the production of new plays, usually by new playwrights and often using workshops as part of the playwriting process. The last two categories contained groups which were often unconcerned about the specific nature of their audiences, only that they had an audience at all.

By the end of the decade there were about seventy groups in the last three categories. Most of these were alternative primarily in the sense of being opposed to the theatrical mainstream. As the other categories tended to include ideologically oppositional companies they are more central to my overall argument, so a brief summary of their growth will be useful. At the start of the decade there were perhaps five overtly political groups in existence. By 1975 the number had risen to fifteen; but the political climate discouraged further growth in the second half of the decade. The growth of the campaign groups – the women's, gay and black companies – provides a striking contrast. By 1975 there were only around five such companies, but by 1980 there were some twenty or so, fifteen women's, two gay and three black. Community theatre grew faster than the political and campaign groups overall. In 1970 there were about five community groups, by 1975 this had grown to some twenty-four groups, and in 1980 there were no fewer than forty-five companies which claimed a serious commitment to community-based performance. By the start of the 1980s, then, there were at least seventy groups producing performances and participatory projects which were informed by policies with a deliberate oppositional socio-political intent.

There were significant developments in both the means of production and distribution of these companies, so that formal and aesthetic inventiveness was matched by organisational and administrative ingenuity. Given the shoe-string economy of the movement, such improvisations were perhaps inevitable. But, more importantly, the innovations were also the result of a broad *cultural* radicalism, allied to the kind initiated by the Arts Laboratory. The fact that the main focus of the movement was cultural in the broadest sense meant that a very varied pattern of practices could be developed without losing the sense of a relatively coherent movement. And the wide spectrum of oppositional ideologies – from Marxist fundamentalism to situationist anarchism – was contained, as it were, within the crucible of a general resistance to the status quo. The formal characteristics of the movement were still encompassed by the carnival–agit prop spectrum, but there were increasing efforts to appeal to new constituencies of spectator, to reach new types of community with ideologically oppositional messages.

The underlying impulse for this overall growth was a desire to improve the match between companies and audiences, to evolve theatrical styles and operational procedures which were tailored to fit very specific constituencies of spectator. Such care was part of a more general trend still, towards an increased specialisation which appears to have had two fundamental functions. Firstly, it underlined the potential utility of performance for particular types of spectator; and secondly, it underpinned the potential survival of a company in an environment that, as far as public subsidy was concerned, was becoming more and more competitive. More positively, from an ideological point of view, if particular audiences/communities/constituencies agree that your theatre is of some specific *use* to them, then it is to be hoped that they will claim it as their own. The embrace of the community – however defined – may thus validate a company's ideological project – however conceived. Such a welcome also, of course, enhanced the potential for performance efficacy. The effect of these trends on the movement as a whole made it increasingly complex in its internal structure.

The new complexity was shaped by several major sub-trends, which both indicate how alternative theatre consolidated its position as part of British culture, and suggest the growing ideological tensions faced by the movement as the 1980s got nearer. The continuous aim to reach 'new' audiences fostered a regional emphasis, as the majority of groups were based outside London and focused their efforts on regional and sub-regional touring. Aesthetic experimentation continued as a common aim for much of the movement, but grew in sophistication as groups drew on a widening range of sources for inspiration, especially in the second half of the decade. For example, the studio companies, influenced particularly by post-modernist and post-structuralist trends in film, developed more complex scenarios and *mises-en-scène*; popular theatre groups drew on the continental traditions of mime and commedia dell'arte; while community-based companies explored new combinations of social and theatrical conventions. Many companies, but particularly the community theatre companies, joined a growing trend to include workshops and other forms of participatory activity in their programming. For studio–touring groups the aim was often to communicate some of the skills necessary to their style. For community-based companies the aim was to get 'closer' to the community, so that the design of projects could be more fully determined by the community as part of the process of empowerment.

The creation of a number of national organisations – the Association of Community Theatres, the Independent Theatre Council, the Theatre Writers' Union – led to the unionisation of the movement in the second half of the decade. This introduced more carefully regulated – and often improved – working conditions, and through that a greater and subtler pressure on the funding bodies to provide increased levels of subsidy. Moreover, unionisation went hand-in-hand with a restructuring of the means of production and distribution of many groups, as the Arts Council and RAAs established national and regional venue circuits and introduced a competitive system for the allocation of grants. This pushed the movement towards an internal hierarchy of groups, in which increasingly the best funded were playing to ghetto-like audiences in specially designed, well-equipped studios. Then towards the end of the decade there was a growing interaction between the movement and mainstream theatre, particularly the regional repertory theatres. Exchanges of personnel and repertoire became increasingly common and some small-scale companies began touring repertory-style programmes. Simultaneously, the movement became even more broadly politicised than before, as a significant number of new feminist and women's groups were established. This encouraged other groups to take on board issues of gender and sexual discrimination. Moreover, many companies extended their commitment to minority groups in the community, so that questions of race, disability, age (or generation), the politics of the personal and the presumptions of the patriarchy moved steadily up the ideological agenda.

It will be apparent that, particularly towards the end of the decade, these trends were pushing the movement in at least two directions at once: towards an encroaching neo-conservatism, and towards a wider range of ideologically oppositional positions – towards incorporation into the right-wing circus, and towards a determined resistance to its distractions. Yet despite these strains many companies developed sound and imaginative socio-politically critical practices in the 1970s. And the work of these groups was a small but significant contribution to the widespread demand, particularly at the level of the local community, for self-determination and participatory democracy. They were often in the forefront of the new oppositional cultural movements, and often their pursuit of performative efficacy led them to make original cultural interventions in places totally foreign to theatre. Together, these companies – the campaign companies, the political and community theatre companies, and a few of the populist companies – created a sub-movement within alternative theatre which placed aesthetic experiment at the service of cultural innovation.

Community theatre in the 1970s

The expansion of community theatre was fuelled by the fact that there were vast tracts of Britain in which live theatre simply was not available, let alone accessible. Cultural experimentation was stimulated by this geographical vacuum. The nature of the audience and its community became a central concern, so that the audience provided the starting point for making theatre, fundamentally influencing policy, programming and the aesthetics of performance.

A brief survey of the main characteristics of community theatre in the 1970s will show that no aspect of its practice remained unaffected by cultural experimentation. For example, the creative process was fundamentally influenced by a desire for accessibility. Performances tended to be tailor-made, often through collective devising, for particular communities or groupings within communities. The devising/writing process often included 'research' into the nature of the target community's history and/or contemporary problems, in order to make shows and projects more 'relevant', authenticating conventions more readable. In an effort to appeal to a broad constituency within the community, the traditions of popular theatre were frequently drawn on to provide rhetorical conventions. Moreover, work across a range of venue types encouraged groups to develop skills in such forms as puppetry, circus techniques and outdoor performance styles.

Similarly, the means of distribution were profoundly affected by commitment to the community. No location was excluded as a potential venue, provided it was accessible to the community. Many groups worked with sub-sections of their particular communities, especially groups which were seen as in some kind of special need: the hospitalised, the disabled, the elderly. Finally, community companies often worked to create an 'open' or participatory ethic, which ranged from the participation of the community in the running of the company, through the booking of performances for the company, to the production of performances by the community itself, enabled by the professionals. Frequently actors took on the role of aesthetic community workers, so to speak, or companies set up sub-units to develop particular participatory approaches.

As a result of these general tendencies, community theatre companies can be grouped according to their position on five main operational spectra. Firstly, all of them defined their target audiences partly in terms of geographical spread, ranging from metropolitan inner-city areas or rural villages or industrial towns, through to counties or conurbations, sub-regions and regions. Secondly, these companies varied in the range of types of venues or community sub-groupings that they tried to reach. On the one hand, some companies aimed to play to 'all community venues' in their area – most typically, schools, youth clubs, community centres, social clubs, pubs, hospitals, day centres, old people's homes, shopping centres, parks, streets. On the other hand, others narrowed their sights on a more precisely identified selection of these: community centres and schools being a common combination, for example. Thirdly, the aesthetics of the contact with the community in particular events ranged from the straightforward presentation of shows to complicated processes of participatory engagement. Fourthly, programming ranged from the almost wildly eclectic – combining participatory projects of different kinds with the production of self-devised shows, specially commissioned plays, existing texts – to the mildly conservative – in which a near-repertory model was adopted in taking theatre to the (assumed) cultural wastes of rural Northumberland or suburban Southampton. Fifthly, the community theatre companies echoed the broadly oppositional ideological tendency of the movement as a whole, though the nature of their preferred communities caused them to be cautious about explicit claims to subversion. Hence, policy statements encompassed a spectrum from mild political radicalism through guarded social criticism to uneasy cultural conservatism.

Within the wide variety of practices we can identify a small number of over-riding characteristics as part of the ideological stock-in-trade of these community theatre groups. There was, for example, a ubiquitous commitment to the idea of theatre as a service to the community, derived by analogy from welfare state institutions, and placing these companies in the tradition of Unity, Centre 42 and the Arden/D'Arcy community dramas. Provided it was specially created for the locality, theatre was thought to have a practical utility value for the local community, an identifiable efficacy. As a result these companies possessed a consciously anti-centrist bias, and this was the product of their commitment to localism and locality, to the creation of grassroots or neighbourhood culture (as opposed to national culture). Thus, even in London, companies were set up in idiosyncratic locations (from a mainstream point of view): Wandsworth and Deptford, for example. This commitment to locality, when combined with a participatory ethic, obviously was anti-hierarchical and tended towards cultural democracy as a socio-political programme. Thus the empowerment of the community was central to community theatre ideologies, whether that was conceived in terms of 'giving a voice to the community', or 'strengthening the solidarity of the community', or 'creating a new identity with the community'.

Finally, the new contexts for performance made many community theatre companies acutely aware of contextuality and ideological relativity, causing radicalism to be framed in relatively inoffensive social or cultural terms. Nevertheless, it is easy to detect the ideologies of egalitarianism, collectivism and participatory democracy in the programmes and policies of the majority of these companies. The overall intent to intervene at least aesthetically, often socially, and sometimes politically, in the production of local and regional culture involved all of them (even the most conservative) in complex ideological transactions with their host communities. Often their policy and programming reflect an awkward balancing act, between the impulse to question the status quo and the need to be accepted by the (often conservative) community. Especially in a period of national crises, these companies frequently had to face ideological contradictions of a high order.

A different class of audience

Some idea of what was felt to be at stake in the development of political and community theatre in the 1970s can be gained from a debate that animated the whole movement in the second half of the decade. The debate was initiated in 1977 by Bruce Birchall in the radical magazine *Wedge*. He argued that the revolutionary ambitions of the political theatre groups had been undermined by 'reformism'. Reformism was defined as co-operation with the state through the acceptance of Arts Council grants, which had caused groups to become more interested in professional survival than in revolutionary action. What is crucial about Birchall's argument, though, is his claim that political theatre which was 'revolutionary' could directly engage with, and have an effect on, the 'class struggles' of the 1970s. By implication, there was a strong suggestion that some groups had failed, and some had succeeded, in achieving such an effect.

For David Edgar the issues centred on the type of audiences to which political theatre was playing. Partly in response to the *Wedge* article Edgar argued that:

> while the scale of socialist theatre is impressive, it is obvious that its intervention in the working-class struggle has been at best patchy and peripheral.
>
> (Edgar 1988: 24)

He concluded that political theatre had failed to attract a working-class audience, and so the best course of action would be to recognise the audience that *had* been created; namely, the people that groups such as Monstrous Regiment played to in arts centre and studio-theatre venues throughout the country. The interests of revolutionary theatre would be better served by adopting the 'modest aims' of 'perform[ing] aesthetically and politically mature plays to an existing audience' (Edgar 1988: 47).

In his turn, John McGrath took strong exception to Edgar's position. He accused Edgar of a 'basic ignorance of what was actually happening' and argued that his position produced a number of debilitating consequences for the practice of politically oppositional theatre

> One of these . . . is indifference to the development of working-class culture . . . Another is that a great deal of writing, acting and directing talent is given a 'socialist' reason for deserting the working class . . . A third consequence is that theatre is seen not as a means of production but as a collection of texts.
>
> (McGrath 1979: 54)

McGrath's counter-proposals argue for a theatre practice that uses its context as an essential part of its productive processes, so that all aspects of a performance become operative in the ideological transaction between company and audience. In other words, simply to accept existing venues and to perform for existing audiences, as Edgar suggested, is a denial of the full radical potential of theatre. A truly oppositional theatre needs to radicalise every element of production, distribution and exchange in order to achieve its fullest socio-political effect.

Now, although these battles were fought out primarily in relation to overtly socialist performance practice, they had extensive implications for all the community, campaign and political theatre companies – that is to say, for at least half of the

alternative theatre movement. For the crisis conditions of the
1970s frequently posed companies with fundamental issues of
survival and integrity. Was it better to go for safe options in terms
of programming, venue type, audience constituency, and so on,
and thus have a greater chance of securing the future, even if that
meant partial ideological compromise; or was it better to
continue the ideological experiment at full pitch, by reaching
out to yet more new 'deprived' or 'working-class' audiences, even
if that placed your individual company, and by extension the
whole movement, at risk? Of course, there were no easy answers
to such dilemmas.

The issues were further complicated by the successful growth
and the ideological vigour of the movement. On the one hand,
the expanding size and status of the movement were bolstered, in
a grudging kind of way, by the state (through the funding
system), by increasing *rapprochement* with the mainstream
theatre sectors, and by the slow but certain influx of alternative
theatre practitioners into posts in education and the media. On
the other hand, the tightening grip of neo-conservatism on the
political arteries of the nation led to a spectacular strengthening
of resistance and ideological opposition, especially when
attempts were made to suppress or censor the work of radical
companies such as Foco Novo (in 1976), North West Spanner (in
1978), and the Newcastle-based Bruvvers (in 1979) (Knight 1980:
21-5). In fact, the increasingly complex dependence on state and
commercial agencies in part reinforced resistance. Hence, the
increased dependence on the state can be read as *both* a prudent
political tactic used to stay in oppositional business *and* a craven
accommodation to the status quo. The *Wedge* debate erupted in
response to these growing ideological tensions within the movement, which in turn derived from its responsiveness to the
culture of crisis and confrontation in the 1970s.

As an integral part of the major cultural formations of the
period alternative theatre could hardly avoid being drawn into
the confrontational socio-political climate of the late 1970s. As
Robert Hewison has argued, alternative theatre in Britain had
become an effective extension of the counter-cultures, an
impressive example of an extended expressive revolution, with its
own ethos, values, codes and institutional infrastructures (Hewison 1986: 225). This was why so many companies, despite the
argument of the *Wedge* article, chose the harder, experimental

option. For there were widespread attempts in political and community theatre to meet the ideological challenges of the decade more or less head-on, with performance projects designed to activate every dimension of the theatre transaction in the interests of efficacy. And this emphasised theatre as cultural production rather than as aesthetic event. Such consolidations were possible because the early experiments of pioneering companies such as 7:84 (Scotland) had laid impressively solid foundations for the construction of a remarkable range of radical approaches to performance.

John McGrath sets up 7:84 (Scotland)

In 1973 the playwright John McGrath moved from London to Scotland to set up one of the most influential companies in the history of British alternative theatre: 7:84 (Scotland). McGrath had already achieved success in the mainstream of BBC television ('Z Cars') and repertory theatre (Royal Court and elsewhere). He had written plays that reinforced the radicalism of the Liverpool Everyman, and he had founded, in 1971, 7:84 (England), one of the first English alternative political theatre companies. His move to Scotland can be read as emblematic of a much more widespread dissatisfaction among young theatre workers with the irrelevance of most theatre to the mass of the populace. The geographic progression from the metropolitan centre to the provincial periphery signalled a decisive break, the final stage in a deliberate shift from the commercial mass-populism of the media, through the subsidised minority-elitism of mainstream theatres, to an ambitious stab at a (to begin with) self-financed popular localism. In moving to Scotland McGrath's aim was to forge a new kind of theatre practice: political community performance.

McGrath's political position is overtly socialist, and he is an activist who for many years has worked for a cultural revolution. He was involved in the early stages of Centre 42, he visited Paris as a representative of British artists during the 1968 *événements*, and this led to an abiding alignment with the counter-culture. In 1975 he was confidently proclaiming:

the importance of the thinking around that whole time, the excitement of that whole complex set of attitudes to life which that para-revolutionary situation threw up, was incredible – the thinking about ordinary life, the freshness of the approach, the urgency and beauty of the ideas was amazing.

(McGrath 1975: 43)

And this impression was still strong even in 1987:

The connection between the way the excitement of '68 was suppressed and what happened afterwards is as important as the connection between the ideas of '68 and what happened in the theater later.

(McGrath 1987: 121–2)

This sustained interest in the meanings of the counter-culture inflected McGrath's thinking and practice even as he became more committed to Marxist ideas through the 1970s.

His most explicitly theoretical use of Marxism occurs in a 1979 article, where he writes about:

the three main areas of activity of 'political' theatre: firstly, the struggle within the institutions of theatre, against the hegemony of the 'bourgeois' ideology within those institutions; secondly, the making of a theatre that is *interventionist* on a political level, usually outside those institutions; and thirdly and most importantly, the creation of a counter culture based on the working class, which will grow in richness and confidence until it eventually displaces the dominant bourgeois culture of late-capitalism.

(McGrath 1979: 44)

McGrath is thus firmly in the ideological tradition of Gramsci, Althusser, Adorno and Williams, which sees cultural revolution as an essential element in the elimination of the state. But his linking of the concepts of 'working class' and 'counter-culture' suggests a rich synthesis of formations that usually have been seen as distinct, or even in opposition. The idea of a working-class counter-culture extends traditional Marxist formulations of class structuring by adding a type of formation that is new to the analysis. Theatrical interventions into working-class locations can contribute significant new expressions of *cultural* opposition to the status quo.

Even a brief survey of McGrath's various theoretical statements reveals an impressive consistency in his balancing of ideas of expressive freedom with notions of ideological coherence. Thus in a 1985 interview he argued:

> if a writer is committed to an over-rigid set of political principles, the end would have been written before the play, and I think that negates the whole purpose of creating the work . . . a political method of looking at the world is what I'm interested in rather than direct political message conclusions.
>
> (McGrath 1985: 396)

The anti-doctrinaire, non-dogmatic bent is a key characteristic of counter-cultural approaches – ideological progress evolves from the interaction of practice and theory – and McGrath has produced a substantial body of theatrical and theoretical work which aimed to sustain this kind of dialectic. In effect, this has amounted to repeated attempts to synthesise Marxist sociopolitical analysis with a libertarian cultural activism, to produce a new programme for revolutionary cultural production.

This extraordinary ambition has generated heated debate with Arnold Wesker and David Edgar in particular. It also ensured that his early work with 7:84 (especially the Scottish company) was particularly representative of alternative theatre practices which sought an overt socio-political effect. By deliberately placing their radical practice in relatively conservative contexts, McGrath and 7:84 crystallised some of the fundamental approaches, and problems, of political community theatre. More importantly, they engaged with social and cultural questions and debates that had implications reaching far beyond the rough, ready and often remote Scottish community venues which welcomed their shows. This is especially true of 7:84 (Scotland)'s first show, *The Cheviot, the Stag and the Black, Black Oil*, which has now achieved a classic status among alternative theatre productions. Probably this is because it seems to have secured the rare distinction of being – in Eugène van Erven's words – 'a paradigmatic radical popular play' (van Erven 1989: 109).

Scotland in the early 1970s

In an ironic kind of way, the move in 1973 to set up the second 7:84 company in Scotland was brilliantly propitious in its timing. The country then was animated by two great and inter-related cultural and political debates which could not fail to touch all Scottish people. First, there was the issue of Scottish independence, the importance of which is reflected in the national election results for the Scottish Nationalist Party. In the 1970 election the party gained only 1.1% of the total votes cast, which gave it just one Member of Parliament. By February 1974 the votes for the Nationalists had more than doubled, giving the SNP 2% of the total poll, seven Members of Parliament and 21.9% of the total Scottish vote. In the second election of 1974 the number of SNP MPs rose to twelve. This astonishing growth is an obvious index of the strength of Scottish nationalism in the period. Sked and Cook argue that it was never likely that the Nationalists would do much better than this because of 'the ambiguity of Scottish patriotism' (Sked/Cook 1984: 226). Having its own educational, legal and religious systems, its own currency, newspapers, television programmes and so on, the national cultural identity did not need a separate political system, a separate state to ensure its vigour and its future. In the early 1970s, though, the second great Scottish issue seemed to suggest otherwise.

An exceptionally lively and wide-ranging socio-economic debate had been provoked by the discovery and development of the North Sea oil fields. The new industry promised an economic growth that would more than replace the loss of the heavy industries of shipbuilding and mining. In addition, energy policy was pushed to the top of the political agenda by the 1972/3 miners' disputes, the 1973 oil crisis, and the State of Emergency which forced stringent restrictions on the use of fuel and electricity. In this context 'Scottish oil' (as it was called by the Nationalists) promised political power, as well as economic regeneration. The fact that in the 1974 elections the SNP did best in the Grampians, which were most directly affected by the oil boom, was an indication of the widespread concern about how the new wealth might be distributed between Scotland and other nations, particularly as most of the oil companies were foreign-owned. So fundamental national and international issues were embedded in how 'Scottish oil' was to be exploited. The central SNP point was that control of the oil industry could be achieved only if Scotland had its own, separate political system.

Here then was a situation in which enormous cultural, economic and political questions bore directly on the future of

Scottish communities, particularly in the Highland villages. The people there had on their coastline a constant spectacular reminder of the issues. The typical twentieth-century juxtaposition of massive advanced industrial–technological complexes against remote, wild and beautiful landscapes was an unavoidable image of what was at stake. The root questions prompted by the development – who owns Scotland, who controls its people's destiny? – went to the heart of the country's future. The issues raised, and the sides joined, were a crucial dimension of the wider culture of 1970s crisis and confontation in Britain.

Popular political theatre – aesthetic strategies

Questions about 'Scottish oil' were at the core of 7:84's *The Cheviot, the Stag and the Black, Black Oil* as an ideological transaction with its audiences. The show aimed to illuminate the situation, and to recommend radical action for the future. It aimed to be politically efficacious in its impact on a region – the Highlands – and, through that, on a nation. And it aimed to mobilise 300 years of Scottish history in order to achieve that efficacy for working-class audiences in the villages of the region. But how could a small touring theatre hope to secure such a result?

In his most explicit theoretical treatment of popular political theatre McGrath puts 'directness' at the top of a list of characteristics liked by working-class audiences. Such an audience 'likes to know exactly what you are trying to do or say to it'. If a show is direct in this way, then:

> The people who *are* actually involved in the meaning of it don't think of it as didactic. They think of it as self-evident – truths being stated publicly, socially, in an entertaining way and that is very much what theatre is about. Uncovering and giving expression to what is there, and to the realities of people's lives.
>
> (McGrath 1981b: 54)

Now obviously such a project is fraught with pitfalls. How can the company be sure it hasn't misread the 'realities of people's lives'? What right has it to represent those realities and what forms would produce an efficacious result?

Short answers to these questions are provided by McGrath's

insistence that, firstly, company members have to identify with the real socio-economic and cultural interests of their audiences, and, secondly, that there is a living tradition of popular (working-class) culture, separate and distinct from the bourgeois culture of mainstream theatre and the mass culture of the media. For 'identity' to exist the company has to let the audience know that it cares about being with them particularly. The performers have to make it clear that they have the interests of the community at heart, whatever fictional devices are used in the show. Hence, McGrath's idea of 'identity' is very different from 'empathy'. It indicates an ideological consonance between performer and audience, company and community. The grounds for such solidarity, McGrath suggests, can be provided by popular theatrical forms.

The popular forms to which McGrath is referring include concert parties, ceilidhs, the entertainments of contemporary working men's clubs. He argues that this tradition is still relevant to the culture of audiences in British communities and it may therefore provide a source of effective forms for use in radical theatre practice. He shares this confidence in traditional forms with no less a luminary than Dario Fo (though Fo was unknown in Britain in the early 1970s). Theoretically, it relates to Gramsci's idea that folklore and the popular arts could form the basis of counter-hegemonic cultural activism.

However, in the context of late-capitalist Britain these propositions immediately produce, in theory and in practice, major ideological problems. David Edgar, famously, has attacked McGrath for claiming that such forms may serve a subversive function in contemporary Britain. Edgar argues that the popular forms which have survived the onslaught of the media 'have been so extensively corrupted . . . that they are no longer useable' (Edgar 1988: 233). That corruption is the result of ideological appropriation: the forms are now used to reinforce the status quo. McGrath, of course, is well aware of this tendency. He notes that working-class entertainments can be simplistic, racist, sexist, anti-working class, mindless, manipulative, trivial and nauseously ingratiating (McGrath 1981b: 59–60). The popular forms achieve these effects primarily through stereotyping; therefore in order to produce an oppositional practice they must be treated critically. However, as we shall see, this approach can lead to results that have an ideological double-edge, with contradictory effects that may reinforce the very values which they aim to subvert.

This problem is not altogether surprising, because the history of popular performance forms is by no means as simple as Edgar suggests, and as McGrath sometimes appears to assume. It is a mistake to suggest, for example, that forms such as pantomime and music hall once *belonged* to the working classes and have been appropriated subsequently by enemies of the class. Those forms almost always were part of a complex dialectic through which conflicting ideologies, conflicting interests, have been staged. A major aspect of that dialectic has been the way popular performers and audiences engaged with ideological tensions set in motion by the interaction between rhetorical and authenticating conventions. For example, in nineteenth-century music hall there was often a tension between, on the one hand, the explicit celebration of working-class values of collectivity through, say, the authenticating stereotypical conventions of a coster song, and, on the other hand, the implicit celebration of individualist and hierarchical values represented rhetorically by the star who sang the song. Such contradictions were part of the ideological spice that made the form attractive (Bratton 1986: 111-30).

However, if these forms are so contradictory, and potentially reactionary, how can they provide a basis for the kind of company–community identity that McGrath has in mind? He suggests that 'localism' is crucial to the effect, because 'the best response among working-class audiences comes from characters and events with a local feel' (McGrath 1981b: 58). In other words, authenticating conventions should be drawn from the immediate socio-cultural environment of the performance. He also argues that the non-fictional aspects of performance – the rhetorical conventions – are central to the ideological transaction between company and community:

> There are elements in the language of the theatre beyond the text, even beyond the production, which are often more decisive, more central to one's experience of the event than the text or the production . . . notably the choice of venue, audience, performers, and the relationship between audience and performer.
>
> (McGrath 1981b: 7)

Clearly, the founding of 7:84 was intended to place these

elements under the control of the company. All aspects of performance were to contribute to the overall ideological purpose of telling a radical tale about 'what is there . . . the realities of people's lives'.

When we add to this the richly creative dialectic set in motion by McGrath's attempted coupling of the working class and the counter-culture in the context of 1970s Scottish history, then it is hardly surprising that the early shows of 7:84 (Scotland) provide especially remarkable and stimulating examples of oppositional theatre practices, warts and all. Given this, and provided that the warts were not too distracting, the company may even have had a particularly good chance of achieving efficacy for its audiences.

Staging *The Cheviot, the Stag and the Black, Black Oil*

The process and progress of creating *The Cheviot, the Stag and the Black, Black Oil* are engagingly described by McGrath in his preface to the published play. There was a five-week devising–writing–rehearsal period with the new company of mostly Scottish performers. The show then toured, in the spring of 1973, to twenty-seven Highland venues, consisting mostly of town halls, village halls and community centres. The success of the show led to a second tour in the autumn to twenty-six similar venues. A third short tour of six venues in Ireland was undertaken in 1974. McGrath estimates that over 30,000 people saw the show live and that several million saw the version that the BBC filmed and broadcast twice as a Play For Today in 1974 and 1975. The film subsequently was seen in many other countries. This distribution span – from the small-scale local community hall to the mass-scale of international television – is a measure of the show's popular appeal. It is also emblematic, perhaps, of how the performances crystallised global concerns in the localised detail of Highland history represented by the play.

The international popularity of the show was partly a result of its ceilidh format. The traditional ceilidh is an evening of songs, stories, joke-telling and dancing performed by non-professionals for their own entertainment, dealing with issues of interest and concern to the community which stages it. *The Cheviot . . .* uses the form to tell the story of the Scottish Highland clearances of the nineteenth century, and to draw a parallel between the clearances and the operations of the new oil industry. The show argues that, just as the people were pushed aside by the introduction of the Cheviot sheep, so their interests are being ignored by the oil companies and the class allies of those companies. Thus, its main ideological aim was to raise issues relating to the ownership of North Sea oil and its effects on the people of the Highlands from a socialist perspective, and to suggest that a revolutionary response was appropriate to the situation in Scotland.

The rhetorical conventions of the tour itself were essential codes for establishing the commitment of the company to its audiences. The routine of such a tour is one of sheer hard graft: load the van in the morning, drive miles to the next village, find the hall, unload the van, set up the set, grab something to eat, play the show. In small communities this amount of effort rarely goes unnoticed. The effect was reinforced by the length of the evening's work: the show ran for two hours, and was followed by a dance to music provided by the company, which usually lasted until well after midnight. This contact with the community was carried through into the staging of the show itself. As the audience entered the hall to the sound of fiddle music, the actors chatted to them or made final preparations in full view. The company toured its own stage, which was only 18 inches high; props, costumes, musical instruments were visible on each side of it. During the show the actors frequently addressed the audience directly 'as themselves'; characters were adopted as costumes were put on, usually in view of the audience; individual actors played more than one character. All these techniques stress the reality of the performer, and the artificiality of performing.

In similar fashion the written text underlines the reality of the context of the performance. Facts about the region's history are presented *as* facts, local references are included for each venue (usually culled from chats in the pub). And the form of the show invites audience participation through singing, panto-style involvement and finally dancing. The overall effect of the rhetorical conventions is one of hard-worked-for informality and intimacy in which the company can be read as friendly, approachable and above all concerned with (and for) the interests of the audience. This is the basis for company–community identity, which then serves two main functions. Firstly, it makes the show more accessible. Secondly, it highlights the co-operative collectivity and organisational egalitarianism of the company. The rhetorical conventions thus aim to place these implicit ideological meanings in a positive light.

The authenticating conventions aim to reinforce this reading. The ceilidh is an important participatory event for the transmission of Gaelic culture, and the singing of Gaelic songs by Dolina MacLennan was a fundamental authenticating element in the performance. It also signalled the company's concern and respect for the history of the people of the Highlands, and this was further reinforced by the documentary authority of the text. The audience could easily see that an enormous amount of research into their region's history had gone into the performance, and the programme noted that the company had managed to acquire previously unpublished statistics on Scottish land ownership by capitalists, aristocrats and international conglomerates.

This concern for documentary history was carried through partly in the ways that character was constructed by the show. Many of the named characters are known historical figures, and their speeches are based usually on their actual words. These characters represent the dominant, official history of the Scottish Highlands. They are the powerful, the oppressors – consequently they are presented negatively, via satirical stereotyping. Set against them, the play constructs an alternative history out of the straightforward presentation of stories based on documentary material and songs which are part of the popular tradition of the Highlands. Usually this material is presented by the performers 'as themselves'. Occasionally it is spoken by generic, un-named characters. Only once does the show directly create a fictional collectivity, in a scene which dramatises resistance to the clearances as a public meeting. Always the material of 'alternative' history is given a positive gloss. Thus the show takes different attitudes to authenticating conventions, depending on the sources of the information which they communicate. This provides a clear overall ideological focus, but the technique may also weaken its potential for ideological efficacy.

A reading of *The Cheviot* . . .

The Cheviot . . . is profligate in presenting the enemies of community, the representatives of the dominant ideology. Its main methodology in this respect is satiric parody through

stereotypes whose dialogue is constructed mainly from contemporary clichés or near clichés. Occasionally real historical
figures are given the idiom of the stereotypes. These techniques
produce some wonderfully ironic and funny passages in
performance. For example, consider the song of Loch and Sellar
– two men who implemented major land clearances for the Duke
of Sutherland – which is sung direct to the audience:

> Your barbarous customs, though they may be old
> To civilised people hold horror untold –
> What value a culture that cannot be sold?
> The price of a culture is counted in gold.
>
> There's many a fine shoal of fish in the sea
> All waiting for catching and frying for tea
> And I'll buy the surplus, then sell them you see
> At double the price that you sell them to me.
>
> (McGrath 1981a: 8–9)

Or compare the comic *tour-de-force* of Andy McChuckemup, a
contemporary 'Glasgow property owner's man':

> So, picture it, if yous will, right there at the top of the glen,
> beautiful vista – The Crammem Inn, High Rise Motorcroft –
> all finished in natural, workable, plastic Granitette. Right
> next door, the 'Frying Scotsman'. All Night Chiperama – with
> a wee ethnic bit, Fingal's Caff – serving seaweed-suppers-in-
> the-basket, and draught Drambuie. And to cater for your
> younger set, yous've got your Grouse-a Go-Go.
>
> (McGrath 1981a: 48–9)

More than a century, as well as historical specificity, separates
these characters, but both types are treated in the same way by the
text. By comic or ironic exaggeration their pretension to positive
qualities – such as honesty, reliability, decency, good breeding
and social concern – is rendered totally transparent. Their claims
to represent the best interests of the Highlands are totally
deflated. These techniques of deflation suggest that the authentic
voice of the Highlands is provided not by such characters, but by
the unrecorded mass of the people.

In deflating the pretensions of the powerful, the main
structural principle of the show is to work through representatives from the major groupings of the dominant classes. The list

looks like an almost complete catalogue of Althusser's institutional state apparatuses: it includes the aristocracy (Lady Phosphate, Lord Selkirk), religion (the Minister), law (the Judge), royalty (Queen Victoria), art (Harriet Beecher Stowe), civil service (Whitehall), parliament (Westminster), and capitalists and their functionaries (Texas Jim, McChuckemup, Loch, Sellar). The iconography of the satire is always hard-hitting, at times a little crude and blunt, at times brilliantly constructed to exploit the intimacy of the actor–audience relationship.

For example, Lord Crask and Lady Phosphate, two Victorian aristocrats, bring on guns for a shooting party. Their costumes are slightly exaggerated but typical plaid and tartan English-aristocracy-in-Scotland, whereas their weapons, anachronistically, are powerful sub-machine guns. The jokes at their expense are deliberately awful:

LADY PH.   Your highland air is very strong – I quite
                fancy a small port.
LORD CRASK   Oh, how would you like Lochinver?
                                        (McGrath 1981a: 40)

The buffoonery is disarming: the characters are presented as a simple mechanism for a broad attack on privilege. They even sing a comic duet:

BOTH   Oh, it's awfully, frightfully ni-i-ice,
                Shoot stags, my dear, and grice –
                And there's nothing quite so righ-it-it
                As a fortnight catching trite.

But as it ends the song turns unexpectedly vicious:

LORD CRASK   But although we think you're quaint
                Don't forget to pay your rent
                And if you should want your land,
                We'll cut off your grasping hand,
LADY PH.   You had better learn your place,
                You're a low and servile race –
                We've cleared the straths
LORD CRASK   We've cleared the paths
LADY PH.   We've cleared the bens
LORD CRASK   We've cleared the glens

BOTH	. . . and we can do it once again
LADY PH.	We've got the brass
LORD CRASK	We've got the class
LADY PH.	We've got the law
BOTH	We need no more –
	We'll show you we're the ruling class.

(McGrath 1981a: 41)

At this climax they turn the guns on the audience, their faces angry and snarling.

The moment is a complex and risky one. Clearly, the audience is being invited to reject aristocratic/capitalist ideologies because of the contradictions between what they pretend to be and what they actually produce. But the moment is risky because its structure – particularly in the relationship between authenticating and rhetorical conventions – allows for quite different kinds of reading. The portrayal of the aristocracy may be rejected as a ridiculous exaggeration, especially as it depends so much on the buffoonery of stereotype and caricature for its comic effect. The image can be read as completely inauthentic. Moreover, the company may invite rejection through its use of rhetorical conventions. For the informality and the intimacy – the friendliness – of the direct actor–audience contact is used to produce its exact opposite. The audience may think that they have been seduced into a trust which is then unjustifiably exploited. Ironically, the better the quality of the performance, the more this effect may be heightened.

Moreover, as this technique of character construction is common to all the other similar figures in the show, a reading of the moment as invalid can be generalised out, as it were, to include all those other signs. The exaggeration of buffoonery through stereotyping may produce signs without signifiers, a kind of theatrical formalism, in which the satire fails to hit any mark in the reality of the audience because it is too crude, too direct, too full of the kind of theatrical and ideological risks signified by this particular moment. In terms of our theoretical perspective: didactic agit prop would have got the better of ironic satire. Obviously, such readings would signify rejection of the egalitarian and collective – the socialist – ideology of 7:84.

The show takes other risks in its treatment of nationalism, and thus the whole question of how 'Scottish oil' should be managed.

Towards the end of the performance a straightforward claim is made:

> Nationalism is not enough. The enemy of the Scottish people is Scottish capital, as much as the foreign exploiter.
>
> (McGrath 1981a: 66)

But (and it is a very large but) the underlying structure of the show aims to generate an ideological identity of *local* community (through rhetorical conventions) in relation to a *regional* history of oppression (through authenticating conventions), and then the region inevitably is defined as part of the Scottish nation. Despite a powerful appeal for a classic Marxist internationalism, the main basis for solidarity proposed by the show is the community of interest formed by *all* the oppressed people of Scotland. This reading is reinforced by the sign systems which are used to construct the stereotypes and caricatures: they are *Scottish* aristocrats, factors, ministers; or *English* royalty, civil servants, politicians; *American* novelists and businessmen.

Together these aspects of the performance implicitly foster a nationalist interpretation of international relations. In other words, the implicit ideologies built into the popular forms of satirical national stereotyping run directly counter to the explicit ideology that the show wished to transact. In this respect 7:84 does not seem to have achieved the critical perspective on the popular forms of entertainment that McGrath recommends for an ideologically sound good night out.

The ideological ambivalence of the show's treatment of nationalism was especially highlighted by an invitation from the SNP to perform at the party's annual conference at the end of the first tour. McGrath makes a vigorous defence against criticisms from the Scottish left for agreeing to do the gig. The reception by the conference itself of the overt anti-nationalist message was very mixed; 'some cheered, some booed, the rest were thinking about it' (McGrath 1981a: xxvi). But in the end the company received a 10-minute standing ovation, to which they responded with raised clenched fists. The image is a piquant one, because – despite the overt rejection of nationalism – the performance *could* be read as a rallying cry for all Scotland's oppressed; which from a nationalist point of view would include all Scottish people. Given the crisis conditions of late 1973, the show could well have contributed to the success of the Nationalists in the 1974 election. So

The Cheviot . . . may have been efficacious in reinforcing an ideology that it aimed to question.

Text, context and ideology

As an ideological transaction, *The Cheviot* . . . can thus be seen as particularly vulnerable to the ideological constitution of its performance context, particularly in relation to nationalist gatherings, or anti-nationalist tendencies in any gathering. Thus McGrath reports on the performance in Lochinver:

> [The town] has many breeds of white settlers, English and Scottish, retired, or living off investments, or just failed gentry come to find a few forelocks that might be tugged at them. Unfortunately for us, those people had appropriated us in advance because we were 'theatre' and they were cultivated. Most of the local people had taken their cue and stayed away.
>
> (McGrath 1981a: xx)

However, McGrath also notes that in villages where an indigenous population came to the performance their real connections to historical oppression, via ancestors or the folk-memory, produced an interest which easily accommodated the variety of forms in the show, from bald documentary fact to the violent buffoonery of Phosphate and Crask.

This was the outcome of the show's successful methods for presenting the 'alternative' history, which deliberately avoid painting a picture of a *typical* Highland community. The Highland 'community' is defined only in outline, and mainly with reference to a common folk-memory. The key reference points are topographical: the land, the soil and especially the mountains are constantly referred to as 'belonging to the people'. Likewise, the croft and the fortitude of labour in the fields, the mistreatment by landowners in the clearances and the bravery of opposition, especially by women, become potent images of a past shared by all communities in the region. Some more specific connections are made for particular communities through a list of documentary passages referring to different localities; the stage directions state that different passages are 'to be selected . . . according to where the show is being done'. For example:

> During the time of the Clearances, the population of the

parishes of Killarow and Kilmenny - in Islay - was reduced from 7,100 to 2,700. The population of the entire island was halved.

(McGrath 1981a: 18)

But, in the main, audiences are free to make connections between their local history and the portmanteau regional history. Thus, McGrath writes of the trial of Patrick Sellar, manager of the Duke of Sutherland's estates, that:

it was, or is, a burning memory, never to be forgotten, and never forgiven. As late as 1970, the Sutherland's factor was greeted with Baas, and cries of 'Men not sheep' when he got up rashly to ask a question at a Labour meeting in Golspie.

(McGrath 1981a: vi)

Such connections enable the audience to use the history presented in the performance to define their own sense of community. The show thus hopes to animate the folk-memory to produce symbols which suggest that the 'people' and their communities must be the basis of an oppositional ideology, or at least an ideology of resistance. Thus, the performance animates a dynamic relationship between the rhetorical conventions - which present the *company* - and the autheticating conventions - which represent the *community* - in order to suggest that the history of the Highlands is told most accurately by the collective voice of the 'people', as represented by the socialist collectivity of the company.

In these contexts the concluding dance could turn into a vigorous celebration of ideological solidarity between company and community, a carnivalesque confirmation of identity:

You can tell a lot about a community from the way they dance. In Orkney, during the eightsome, couples pass on from group to group automatically all round the floor, so the whole crowd is in one big integrated routine.

(McGrath 1981a: xxi-ii)

The dancing becomes an expression of the ideological identity of the local community. If it is an authentic celebration, we may suggest that, in the context of a performance of *The Cheviot . . .*, the expressivity of dancing could be inscribed with the ideology transacted by the show: a shared celebration of collectivism,

egalitarianism and a will to self-determination. If this occurred –
and McGrath suggests it was not uncommon – then perhaps we
may read the dancing as the point at which the links between
Marxism and the counter-culture, agit prop and carnival are
most firmly forged in the practice of 7:84, where the class analysis
of the show merges with expressive libertarianism to create a
concrete experience of oppositional participatory democracy, if
only for an hour or two.

Contextuality and efficacy

Paradoxically, the show's potential for alternative readings, its
acute contextuality, as demonstrated in the different reactions at
the SNP conference and in the villages, may have *increased* the
overall efficacy of *The Cheviot* . . . . McGrath reports how the
show 'helped to create pressure within the Labour Party from all
over Scotland for some measures to reform estate ownership and
land use in the Highlands' (McGrath 1981b: 71). But, ironically,
the potential for ambiguous readings of its treatment of nationalism may have had more effect in relation to the issue of North
Sea oil. In 1975 the minority Labour government, with the
support of the SNP MPs, created the British National Oil
Corporation, thus effectively reinforcing (admittedly via a
Glaswegian forum) central control of the development of
'Scottish oil'.

It appears that the show could well have been efficacious
because of its unflinching animation of the key debates
surrounding the future of Scotland, but that its fundamental
ideological power issued from the ways in which it permitted
different communities of both location and interest to make
variant readings. In other words, the extent to which it fell short
of consistent didacticism, the degree to which its messages were
available – within clear parameters defined by the obvious nature
of its central concerns – to alternative readings, was the foundation for its potential actual influence on Scottish history.

Of course, shows such as *The Cheviot* . . . are never likely to
have an unmediated effect on the ownership of Scottish land or the
operations of the oil industry. Their efficacy is primarily cultural;
only under exceptionally propitious circumstances may they
directly foster social or political change. McGrath argues that:

The theatre can never *cause* a social change. It can articulate pressure towards one, help people celebrate their strengths and maybe build their self-confidence . . . Above all, it can be the way people can find their voice, their solidarity and their collective determination. If we achieved any one of these, it was enough.

(McGrath 1981a: xxvii)

This was written in 1981, when 7:84 had much more experience of making popular political theatre under its collective belt. By then the rhetoric of revolutionary vanguardism sometimes heard from radical theatre groups in the early 1970s (but never from McGrath) had been tempered by hard experience and major changes in the socio-political constitution of the nation. Large claims about stirring the working classes into action through radical theatre were no longer acceptable currency. Such claims could be seen for what they really were: romantic fantasies, based on a weak grasp of the social realities of life near the poverty line and misguided notions of the power of performance.

Judged in relation to the optimism of the early 1970s, when many political theatre workers proclaimed ambitions for a real revolution, the subsequent work of 7:84, and of many other overtly political alternative theatre companies, must be pronounced a failure. However, a more realistic assessment produces a kinder result. For example, alternative theatre companies have learned that the differences between political, social and cultural activism cannot be glossed over in a generalised appeal to revolutionary action. Radical work in each of the three spheres can be mutually supportive, but the procedures demanded – and the types of effect produced – are by no means the same. The years of contact with specific audiences in specific communities have taught an important lesson to radical theatre workers: each type of community, each kind of constituency, requires a tailor-made approach – in order to become culturally and, perhaps, sociopolitically efficacious.

In the early 1980s 7:84 (Scotland) toured McGrath's *Blood Red Roses* to a few of the Highland venues first visited by *The Cheviot* . . . . This was done, according to McGrath, 'as an experiment' because the play had been written for the industrial towns of the lowlands. McGrath reports that:

In the quieter, rural areas there was some disappointment; this

is not one for us, they told me – and they had different
attitudes to industrial battles, and to the abrasive character of
Bessie, the heroine. There was, in plain words, a clash of
cultures.

(McGrath 1990: 72)

This led to a confirmation of existing policy for 7:84, in which
different types of show were staged for the variety of Scottish
audiences that the company had identified. McGrath maintains,
rightly, that such responsiveness to cultural pluralism does not
entail ideological fragmentation in a company's programme. In
fact the range of cultural contexts may enable the evolution of a
subtler use of conventions, and may clarify the overall socio-
political orientation of a group's cultural production.

Despite this advance through nearly fourteen years of dedicated
experimentation, McGrath was forced by the Scottish Arts
Council to relinquish his control of 7:84 in 1988. In the late 1980s
he developed an interest in spectacle and carnival, and, with
Wildcat Theatre, he staged a series of large-scale pageant-style
events at the Glasgow Tramshed Theatre. In these shows he
again essayed an historical panorama of Scottish political struggle, but this time on a grand scale. In aesthetic terms, and in
terms of the constituency to which they made their appeal, these
shows were light years away from *The Cheviot*. . . . But from the
point of view of their ideology as part of a wider programme of
cultural activism they demonstrated an impressive consistency
with the first 7:84 Scottish tour.

Watching John Bett in the Wildcat productions, it was easy to
recall his work as Crask and other characters in *The Cheviot*. . . .
This was not simply a matter of a remarkable performance; it was
also a reminder of how influential that first show had been. With
The Cheviot . . . McGrath and 7:84 created a flexible model that
was adopted and modified by a wide spectrum of political and
community theatre companies throughout the 1970s and even into
the 1980s. Of the earlier ones pursuing parallel practices we can
list CAST, Red Ladder, Portable Theatre and General Will. And
the later ones would include Belt and Braces, Foco Novo, Joint
Stock, Broadside Mobile Workers' Theatre, North West Spanner,
Monstrous Regiment and many of the other late-1970s feminist
groups. Among the community theatre companies we might
mention Pentabus, EMMA, Live Theatre, Bruvvers, Perspectives,

Medium Fair and many more. There is no doubt that *The Cheviot* . . . crystallised a form of cultural production that became increasingly important in the 1970s.

Throughout the country, groups were set up to explore new interfaces between theatre and community. A widening range of practices searched for ideological efficacy through performance. The majority were concerned to empower their audiences, and there can be no doubt that many of their performances were greeted with enthusiasm by all kinds of communities. For in periods of social and political crisis, such as the 1970s, there is often an ever-present need for self-determination and a deep desire for cultural autonomy. The political and community theatre movement grew and prospered because it addressed, and sometimes perhaps even satisfied, those needs and desires. A new and often effective form of cultural production was created and consolidated on a national scale.

Chapter 6

Reorientation in the 1980s
The community plays of Ann Jellicoe and the Colway Theatre Trust

The divided nation of the 1980s

In Britain the 1980s began in 1979, when the Conservatives won the general election and Margaret Thatcher became the first woman Prime Minister. The Tory's landslide victory was a foregone conclusion. The Labour Party was in ideological disarray and its policies had produced economic and social instability. Thatcher's promise of a return to strong government leadership had wide public appeal among a populace fed up with the repeated crises of the 1970s. The new Tory policies inaugurated the most fundamental redirection of British society since the second world war. All spheres of social and cultural life were to be judged first in economic terms. Monetarism meant the dismantling of the welfare state, privatisation of the nationalised industries, radical curbing of trade union power, 'structural' unemployment, a strengthened police force, a pro-nuclear defence policy, and a new moral order based on self-interest. Private enterprise was to replace public dependency, so cuts in government expenditure, including that on the arts, were inevitable. In effect, the values of 'community' which informed the 1970s were to be replaced by those of the nuclear family and the individual. Co-operation was to be supplanted by competition. Thatcherism was bound to exacerbate confrontation, and produce a divided nation (Sked/Cook 1984).

In 1980 unemployment rose above 2 million for the first time since the 1930s. School leavers and other young people made up a large proportion of the unemployed, so it is hardly surprising that in 1981 'youth' riots broke out in several major cities. In the same year IRA prisoners in the Maze went on hunger strike, the women's peace camp at the USAF Greenham Common base was set up, and unemployment passed the 3 million mark. Public attention was deflected from growing domestic protest in 1982 by the Falklands war, which Thatcher skilfully used to muster support for the government in the 1983 election. The Tories won again, with an increased parliamentary majority but a decreased popular vote. The first American Cruise missile was delivered to Britain in election year and massive anti-nuclear demonstrations followed in London and other major European cities. The same year also saw massed protest in the People's March for Jobs, replicating the 1930s Jarrow Marches, but on a much bigger scale. The bitterest strike in the history of the mining industry followed in 1984/5, but new trade union legislation ensured a humiliating defeat for the miners. Another blow against unionism was struck in 1985 when workers at the Cheltenham GCHQ government communications centre were banned from union membership, causing widespread protest.

Organised resistance to Thatcherism in the local authorities grew throughout the decade. Particularly in the metropolitan boroughs there had been a sustained effort to counter the erosion of public services caused by central government rate-capping. The Greater London Council (GLC) was spectacularly successful in this respect, evolving a socio-cultural policy based on the ideology of cultural democracy. But new legislation abolished the metropolitan boroughs in 1986, producing vigorous public protests. In 1987 further disabling legislation began its progress through Parliament, in the form of the notorious Clause 28, which banned local authorities from doing anything which might 'promote' homosexuality. Again there was widespread opposition to the repressive implications of the bill, but again the Tory majority ensured Clause 28 became law. The following year saw a radical revision of the rating system in the form of the Poll Tax, or Community Charge. This proved to be massively unpopular, as it undermined local democracy by introducing more centralised control of local government budgets and as it was more expensive than the old rating system. As the decade came to an end civil disobedience reappeared across the land. Millions of people refused to pay the new tax and demonstrations erupted in many cities and towns. Perhaps few really believed it would happen, but the dissent proved to be the beginning of the end for Margaret Thatcher's rule.

The catalogue of protest highlights the popular resistance to Thatcherism, which was fuelled by a crucial contradiction in the government's ideology, between a centralised authoritarian control and a commitment to individual freedom. This contradiction produced a cultural ethos mainly characterised by polarised attitudes: between the rich and the poor, between black and white, between the north and the south. It became increasingly impossible to be neutral in the face of the massive changes that the government was inducing in British society. This had two main effects that are centrally relevant to this study. Firstly, it gradually strengthened the resolve of oppositional movements, so that ideological clarity became increasingly important. Secondly, it encouraged the theatricalisation of protest and resistance. Deprived of real power, oppositional movements – from the Labour Party to the local ginger group – rediscovered the power of the quickly read symbolic gesture. The best examples perhaps are provided by the fence decorations of the Greenham Common women, closely followed by the iconography of the young unemployed, with its pop-parodic pseudo-militarism of shaved heads, leathers and Doc Martens (Campbell 1984). The political potency of carefully selected oppositional signs added visual spice to the culture of confrontation. The 1980s saw a return to the society of the spectacle.

Versions of 'cultural provision' in the 1980s

The economic, social and political divides in Britain were reflected at every cultural level, but nowhere more clearly than in the opposing policies of the Arts Council and the Greater London Council. In January 1981 the Arts Council, for the first time in its history, announced the withdrawal of funds from forty-one of its 'clients'. This was the first major public signal that the funding body was intent on assuming a new operational stance in the 1980s. Personnel changes in the top ranks of the Council reinforced its change of identity. In 1981 William Rees-Mogg (later Lord Rees-Mogg), a former high-Tory editor of *The Times*, was appointed Chairman of the Council. Then in 1982 Richard Hoggart's tenure as Council Vice-chairman was not renewed (as had been standard practice). According to Roy Shaw (the Secretary General of the Council) he was dismissed because 'Number 10 doesn't like him' (Shaw 1987: 43–4). Hoggart, of course, was broadly sympathetic to the left. In the same year Shaw himself retired and was replaced by Luke Rittner, who, through ABSA (Association for Business Sponsorship of the Arts), had been a national leader in the promotion of commercial and industrial sponsorship as a partial replacement for state subsidy of the arts. Rittner was not sympathetic to the left. The liberal role so far played by the Council was abandoned in favour of a harsher, more interventionist, public image. Cut clients were denied any right of appeal.

The new interventionism was spelled out in a major document in 1984, hubristically titled: *The Glory of the Garden: The Development of the Arts in England – A Strategy for a Decade.* The chief strategy outlined for English theatre was the setting-up of a 'national theatre' in each major region of population, based on producing companies in existing repertory theatre buildings. As well as providing 'centres of excellence', these theatres would also be responsible for co-ordinating alternative theatre and theatre-in-education in their areas. The plan ran into immediate trouble, not least with the very Regional Arts Associations that it was supposed to benefit. For example, following a one-day conference on the new policy, North West Arts published a critical response, wittily dubbed *Haughty Culture* (North West Arts 1984). This title nicely captures the real attitudes behind the 'strategy' of *The Glory* . . . . The regions would be supported by the metropolitan centre if they reproduced the principles of centrism and hierarchy which were the root of their subjugation to the centre. For once, regional resistance to the Arts Council was generally successful. By 1986, according to the Cork Report (a major ACGB enquiry into professional theatre in England), not one of the strategy's main recommendations were 'in place' (Cork 1986). But the new regime was not to be deterred.

In the mid-1980s the Arts Council increasingly looked like a central government clone. For a start it spoke the same language as its paymaster. Consider the following from William Rees-Mogg in 1985:

The qualities required for survival in this age are the qualities of the age itself. They include self-reliance, imagination, a sense of opportunity, range of choice, and the entrepreneurial action of small professional groups. The state should continue to help the arts, but the arts should first look to themselves, and to their audiences for their future and their growth.

(Rees-Mogg 1985: 8)

A new series of funding schemes was introduced in the second half of the 1980s, which fostered the kind of 'entrepreneurial action' preferred by neo-conservatism. These promoted commercial and industrial 'investment' in the arts though sponsorship deals, through 'partnership funding' (equal monies from different funding bodies), and as part of major city-centre redevelopments, where the American 'percent for art' idea (1% of development costs to be spent on art) was embraced with dubious fervour. The Council also up-graded the business performance of arts organisations through enhanced training for administrators and managers, and through 'business incentive' programmes. Whilst some of these schemes brought much-needed 'new money' into the arts and welcome increases in efficiency, they also all demanded an ideological pay-off. In drama, for example, there was a major shift in funding patterns, from revenue (annual) grants to project (short-term) grants, making long-term community-based cultural experiments increasingly rare. By the end of the decade neo-conservative values were inscribed deeply into the structures of the state funding system and the operations of many of its clients. A centrist and elitist subsidy superstructure cast long shadows over the arts landscape.

The conversion of the subsidised arts sector to a neo-conservative business ethic was achieved in the face of spectacular radical alternatives. Especially in Tyne and Wear, Merseyside and, quintessentially, Greater London, the metropolitan boroughs had funded many new initiatives in grass-roots cultural production. The most radical of the metropolitan programmes was pursued cheek by jowl with the Arts Council. The Greater London Council built a complex edifice of cultural innovation, based on a number of straightforward policies. These included: defining audiences in terms of communities of interest – the unemployed, women's and gay groups, the elderly; fostering active participation by non-professionals in cultural production; encouraging grass-roots participation in the cultural industries – such as radio, video, recorded music, publishing; and support for ideologically controversial events, such as the 1982 festival of lesbian and gay-male arts. In the four years that these policies were pursued (1981-5) theatre received more funding from the GLC than any other category of activity, with money distributed among seventy-five alternative groups (Greater London Council 1986; Mulgan/Warpole 1986). Two of these were overtly political companies which had been cut by the Arts Council's *Glory . . .* strategy: Broadside Mobile Workers' Theatre and our old friend CAST. The GLC Arts Sub-Committee was nothing if not witty in its strategic use of cultural politics. The government, and the tabloid press, were suitably affronted.

A more puckish riposte to Arts Council elitism was made by the GLC in 1985, in its role as landlord of the Hayward Gallery in the South Bank arts complex. The GLC threatened to evict the sitting tenants of the gallery, namely, the Arts Council, on the grounds that the exhibition programme was not in harmony with its cultural policy. According to the GLC, the Arts Council's shows had not sufficiently represented the works of women and black artists, and so its policy was implicitly sexist and racist. In the event, the eviction did not take place, as existing contracts took the tenancy to May 1986, only a month before the GLC was finally abolished by the government. Overt repression seemed to be the only tactic that the Tories could muster against local democratic movements such as those represented by the GLC. However, the GLC - and other councils - had demonstrated how culture could, spectacularly, be a site of ideological resistance.

The divisions in British society were also reflected in the growing distance between the top and bottom of the theatrical pyramid during the 1980s. In 1982 the Royal Shakespeare Company had moved into the huge concrete edifice of the Barbican in the City of London. The following year a government-ordered investigation into the RSC (the Priestley Report) concluded that - counter to government suspicions - the company was efficient but underfunded to the tune of £1 million a year. A similar inquiry into the National Theatre (the Rayner Report) followed, but concluded that the levels of grant aid were appropriate to its needs. As the decade progressed the two nationals took up an increasing proportion of the total grant aid allocated by the ACGB for theatre, averaging around 47% (though their grants fell in value in real terms) (Cork 1986: 98-101; Feist/Hutchison 1990: 12). By the late 1980s the annual subsidy to the National Theatre was approaching £10 million and the RSC was not far behind at £8 million.

The customary justification in the 1970s for such high levels of subsidy was that they enabled the two nationals to set the artistic standards by which the rest of British theatre could be judged. But in the 1980s two further arguments were increasingly heard, and these were symptomatic of the ideological shifts influencing the whole history of British theatre in that sad decade. Firstly, it was claimed they were of significant economic value to the nation through their contribution to Britain's tourist trade. Secondly, it was frequently suggested that they were essential to the maintenance of the nation's 'heritage'.

Now Robert Hewison's analysis of the 'heritage industry' provides another suggestive piece to the hegemonic jigsaw in 1980s Britain. Hewison argues that the heritage industry:

> conspires to create a shallow screen that intervenes between our present life and our history. We have no understanding of history in depth, but instead are offered a contemporary creation, more costume drama and re-enactment than critical discourse.
>
> (Hewison 1987: 135)

In other words, the heritage industry – including to some extent the major theatres of the land – produces a *decontextualised* culture, a culture without roots. Some of the processes used to make such a culture can be detected in the practices of the two national theatres in the 1980s. They include: a merchant bank sponsoring Brecht's *Threepenny Opera* at the National Theatre; a community play re-staged by the nation's 'top' actors in the National's Cottesloe auditorium; the transfer of the RSC's *Nicholas Nickleby* (which used techniques developed in alternative theatre) to Broadway. What seems to determine these events is not cultural need, the situation of any particular community of spectators, but the demand placed on the national theatres in the 1980s to play the role of market-leaders, on the international arts scene and to a range of home markets. Now the nationals not only were setting 'artistic standards', they were also the model for a new consumer-oriented attitude to cultural production in the subsidised theatre. The dominance of such models placed ideologically oppositional theatre practices under increasing pressure as the difficult decade wore on.

In addition, the national theatres pursued their policies of cultural appropriation, but with greater intensity. Talented actors such as Alfred Molina (who had performed with Belt and Braces Theatre Company, an offshoot of 7:84), and innovative directors such as Deborah Warner (who had founded the Kick Theatre Company to produce modern classics), were offered contracts by the top two as soon as news of their outstanding qualities spread beyond the alternative circuit. The theatre reviewers – especially those working for the 'quality' national newspapers – acted as quasi-talent-spotters. The repertory theatres devised joint projects which absorbed some subversive theatre practices. Many alternative theatre groups and practitioners colluded in this process, which has been described by Gramsci and Williams as the incorporation of emergent ideologies into the dominant means of cultural production (Gramsci 1971: 59–61; Williams 1981: 203–5). Ironically, the impact of Thatcherism on alternative theatre in the 1980s certainly supports their analysis.

Alternative theatre in the 1980s

Any review of alternative theatre in the 1980s is certain to be mixed. On the one hand, many of the new companies which appeared were aesthetically unadventurous and ideologically reticent (to say the least). On the other hand, there were some especially successful efforts to devise new and subversive approaches to audiences and their communities. For example, in the late 1970s a number of groups had begun to address the 'problem' of the ubiquitously small audiences that traditionally had turned out for alternative theatre events. Foremost among these was Welfare State International, which by 1981 had scaled up its annual Guy Fawkes bonfire spectacle, *Parliament in Flames*, to attract an audience of 15,000 at Catford, South London. Meanwhile, in the South West of England, the playwright Ann Jellicoe had discovered what almost amounted to a new genre: the community play. The tone of excitement that always attaches to the scale of these events came across loud and clear in a BBC *Arena* documentary about the 1981 community play for Bridport, in Dorset:

> Now we involve at least 150 people as actors, but around that we shall involve a further 350 or 400 . . . making costumes,

helping with transport . . . Not just that, because we work
through the school . . . and one-third of the households in the
town are directly affected by the school . . . the play goes
directly into one-third of the households in the town . . . what
we know from past experience will happen, is that enormous
amounts of small contacts are made, the town is irrigated with
a kind of creativity.

(Jellicoe, *Arena* 1981)

The large numbers seem to generate excitement in their own right.
Welfare State and Ann Jellicoe were particularly influential in
1980s alternative theatre in large part because the scale of their
projects almost guaranteed an impact on the community.

In the first half of the 1980s, alternative theatre continued to
expand at an impressive rate, so that by mid-decade the total
number of companies exceeded 300 for the first time, growing
from 142 in 1980 to 313 in 1987. This was the result of a
remarkable boom in the founding of new companies: in 1979
about 34 new groups began work; in 1980 an astonishing 54 or so
were set up, and the rate was increased over the next three years
(1982: 54; 1983: 64; 1984: 70). The geographical distribution
begun in the 1970s was extended, and most areas of Britain were
within the reach of an alternative group. The proliferation was
sustained by a number of factors, including: a now well-
established studio-venue system; consolidation of the movement
as a recognised element of the subsidised theatre system; strengthened national organisations (particularly the Independent
Theatre Council and the Theatre Writers' Union); a growing
number of new graduates trained to work in the field; a widening
range of approaches to theatre as cultural production; and,
crucially, a tradition of self-help and survival against the odds
that ironically enabled groups to benefit from the Thatcherite
'enterprise culture'.

Despite these advantages, from about mid-decade there was a
falling off in both the number of new groups founded and the
total size of the movement. In 1985 only 45 new companies were
started up, signalling the start of an erratic downward trend
(1986: 39; 1987: 48; 1988: 30; 1989: 38; 1990: 13). More significantly, the total number of groups fell from 313 in 1985 to 272
in 1990. The brunt of this reduction was borne by the small-scale
touring groups, which dropped from 220 to 187, and by

community theatre. The one notable exception to the decline was in the number of middle-scale groups, which expanded from 37 (1985) to 49 (1990). This growth reflects the consolidation of ACGB revenue funding for a small number of favoured companies at the top of the alternative tree. However, there can be little doubt that the overall decline was the result of new policies in the funding system. Firstly, there was a fall in real terms in the total grant available for theatre, forcing increased reliance on sponsorship and box-office income. Alternative theatre, not being a particularly attractive site for advertising, made little headway in raising sponsorship money, though there was an improvement overall in box-office takings (Feist/Hutchison 1990: 19). Secondly, greater competition in the movement was encouraged by the general shift away from annual revenue grants towards short-term project grants and 'incentive' funding schemes. Thirdly, the distinctions between alternative and mainstream theatre were increasingly blurred, as financial shortage in both sectors encouraged a variety of collaborations and transfers. All this destabilised alternative theatre, undermining subversive practices, and causing many companies to 'go dark' for part of the year, sometimes never to see the light again.

The overall trend towards a less ideologically radical orientation in alternative theatre can be detected, to a greater or lesser degree, in eight categories of approach – a few of which were new to the scene. Three categories were most significant to the process of ideological weakening, as their programmes simply tended to reproduce mainstream practices in miniature, by focusing on either (a) modern plays/new writing, or (b) the classics, or (c) repertory-style seasons combining both. Typically, these groups talked about the 'artistic quality' of their shows with little indication of the reasons for producing them, and when they mentioned touring patterns they referred to *venues* rather than *audiences* (a habit picked up from the Arts Council). Companies such as Remould, Eastern Angles and Red Shift were characteristic of these groupings, which enjoyed a significant growth as the arts centre venues demanded more middle-of-the-road products.

Groups in the fourth category continued the trend started in the late 1970s by companies such as Hesitate and Demonstrate and Impact, concentrating on aesthetic innovations for studio settings, usually with an emphasis on visual and physical effects.

The new groups (such as Optik, Theatre Babel and the Shadow
Syndicate) were committed to the subjective as the determining
domain of theatrical conventions, so they could justifiably be
called 'neo-expressionist'. Despite occasional nods towards
populism, most of them were wedded to ritualism and montage
post-modernism, so their ideological orientations were opaque
or even invisible. The fifth and sixth types of group were
relatively new to alternative theatre: these were the music-theatre
and site-specific companies. At one end of the ideological spectrum, music-theatre included scaled-down adaptations of mainstream operas which merely added a populist gloss to the elitism
written into the form (for example, Opera Restor'd); while, at the
other end, site-specific groups such as Emergency Exit Arts
(which made one-off shows in response to particular locations)
sometimes worked closely with local communities to make
participatory spectacles in celebration of grass-roots identities.

  This kind of implicit, somewhat unfocused ideological opposition was reproduced by a number of the populist theatre
groups, which formed the seventh type of company. Most of these
groups chose to perform in streets, parks, pubs, shopping
precincts, on beaches, promenades and docksides. Some of them,
such as Mummerandada and Fortunati, derived a sophistication
of style from the European traditions represented by Jacques
Lecoq and Dario Fo, and gained a further boost towards the end
of the decade from the humanist orientation of 'new circus'.
Some simply provided escapism (there was a boom in street
entertainment), but others were by no means ideologically
neutral: sometimes the down-trodden clown's exposure to
ridicule paralleled the plight of the millions of unemployed
people, and her/his resilience in adversity suggested a dignified
survival against the odds.

  But it is the eighth type of company which most clearly signals
a major ideological refocusing of alternative theatre. We might
call them the 'soft ideology' groups, on account of their general
tendency to soft-pedal socially critical issues. The more tentative
of these groups, such as Meeting Ground, aimed to 'explore
common visions, desires and fears' or to 'provoke thought', or to
'stimulate imagination'. Their more radical compatriots, such as
Communicado, produced shows which investigated more problematic areas, most commonly issues of gender, sexuality, race
and, increasingly, the environment. They aimed to uncover

hegemony by 'raising questions' or by 'challenging received attitudes/opinions/prejudices'. Their work often reflected a general perception that the issues to be dealt with are as much embedded in the consciousness of the group as 'out there' in the social sphere or political arena. Their aesthetic eclecticism – they drew on a broad spectrum of genres and forms – aimed to appeal to a wide range of venues, part of the go-getting ethos of the times. Thus the 'softest' seemed simply to be reinforcing the wider trend towards ideologically innocuous programming. However, for some of them the soft ideological line was camouflage for a more radical reaction to the harsh political environment of the decade.

On the positive side, these new categories of company added a rich diversity and a lively ideological chaos to alternative theatre. They shifted it away from the grant-induced complacency and settled patterns of programming which threatened too many practices in the late 1970s. On the negative side, the new variety was more apparent than real as the survival of new groups often depended on the marketing of 'safe' products, particularly for the arts centre circuit. More fundamentally, the increased competition induced by their expanding numbers exacerbated the stratifying effects of the re-jigged subsidy system. The reduction in revenue grants ensured that any new companies would add to a growing 'underclass' struggling to make a unique mark in the alternative theatre market-place. The general effect of such commercialisation was to push alternative theatre further into the de-radicalised fragmentation that had started in the late 1970s.

It is depressingly clear that, as a result of these trends, overt political theatre became increasingly hard to sustain in the 1980s. A number of leading companies had their grants cut and were forced to close down, including 7:84 (England), Foco Novo and Joint Stock. Hence, the key focus of explicit ideologically oppositional practice shifted to the women's, gay, black, and special needs groups (such as Scarlet Harlets, the Theatre of Black Women, and Graeae Theatre Company), and to some of the community theatre companies. Together these made up a shrinking proportion of the whole sector, hovering at around a third of the total. Overall, there was a fall in the number of political and community companies, though this was partly offset by increases in the number of special needs and women's/

feminist groups. These last led the way to a partial rejuvination of the movement, producing shows which ranged in style from naturalism to cabaret, and from multi-media spectacles to theatre-in-education. The shrill and aggressive conventions of the 1970s separatists were mostly left behind, to be replaced by a more carefully considered concern for the ideological identity of the audience. There was a new variety of oppositional philosophies, ranging from the abiding separatism of the more radical feminisms, through the emancipationism of bourgeois feminism, to the contradictions of socialist feminism. Overall, in this whole group of companies, there was greater subtlety in the promulgation of subversive ideologies.

The success of the women's groups encouraged the refinement of practice by other oppositional companies in two main ways. Firstly, they boosted a trend that located the big political issues in the everyday consumption of cultural artefacts (especially those made by the media), so that the ideological meanings of personal choice were subject to critical scrutiny in performance. Secondly, they fostered a more determined approach to a deconstructionist aesthetic, which aimed to dismantle theatrical stereotypes and to substitute alternative codes that were clearly in opposition to the hegemonic status quo. Both tactics aimed to empower the audience by subverting the post-modernist retreat from ideology. But perhaps most important of all, the best of the women's groups led the way towards a new theatrical playfulness which combined good fun with ideological analysis. Amid the general fragmentation of alternative theatre, remarkably, there was a partial re-animation of the original counter-cultural impulse towards celebratory protest.

The overall expansion in the first half of the decade had produced greater sophistication and specialisation in the aesthetic and operational diversity of alternative theatre. The original oppositional ferment of the movement was at first diluted by the growth of neo-conservative groups, forcing a retrenchment. This then turned into a reorientation as new ideological perspectives came into play. Hence, throughout the 1980s the internal trends of alternative theatre pulled it, increasingly, in two opposing ideological directions at once: on the one hand, towards a reformulated radicalism, in the weak version represented by the soft ideology groups, and in the stronger version by the campaign companies, especially the women's/

feminist companies, and by some of the community theatre groups; on the other hand, towards a reactionary neo-conservatism, in reproductions of mainstream practices and through the introduction of market-place ethics in the operation of many groups.

Ironically, the movement had spawned a large number of companies that could be called 'alternative' only in the sense of being different from, but not in ideological opposition to, the mainstream. Thus the 1980s can best be described, first, as a period of diversification and fundamental fragmentation for alternative theatre as a whole, and, second, as a period of retrenchment and reorientation for the oppositional cultural movement which had fostered its growth. The net result is that, for the first time in its history, a clear distinction can be made between alternative theatre as a cultural *movement* and as a new *sector* of the British theatre industry. This is another development which can be read as a reflection of the widening divisions in society as a whole.

Community theatre in the 1980s

At the start of the decade, community theatre offered a reassuring panorama of mini-welfare-stateism, providing a theatre service, mainly through small-scale sub-regional touring, for parts of the nation that other approaches could not reach. In the brave new world of Thatcherism such a phenomenon was bound to face disruption. The overall number remained stable at around forty-eight companies up until 1987, but these declined to thirty-seven in the final years of the decade. The majority were located in the regions, mostly in cities and towns, though a few were rural-based. Localism and anti-centrism were still high on the ideological agenda. However, community theatre was subject to its own kinds of retrenchment and fragmentation as the 1980s progressed.

A number of older groups – such as Medium Fair and EMMA – were disbanded in the early 1980s because of financial shortages in the regional funding system, and both the survivors and the new companies subsequently were placed under contradictory pressures by the funding bodies. On the one hand, they were encouraged to increase box-office income, most often by touring shows outside their base region. On the other hand, the success of the community play movement (of which more below) led to demands for more long-term participatory projects in single locations. Many companies simplified their annual programming by producing fewer shows and projects for a narrowing range of constituency; new groups tended to concentrate on specialist areas of work. These pressures allowed less time for group research into local issues and histories, and there was greater reliance upon playwriting commissions. The range of skills required of community theatre workers narrowed, so actors increasingly were hired for individual shows or seasons, undermining the idea of the ensemble and placing more power in the hands of directors and administrators. This trend also caused more practitioners to operate on a freelance basis. The underlying trend followed alternative theatre generally towards a search for cost-effective efficiency, putting more emphasis on theatre-as-aesthetic-product and leaving less creative space for cultural experimentation.

Hence, the idea of a company able to respond flexibly to a range of community needs gradually gave way to a plurality of more or less specialist practices, with groups set up to pursue particular techniques or themes. The boundaries between community theatre and other categories of approach, while never that clear-cut, were subject to even more blurring, as groups, for example, combined small-scale national touring with sub-regional specialist tours, or were prepared to shift from region to region in order to secure a full year's income for their particular specialism. Most groups became more cautious about claiming even the mildest oppositional intent for their work. Radicalism usually retreated into highly coded forms, implicit in the total approach to performance rather than explicitly stated in individual shows. The contextuality of community theatre rendered it especially sensitive in this respect, as conservatism in local communities was legitimised by the wider socio-political climate, and grass-roots activity which challenged the dominant ethos had to tread carefully in a minefield of potential rejection.

All this could be seen in the new companies set up during the decade. Some were devoted exclusively to the development of particular techniques, such as community plays, reminiscence theatre or new circus, thus introducing a sub-trend towards specialist participatory projects. Others were established to pursue particular themes. Some of these reinforced conservatism through such forms as museum theatre, and other projects latched onto the heritage industry. A few assumed a more aggressively new-age stance through alignment with 'green' campaigns against global environmental pollution or local ecological degradation. A related orientation appeared in the small number of companies created to investigate new notions of internationalism, especially through multi-racial projects, a number of which involved cross-cultural collaborations with artists in 'third world' countries.

It is refreshing to reflect, then, that despite the glaring signs of conservatism, the *main* drift of the community companies was towards a more thoroughgoing concern with social issues. This appeared through a range of styles which mirrored the greater formal sophistication of the sector as a whole – from cabaret to storytelling, and from neo-expressionism to environmental theatre. It can be detected in the increased tendency to devise programming which matched particular shows to specific audiences. It can be found also in the growth of more carefully structured approaches to participatory practices, whether they stem from influences as different as Ann Jellicoe or Augusto Boal, or from the European experiment of Odin Theatre or the British community arts movement. Hence, many of the community theatre companies refined their practices in order to maintain a broadly oppositional ideology in line with the political, campaign and special needs groups. The fact that community theatre achieved this in predominantly conservative contexts in a period of political, social and cultural reaction is especially interesting, as it indicates performances which involved subtle ideological negotiations – for almost all these new approaches to community theatre were implicated in contradictions deriving from the widening divisions fostered by Tory national policies.

Cultural democracy versus the democratisation of culture

Some sense of the ideological strain that the culture of division placed on oppositional theatre can be gauged from a cultural debate that erupted in the mid-1980s. The two main protagonists were Sir Roy Shaw, then retired Secretary General of the Arts Council, and Owen Kelly, a London-based community artist. They stood for two fundamentally opposing attitudes towards cultural production: Shaw was on the side of the democratisation of culture; Kelly supported cultural democracy. As we have seen, these two positions were reproduced institutionally by the Arts Council and the Greater London Council. The argument, therefore, is worth further brief investigation.

Roy Shaw claims that the meaning of the democratisation of culture is best summed up by the aim of the Arts Council's precursor, CEMA (Council for the Encouragement of Music and the Arts), which wished to provide 'the best for the most'. Thus the democratisation of culture is about 'making the "high" arts more accessible to working people', on the premise that these arts are more 'relevant to our common humanity rather than to our particular job, or social class'. However, the 'difficulty' of these arts means that 'to inherit culture, you have to make an effort, sometimes a considerable one', and it then follows that education 'is the prime factor in facilitating greater access to the arts'. Shaw stoutly maintains that his belief in the democratisation of culture does not rule out support for cultural democracy: 'I have never been able to see why we should not do both.' To Shaw the inclusion of cultural democracy on the agenda is evidence that Britain is a (relatively) free society (Shaw 1987: 131-2).

Owen Kelly sees the democratisation of culture as a system for 'the popularisation of an already decided cultural agenda'. This agenda is a means for legitimising an 'agreed hierarchy of values which is the necessary precursor of the centrally co-ordinated cultural package, more usually referred to as "serious art" ' (Kelly 1984: 100). By 'serious art' he means the mainstream arts – the repertory and national theatres, opera, art galleries, symphony orchestras. The consumption of the package's contents 'can be seen as the imposition, on society at large, of the values of one particularly powerful group', and 'these values appear as neutral, or natural'. But in fact the 'compulsory imposition of centrally controlled systems of value is poisonous' (Kelly 1984: 101). To Kelly, then, the democratisation of culture is a hegemonic procedure that aims to cheat the mass of people of their right to create culture, and that conspires to hold them in thrall to their own uncreative subjugation.

Similar oppositions animate their versions of cultural democracy. For example, Roy Shaw claims that the term means:

> working from the grass-roots upwards rather than from the top downwards. It involves encouraging working people to

develop their own creativity, preferably by collective action rather than individual action . . . [It tends to] underestimate the difficulty and exaggerate the value of self-expression in the arts . . . [so that] relevance has become more important than quality.

(Shaw 1987: 133–5)

Kelly's account is couched in an entirely different language. He calls for widespread 'direct participation in the production of a living culture', because:

> Cultural democracy . . . is an idea which revolves around the notion of plurality, and around equality of access to the means of cultural production and distribution. It assumes that cultural production happens in the context of wider social discourses . . . it will produce not only pleasure but knowledge [which] will accrue to the primary understanding of community.

(Kelly 1984: 101)

This chalk and cheese debate re-animated issues surrounding the production of culture which had been raised as early as the mid-1970s. However, the debate had a new urgency in the 1980s as all areas of social life were politicised by the Tory reforms. The question of who had access to which resources became more crucial in the battle for the ideological high ground. And even when cultural democracy seemed to be secured by particular projects, the great divides of the decade rendered the results by no means ideologically unambiguous, as we shall see next in the case of the first community plays.

The politics of community plays

In 1978 the playwright Ann Jellicoe approached the Exeter-based community theatre company Medium Fair with a proposal. She had written a new play for the comprehensive school in Lyme Regis, where she lived, which she planned to put on in the school hall. The play was about the Monmouth rebellion, which began in Lyme in 1686, it had a cast of over 100 and was written for promenade staging. Would the company like to be involved in the project, as actors, as technicians, stage managers, facilitators? Three years earlier Medium Fair had done a similar participatory project in six Devon villages (Kershaw 1978). The proposal offered a further extension of this trend, so the company became involved in *The Reckoning*, which Jellicoe called a 'community play'.

The project was a great popular success in Lyme Regis, and it became a model for the production of more large-scale events. These have involved up to 150 non-professional performers and many more helpers and supporters, guaranteeing an impact on the host community. Moreover, the model has been adopted and adapted by many towns and villages, so that nine years after *The Reckoning* Ann Jellicoe could confidently write:

> All over the country community plays are being produced. Now they are being set up abroad. The movement is flourishing.
>
> (Jellicoe 1987: 41)

What had she discovered in the Lyme Regis project about cultural production that would be so willingly taken up by many other communities? And what was the ideological nature of her total project?

Ann Jellicoe's first theatrical success was as a playwright and director at the Royal Court Theatre in the late 1950s and early 1960s. With *The Sport of My Mad Mother* and *The Knack* she gained a reputation for being in touch with the younger generation (Marowitz *et al.* 1965: 222). She now speaks fondly of a commission in 1960 from the Girl Guides Association to write a play for 400 girls, in celebration of the Association's 50th anniversary. It was to be staged at the Empire Pool, Wembley, and showed 'all the older women in the world suppressing men and finally destroying the earth with an atomic bomb' (Jellicoe 1987: 2). Not surprisingly, the Guides found the play too ideologically challenging to produce, but it makes an interesting comparison with Arden and D'Arcy's much more modest effort with the Guides of Kirkbymoorside some five years later. Unlike Arden/D'Arcy, Jellicoe has never overtly professed an ideologically radical position, though her plays demonstrate egalitarian sympathies. These mostly take the form of a liberated attitude to sexuality and an untheorised feminism, both reminiscent of the 1960s counter-culture. But Jellicoe had little direct involvement with the counter-cultural movement, or with alternative theatre before the late 1970s.

Given this, it is especially interesting that she has often invited playwrights of a more explicitly radical persuasion – and of a younger generation than her own – to provide scripts for the Colway Theatre Trust (the organisation she created in 1980 to manage her community play projects). This practice began with Howard Barker in 1981. By then Barker's plays had been produced at the Royal Court, by the Royal Shakespeare Company (in the Warehouse studio theatre), and in regional repertory theatres. But he had also had plays staged at alternative venues in London (the Open Space and the King's Head), and by the early 1970s radical touring group Recreation Ground. He has been grouped frequently with other radical playwrights of the counter-cultural generation, such as Hare, Brenton and Edgar. But unlike these he has always been 'suspicious of, and ignorant of, the politicisation of 1968'. This was partly because he learnt about politics earlier: 'I had a fundamental Stalinist education from my father who was a shop steward' (Barker 1981a: 3). And the lessons were lasting: by the late 1970s he was still committed to socialism, but it was a socialism inflected by a distinctive personal vision:

> What I . . . rarely show is the bold, confident projection of left wing ideology, flashed at the audience in the expectation of instant support . . . What I celebrate is energy and the small discovery of dignity. I think that is socialist. From confronting the pessimism comes the will to change.
>
> (Barker 1981a: 14)

The aversion to working to a tight ideological programme is reminiscent of John McGrath; and perhaps we can read in Barker's iconoclasm at least a trace of counter-cultural expressivity. The impression is reinforced by his willingness to take stunning aesthetic risks, which has resulted in an uneasy relationship with critics and the public.

Consequently, Ann Jellicoe's invitation to Barker to write a community play for the relatively conservative town of Bridport in Dorset was especially audacious. It was politically audacious, because of his iconoclastic socialism. It was socially audacious, because his work was far from populist in appeal. It was aesthetically audacious, because of his predilection for subverting conventional theatrical codes. In addition, Barker was well known for his lively interest in state-of-the-nation plays, and the state of the nation in the early 1980s was far from reassuring, especially perhaps from the perspective of communities such as Bridport.

The socio-political context

On April 11, 1981, the first of a series of inner-city riots erupted in Brixton, South London. The riot lasted for three days, leaving 279 policemen and 45 members of the public injured, hundreds of shops looted and burned out, many more vehicles destroyed, and unforgettable images of police dodging firebombs on the nation's television screens. Further disturbances on a similar scale followed in Southall (London) and Toxteth (Liverpool) in July. This time the pictures included police firing CS gas canisters at English civilians – for the first time in British history. So-called copy-cat riots occurred a week later in Moss Side (Manchester) and Handsworth (Birmingham); then a few days after that there were more serious disturbances in Birmingham, and in Blackburn, Bradford, Derby, Leeds, Leicester and Wolver-hampton. It seemed as if England's youth had taken to the streets in a determined attack on law and order, and even, perhaps, on Thatcherism.

There was plenty of circumstantial evidence to support this last political reading. The immediate cause of the Brixton riot was the unpopular 'sus' laws introduced by the Tories, which empowered plain-clothes policemen to stop and search anyone they suspected of illegal activity. In the week before the first riot 943 people had been questioned on the streets of Brixton, but only 93 were charged, in a police exercise code-named 'Operation Swamp'. Other acute social problems were lined up by the press as potential causes of the trouble, including: the decline of the inner-cities, immigration and racial prejudice, and the rapidly rising crime rate. Yet the riots and the crime rate were surely a symptom of a deeper malaise, and one most directly affecting the nation's young people.

Between 1979 and 1982 unemployment in Britain increased by 141%, from 1,253,000 to 3,021,000. Half of the unemployed were under 25, and some 134,000 school leavers had never had a job. In the same period, state spending on education fell by 6%, on child benefit by the same amount, and on local authority housing programmes – which affected working-class families most – by an astonishing 55%. These cuts were exacerbated by the abolition of earnings-related benefits to the lowest paid and by the fixing of unemployment and related benefits at 5% below the level of inflation. In order to improve the unemployment figures, and to school the young in work disciplines, the state's Manpower Services Commission 'youth training schemes' were expanded; but these were widely regarded as simply a source of cheap labour for employers. The new measures forced many young people into economic reliance on family and state just at the point when they might reasonably have hoped for more independence. Widespread frustration and anger were a predictable response.

In 1981 a *Sunday Times* MORI poll found that a majority of unemployed young people thought that violence was justified in order to change society. A further study in 1982 found that few young people had any confidence in the ability of traditional party politics to improve their future. Not surprisingly, the study claimed that its findings indicated a 'lost generation'. Yet it is clear that the young were simply the most visible part of a much more malignant social disease, and one which was worsening. In 1983 a further MORI poll revealed that some 7½ million people in Britain – about 8% of the total population – had inadequate supplies of the basic necessities of food, warm clothing, heat. For every unemployed young person there were another four or more people living in poverty. Here was a great reservoir of mostly hidden misery, the ugly underside of modern capitalism. So if the youth riots were a threat to law and order, what action might the new poor take in order to secure a greater social justice?

Ideological tensions

Such was the broader socio-political context of Howard Barker's *The Poor Man's Friend*, which opened in December 1981. The more immediate setting was the small market town of Bridport. In the early 1980s the town was relatively prosperous, weathering the recession on a mixture of old agricultural and new light-manufacturing industries, though it did possess one dominant manufacturing industry: rope-making. It had a population of some 6000, comparatively little unemployment, and an active social life; for example, it had five amateur dramatic societies and its own Arts Association. Politically – and predictably – it voted Conservative. It seems hardly surprising for Ann Jellicoe to

report that 'Everyone who lives in Bridport speaks well of it. A fortunate little town' (Jellicoe 1987: 15).
The conjunction of Barker and Bridport produced an inevitable uneasiness for Jellicoe.

> Howard seized upon the rope-making industry, noting with some glee that Bridport rope had been used to hang criminals all over the British Empire. How my heart sank when he told me this! I was acutely anxious until the script was delivered in case the play would be too much for Bridport.
>
> (Jellicoe 1987: 17)

And even then she was nervous of its progress into the public domain, because 'I knew the town would throw it out if they realised what it was about'. In the event the town was big enough to accept the play. Even though *The Poor Man's Friend* offered a profound ideological challenge to the community's good fortune, the final outcome of performance was unifying.

The celebration of unity – of a common identity over-riding internal differences – is a fundamental aim of Jellicoe's approach to the staging of community plays. This tends to push overt political debate into the background.

> Politics are divisive. We strongly feel that the humanising effect of our work is far more productive than stirring up political confrontation . . . While the extreme left would doubtless say there is no possible ground where anyone in a given community can meet without dishonesty, we [the Colway Theatre Trust] strongly feel that these plays do provide such a ground.
>
> (Jellicoe 1987: 122)

Thus, her community plays aim to transcend social differences, at least temporarily, and to use participation in creative work to strengthen the networks of community. As a key component in that effect, participants, audiences and critics have frequently reported experiencing overwhelming emotion in these events. The celebratory, carnivalesque atmosphere which they create appears to eliminate day-to-day divisions: in this particular performative equation celebration equals community cohesiveness.

Of course, the exact complexion of that unity may then depend on the existing ideological identity of the community: the event may be simply an expression and a reinforcement of an existing state of affairs. This has led some commentators, particularly on the left, to accuse Jellicoe of ignoring the realities of capitalist society. Hence Graham Woodruff claims that:

> Ann Jellicoe appears to think that this formulation of community avoids politics. Of course, it does nothing of the kind. It reinforces an idealised notion of community as an unchanging unity. It challenges none of the inequalities which exist in a West Dorset town which by her own admission is 'very right-wing, even feudal'.
>
> (Woodruff 1989: 371)

From this perspective Jellicoe produces an opportunity only for a quasi-egalitarianism, a short-term fantasy which provides an escape valve for the resentments of the oppressed and an outlet for the privileged to express a wholly duplicitous largess. The methodology of community plays does not solve any ideological problems in the community's identity, it simply side-steps them.

The differing interpretations, of course, raise fundamental questions about the potential efficacy of these community plays. Are they simply reactionary – reproducing the existing ideology of the predominantly conservative South West communities which have staged them – or can they serve a more radical purpose – a questioning of the ideology of the community and through that the status quo? The answers to this question may extend our discussion about the interaction of analysis and celebration, socio-political criticism and carnivalesque excess. Perhaps the participatory processes of community plays – and perhaps therefore of other participatory approaches to performance developed in the 1980s – open up new aesthetic possibilities which promise a fundamentally dialectical form of efficacy for community play performance.

The conventions of community plays

The chief rhetorical conventions of Ann Jellicoe's community plays offer an unusual combination of mainstream and alternative theatre practices. On the one hand, she subscribes to the aesthetics of character and plot construction that can be witnessed on any night in the West End:

We identify with the heroes and heroines and are swept along by the story through the switchback of the play and building and release of tension to the climax.

(Jellicoe 1987: 120)

She sees this type of experience as at the root of drama's popularity, though she increasingly felt that community plays should have groups rather than individuals as the heroines and/ or heroes. On the other hand, she has developed the conventions of promenade performance – most recently revived in the 1970s by alternative companies such as Welfare State and Joint Stock – in the staging of her shows. Thus, the school halls, community meeting-rooms and churches where they are performed are transformed into carnival-like environments.

The celebratory atmosphere is established at the very start by the traditional fair or market (every town had one) that precedes the show:

the initial impression is one of chaos: there are many people standing and moving everywhere, some in costume, some selling things, some obviously setting up for the performance. The only seating – for the elderly and people with disabilities – is in rows on rostra scattered round the edge of the space. The rest of us must stand and promenade, following the action round and between the four or so stages of different sizes, placed strategically to encourage circulation . . . The play does not so much *begin* as *grow out of* the fair, the first scene starting among the combined chatter of the audience and performers.

(Kershaw 1983b: 114)

These techniques clearly are designed to make the performances more accessible, by blurring the distinction between 'reality' and 'play', so that the transition into performance consciousness is modulated by conventions drawn from non-theatrical, social occasions. Our role as audience is made ambiguous: we are both a part of, and apart from, the action.

Other conventions reinforce the ambiguous audience role. As far as possible all the performers are 'on-stage' all the time; they do not drop out of character or leave the space but remain visible and attentive to the action, constant reminders of the community which the play is about. Scenes are sometimes played simulta-

neously in different parts of the space. Particularly effective have
been juxtapositions of real games and work – such as rope-
making – with acted scenes. The old technique of casting the
audience as a crowd has been used often, with the difference here
that characters standing next to you will urge you to action, to
join in the arguments. Thus the rhetorical conventions of both
the gathering phase and performing phase of community plays
were designed to promote accessibility, involvement, identification: the keynotes of successful community theatre.

Participation is paramount in all aspects of community play
production, and normally starts two years or so before the show is
staged. Anyone who wants to act in the play is accepted, anyone
who wants to help is welcomed. The show itself will run for ten
to fifteen performances; audiences number 300 or more; ticket
prices are kept low. The complex business of steering the project
is undertaken by a 'core group' of professional theatre workers
which normally includes a director, a writer, a stage manager, a
designer, a musical director. The dynamic between the professionals and non-professionals raises interesting ideological issues
in community play production, particularly in relation to the
empowerment of the participants. Unsympathetic observers have
noted the potential for mystification and manipulation in the
relationship, for the professionals are in control of the event in
that they write the play, direct it, design it. But the relationship
also can be characterised as one of *barter*, in the sense that
Eugenio Barba employs the term. That is to say, the skills of the
professionals are exchanged for performances (and other types of
work) by local people, not as equals but as a way of achieving
equality (Barba 1979). Both types of relationship are possible
within the Jellicoe model, and only careful analysis of individual
projects can show the likely ideological outcome of the balance
of power.

The authenticating conventions of community plays are a
major source of power for the non-professionals, as they usually
derive from *local* culture and history. By animating history,
community plays aim to make the past vividly alive in the
present. Many scenes are set in known local locations, so local
geography and topography gradually emerge as significant to the
action. Local dialects and turns of speech are used extensively. In
the later plays, when work or pastimes were presented they were
done 'for real'. Similarly all props and costumes are either really

from the period of the play or accurate reproductions, great attention being paid to the detail of design. The overall aim is to convince the audience that a slice of history is being represented as accurately as possible. Thus the town witnesses the reincarnation of its ancestors through performance (in some cases particular performers may be playing their forbears). Moreover, the primary network represented by the shows is the family, and family units serve as a kind of key to the structure of relationships in the play, so that it becomes obvious that all characters, however minor, are part of a complex series of interdependencies. This serves as a fundamental authenticating convention, for it reproduces the way in which we experience community in reality. In relatively homogeneous communities, such as market towns in the South West of England, this may suggest an identity between the community networks of past and present which validates the representation. The community may be strengthening itself in the present by representing its past.

The majority of community plays have dealt with *hidden* histories – episodes in the past of the community which are little known or have been forgotten. This is one main source for any ideologically oppositional thrust in performance. For often hidden histories are suppressed histories and their discovery implies an act of liberation. More fundamentally, such histories are frequently histories of oppression, so a community play which tells the tale of the underdog from a sympathetic point of view may mount a criticism of oppression in the present. In such cases historical parallelism can become a powerful tool in the hands of contemporary radicalism.

Ironically, Ann Jellicoe reinforces this potential in community plays with an injunction that was designed to keep politics *out* of them:

> organise your villains so that if possible they come from out of town: people whom the community can comfortably unite against.

> (Jellicoe 1987: 125)

So a further potentially subversive strategy arises from the conflict between the community and 'outsiders' – who may, of course, represent society, or even the status quo. If we want to understand why socialist playwrights have been attracted to community plays – apart from the fact that large casts are needed for state-of-the-nation shows – perhaps we need look no further. They may provide the means whereby she or he can present the historically subservient as in necessary opposition to the contemporary status quo. In order to celebrate unity the community may have, first, to look at itself – through the prism of history – self-critically, and, second, to oppose the oppressions of the dominant order, at least by implication. In this respect Howard Barker's *The Poor Man's Friend* offers an object lesson in ironic oppositional practice.

Resignation and resistance in *The Poor Man's Friend*

Three years after the play was staged, to great acclaim, Barker offered the following interpretation:

> in essence it was a parody of Thomas Hardy – fatalistic tragedy, with a mute victim. My real heroes are people who act, not people who suffer . . . I thought the play was about resistance, and at the first glance it is. But now it's more about pity.
>
> (Barker 1984: 43)

What is at issue now is whether such a reading of the performance (as opposed to the play) is inevitable; or whether the complexity of the event – particularly in animating the relationship between rhetorical and authenticating conventions – made other, more subversive, readings available? How did *The Poor Man's Friend* represent the dynamic between resignation (pity) and resistance, and thus how might it have been efficacious in stimulating either?

The show opens brilliantly as the hanged of the British Empire return from the dead, nooses still round their necks, mingling among the standing audience and vigorously justifying their crimes. This is a fitting frame for a play which focuses on the hidden history of Sylvester Wilkins, a 14-year-old Bridport boy who in the nineteenth century was hanged for stealing flax. Significantly, Barker changes his crime to rick burning, no doubt to evoke the bright television images of the recent riots. And he ranges around Sylvester a trio of characters whose contrasting attitudes to his fate raise fundamental questions of law, justice and order. First, Doctor Roberts, a Bridport physician who sold a patent ointment to the rich – the Poor Man's Friend of the title –

and penny pamphlets to the poor. These last combined Christian homilies advising patient acceptance of poverty with basic health-care information. Second, Barefoot, a figure fired – literally, as he burns hayricks in protest against privilege – by the insurrectionary and egalitarian ideas of the French Revolution. And third, Vanstone, the county hangman, who claims:

> Because this is a world of pain, because the worse overcome the better, because boys suffer for old men, I do this, I do evil better than most. There is none brings more pity to his task than me . . . I am . . . an artist in relief of sorts . . . I am – top physician.
>
> (Barker 1981b: 77)

Thus Roberts represents a kind of pseudo-scientific hope that learning and religion can cure the inequities and iniquities of a social system that produces poverty and disease, a kind of liberal humanism. Barefoot stands for the imperatives of necessary resistance against an unjust hierarchy, in favour of a utopian egalitarianism, a kind of primitive Marxism. Vanstone represents a fatalism that accepts the world as it is with all its flaws, a kind of tortured conservatism. In their different ways each claims to be the poor man's best friend.

Barker is at pains to stress the wider historical situation of the debate, though he does it indirectly and very wittily. The key figure in this respect is the lawyer, Gurney. He rightly identifies French revolutionary ideas as the source of the rick burning, though his belief in the manner of their transmission is wild and comic, as is his solution to the problem:

> It's the French wind does it . . . I believe the revolutionists put something in the breeze . . . I am thinking, this is a rope town, ain't it? We might hang nets along the cliffs, to drive them down the coast. Let 'em get the French ideas down in Devon. If Devon starts to smoulder, we can sell 'em nets. The trade's been dead as a doornail since the war.
>
> (Barker 1981b: 24)

The inter-dependence of trade and war, and of the rope workers of Bridport and the exploitations of the Empire, is a continuous thematic undercurrent in the show. But perhaps it surfaces most brilliantly in a scene which stages a rope walk, using authentic rope-making gear borrowed from Bridport museum, when the rope-makers discuss how the economics of recession cause suffering for people at the bottom of the social ladder. The discussion focuses on production slow-downs and diversification: it is unlikely that the similarities between past and present would be missed by an audience in 1981.

Barker's skill in drawing historical parallels raises a fundamental issue about the use of history in community plays. For techniques of parallelism can suggest powerfully that nothing changes much, that the hierarchies and injustices of British society will always be with us. Moreover, Barker's depiction of the 'mute victim' Sylvester may be read as reinforcing resignation, for he has nothing to say in self-defence at his trial. This silence, though, produces a fundamental irony that informs the rest of the performance, for we know that Sylvester is both innocently blind to the seriousness of rick-burning and, more importantly, incapable of any seditious intention. This gives Barker the opportunity to expose the contingent nature of justice, and thus of the whole social structure which justice – through the application of law and the maintenance of order – purports to validate.

The point is established particularly powerfully through the kind of scenic contrast which only promenade staging can make available to performance. Thus, Sylvester's trial at the Dorchester Quarter Assizes is played out between performers on several stages with the mass of the audience in between, a marvellous metaphor for how the law operates in the public domain. But we also get a bright behind-the-scenes look at the magistrates' private attitudes to the wielding of power, through scenes set in their dressing-room:

1st MAGISTRATE	Mercy, I say, is conditional on needs of state. I say the same boy could have mercy on Tuesday, but not on Friday. Why?
3rd MAGISTRATE	Why, Billy?
1st MAGISTRATE	Because on Tuesday, England was a calm place, but on Friday very wild. And today is Friday, I suggest.
2nd MAGISTRATE	We will lose old England if she slips much further. There are fires in Dorset every hour.
1st MAGISTRATE	I say we must resist the inclination to be soft. How I long to be soft! You know I

	do, I am a grandfather with rolling children on the grass –
3rd MAGISTRATE	Billy could not be gentler.
1st MAGISTRATE	I could not. But my children will be cut up on the lawn if this does not stop. If I did not love boys, I would not say – let this one swing. I argue this from love.

(Barker 1981b: 67)

Such writing is worthy of Brecht at his best, I think. And the possibility of oppositional readings is brilliantly reinforced by the rhetorical conventions of promenade staging. For our proximity to the small, tightly lit stage on which the scene is set determines whether we are cast as distant onlookers or conspiratorial witnesses. In either case our awareness of other audience members highlights our relationship to the action; it is difficult to be simply sucked into the drama of revelation. So the ideological significance of the scene – especially as it is clearly Friday in contemporary England – becomes inescapable.

Yet whilst it certainly succeeds here in a Brechtian exposé of the iniquity of inequality, the performance has still not yet shown us the seeds of a greater justice. For the death sentence, especially as it is based on such a horrific rationale, underlines the powerlessness of Roberts – 'Gentlemen, I am a quack' – and of Barefoot. It would seem, then, that Vanstone has the greatest claim to be the poor man's friend, especially as he is shown dispatching Sylvester with mercy, both figuratively and literally – by means of two weights tied round the boy's ankles so that his neck will snap cleanly. Right up to the final minutes of the performance it appears that resignation is its most forceful recommendation, pity its predominant emotion.

Cries of opposition

This reading derives from the overt ideological dynamic of the text as it is focused in the central dramatic conflict between characters, and as it was reinforced by extremely skilful use of the promenade staging conventions. Given the relatively traditional rhetorical conventions of the play's plot (characters apparently caught in a tragic inevitability), this could well be the dominant message taken home by the audience. But the reading fails, I think, to take into account Ann Jellicoe's skill in using the kinds of rhetorical conventions that are available perhaps only to community plays with promenade staging, in order to create authentic oppositional meanings. For, having uncovered the hegemony of the judicial process as a lynch-pin supporting oppression and privilege, the performance (and the community as represented by the play) goes on to suggest sources for a more effective revolutionary movement than Barefoot could muster. Not once, but twice.

The announcement of Sylvester's death sentence leads to a cry for a 'general strike' by the workers of Bridport. And as Sylvester's body is brought back to the town, on a real cart that pushes its way through the standing audience, a stunning subversive image is created. The many women of the cast have disappeared during the execution scene, but now they 'emerge from all corners in dazzling white'. The effect is astonishing, for there are many of them and we have not seen such pristine crisp costumes all evening. From a high platform to one side Roberts reinforces the potential significance of the moment.

ROBERTS   I never saw such a field of skirt, and not one man
             among them –
SPARK   They would not have one –
ROBERTS   Like a sea of pity washing the boy in . . . the boy
             will be forgotten, swept down some drain of
             history. His memory won't last much longer
             than the flowers on his grave.
SPARK   Why so, sir? The town is stricken.
ROBERTS   Why so? Because the people do not write books,
             Mr Spark, nor name streets, that's why . . .
                                             (Barker 1981b: 80)

But the women have a different kind of writing in mind, one that gives the most fundamental potential for opposition to the dominant order:

MRS FLAG   Go 'ome now, ladies, go 'ome and get
                children!
MRS DINT   They shall not take our boys! Make others!
MRS STRANGE   Yes, fill the town with babies!
MRS TUTT   Men 'ave their uses.

| MRS STRANGE | We will fight with our bodies. We shall not be scared as long as we are women . . . |
| MRS CRANE | Make the town grow! |

(Barker 1981b: 80)

This then is the reproduction of 'history', not as a tragic round of inevitable oppressions to be greeted with resignation, but as the starting point for a new future to be founded on resistance. For of course the real actors, the community today, are both rereading history (through Barker's eyes) and rewriting it themselves. Because this is decisively *not* a re-enactment, but a new statement of subversive refusal made in the light of the liberationist women's movement of the 1970s and 1980s.

However, the performance has so far still mainly identified the 'villains', in the shape of the Quarter Assizes judiciary, as from out of town. The fact that the town made the rope that hanged one of its sons is still, so to speak, hanging in the air. This is where Barker's willingness to look firmly into the face of horror comes to the fore. For he repeats the marvellous opening of the show by again bringing back the ghosts of all the Empire's hanged, ropes still round their necks, still justifying their lives. But there are two crucial differences to the re-enactment, which offer a fundamental rereading of their potential significance. First, we now know that they are called up by a young witch, Deirdre, who is the daughter of Barefoot (the use of the family unit in community plays ensures that this is a point we are not likely to miss). So the insurrectionary family is responsible for the resurrection of the absolutely oppressed. Second, the dead Sylvester also appears with a rope round his neck and the weight inscribed 'Mercy' round his waist, and the ghosts lift and carry him in a triumphal march, singing a song of profound irony:

It was well done, it was very well done,
Oh, bloody well done, Oh, expertly done,
I never saw it so bloody well done,
Lucky ol' Sylvester.

I wish I'd been done the way 'e was done,
It was beautifully done, it was gorgeously done,
The Bridport knife was never better done,
Lucky ol' Sylvester.

(Barker 1981b: 87)

The singing and the procession are exceedingly uplifting, power-fully instilling a wierd joy, a sense of dangerous unity. Part of what is being celebrated here is an astonishing convergence of the 'real' and 'not real' levels of performance, a merging of rhetorical and authenticating conventions which is the source of the extraordinary energy and emotional charge.

On the one hand, on the 'fictional' level of authenticating conventions, the song can only be read as explicitly ironic because of the way that the contingent nature of 'justice' has been exposed by the show, and because of the way that Bridport rope has been shown as finally supporting the system of 'justice'. The irony of the song strongly suggests that today's community needs to review its part in maintaining the social order, the status quo. Thus the ideological reading encouraged by the song's irony is deeply subversive. On the other hand, on the 'real' level of rhetorical conventions, the song can also be interpreted as a non-ironic, carnivalesque celebration of how well the show itself was produced and performed. On the nights that I saw it there was little doubt that many of the cast were singing it in this spirit. So the song was *also* a joyous reflection on the creative ability of the community as expressed in the staging of the play. From this perspective the song celebrates the cohesive power of a commun-ity to remake itself, in whatever image. It celebrates self-determi-nation in the creation of ideological identity.

These two readings – the subversive and the celebratory, deriving from the satiric 'agit prop' and the carnivalesque elements of the production – co-exist and reinforce each other. They achieve this because of the exceptional ways in which community plays allow authenticating and rhetorical conven-tions, and the ideologies inscribed explicitly and implicitly in them, to interact. It is at moments like this, through the careful construction of a radical text in a relatively conservative setting, and through a sensitive animation of the relationships between the play and the event of which it is a part, that socio-political criticism and community celebration, that analysis and the carnivalesque, can work to each others' mutual benefit. The full ideological efficacy of community plays, and maybe of other forms of community and political theatre, rests fundamentally on this dynamic possibility.

The event and the play in the event

It is important to stress that the readings offered by the final moments of *The Poor Man's Friend*, like all readings of all texts, are held only in potential by the performance. Hence, the ambiguity produced by the song's irony proffers a series of choices to the audience. At its crudest, the choice may be between a reactionary self-satisfaction with the creative achievement of the community ('Who would have thought amateurs could have done so well!'), or a revolutionary insight into the fundamental injustices in the hegemonic hold of the current socio-political status quo ('My god, we're still producing it!'). So it is entirely possible, perhaps even likely, that audience members might prefer one reading and ignore the other.

In either respect, though, the scale of community plays as events virtually guarantees an effect on the networks of the producing community. There is both circumstantial and statistical evidence for this in respect of David Edgar's *Entertaining Strangers*, written for the town of Dorchester in 1985. A questionnaire was distributed to the cast after the production, to which there were eighty replies. Over 75% thought that the play had been very successful as a social catalyst for the group/cast, and 50% made positive comments about the whole experience. So there is little doubt that a fairly high level of cohesiveness was achieved for the cast and group. Ann Jellicoe tells the story of the retired colonel who became friends with an unemployed youth. Even more tellingly, she describes how an employee of Eldridge Pope (the brewers who sponsored the event) was moved to tears when, as a result of their involvement in the play, Christopher Pope (the brewery director) called him by his first name for the first time in fourteen years. The claim that community plays can make people more friendly and open towards each other seems to be borne out. But of course the increased friendliness may obviate a critical attitude to the ideology of the community. In the case of Dorchester, local capitalists may become a little more paternalistic. The project puts a slightly more human face on the status quo.

What is striking, then, in Ann Jellicoe's practice, is the contrast between the efficacy of the *event* and the function of the *play* within it. In fact, Howard Barker employed the conventions developed by Jellicoe to mount an especially powerful critique of the contemporary status quo through extremely skilful use of historical parallels. The parallels were so clearly drawn, and the use of conventions so powerful, that it is unlikely that Bridport people would have been unaffected – especially given the broader context of riots and instability. Moreover, as the impact of the oppositional ideology inscribed in the play derives much of its power from imagery that reinforces a widespread cultural movement already well under way – the women's/feminist movement – then it is not unreasonable to assume that the production of the play represents a serious encounter between the community and an oppositional ideology. (This is doubly remarkable in view of the fact that the main characters of the play are male.) We may interpret the wider cultural movement as, in a sense, preparing the ground for the encounter. But also the play, in this context, is taking a lead by initiating a new kind of ideological transaction in the community. Thus radical texts might still harness the energy of the project in opposition to injustices in the wider society.

Less skilful writers may fail to animate this type of inter-textuality through historical parallelism, so that the event will not be inflected by radicalism. But in any case, the way that a community play is 'nested' in the networks of the producing community – its contextuality – is the source of a potentially successful combination of celebratory cohesiveness and critical consciousness. Indeed, it is the cohesiveness which ensures the capacity for effective self-criticism. In reviewing the show the *Observer* reported that:

> The real feeling you get emerging from a triumphant evening
> . . . is that a community has been confronted with a slice of its
> own past; and that in the process it may have learned
> something vital about the turbulent recessive present.
>
> (Jellicoe 1987: 17)

The crucial dynamic for the efficacy of community plays is that the community is being confronted by the community, in large part through the dialectical interaction of celebration and criticism. If and when this occurs, the plays are not simply giving the community a voice – they may be contributing to its ideological development by prompting a crisis in its identity which may have to be resolved in its 'real' relations in the socio-political present.

David Edgar has praised Ann Jellicoe (and Welfare State

International) for imaginative uses of the carnivalesque, whilst warning against the potential for reactionary escapism in the carnival model. He describes the potential dialectic of carnival and criticism by a neat theoretical conjoining of Brecht and Bakhtin, and stresses the forever nascent nature of the project to combine their contrasting perspectives in practice:

> What I suppose most of us [radical theatre workers] are striving for, is a way of combining the cerebral, unearthly detachment of Brecht's theory with the all too earthy, sensual, visceral experience of Bakhtin's carnival, so that in alliance these two forces can finally defeat the puppeteers and manipulators of the spectacle. We are doing so in full knowledge of the dangers of incorporation, of becoming no more than a radical sideshow to divert the masses and dampen their ardour.
>
> (Edgar 1988: 245)

The community play model as developed by Ann Jellicoe *could* be used to stage sideshows to divert the masses, and sometimes it has no doubt served this purpose. But also it has offered new opportunities for subversive cunning in conservative communities, and for the overt reinforcement of opposition to the status quo in others. At a community play seminar held in Newcastle-upon-Tyne in 1986, over eighty theatre workers – professional and non-professional – gathered to discuss projects they had mounted. Some reported successful events in a number of inner-city and new town locations, where communities of the new poor had celebrated their own brands of resistance to Thatcherism. If overt political performance had been knocked off the national touring agenda of alternative theatre, then it would seem that a powerful replacement had been found – and one which involved whole communities in active development of their own ideological identities.

Hence, radicalism did not disappear from alternative theatre in the 1980s. Rather, it had gone to ground, in the sense of adopting subtle, and sometimes heavily disguised strategies of resistance at a localised level. A similar tendency can be detected in the tactics of the campaign and special needs groups, and even in some of the soft ideology companies. These subversive manoeuvres ironically added to the sense of fragmentation in the alternative theatre movement, whilst often achieving a subversive

directness by incorporating non-professionals in the production
of oppositional culture. In this, and in other less direct ways, the
oppositional practices of alternative theatre contributed a positive dimension to the divides of the decade, by finding new ways
of successfully engaging with a widening range of ideological
communities, including some of the most conservative. In such
contexts – in the market towns of South West England, for
example – we are not talking about revolution, of course. To
expect that would be ridiculously optimistic. But we are talking
about a liberalisation of attitudes, a potential in community
plays (and related forms) for producing emancipatory and
egalitarian results, for reinforcing local democracy. If this
occurred even to a small extent – and *The Poor Man's Friend*
offers a very good case for that – then in the context of the neo-
conservative 1980s we must question any interpretation which
sees alternative theatre primarily as a lost cause. Such reorien-
tations do not necessarily lead to incorporation.

So it seems to me that Ann Jellicoe perhaps has done more
than her critics allow to solve some of the creative and ideological
problems posed for radical practitioners by conservative communities, and perhaps even by eras as reactionary as the 1980s.
Within a broadly liberal practice she has pioneered a model of
performance which is both popular and, in its use of contextuality to sometimes insinuate oppositional readings,
potentially socio-politically critical. The audacity that invites
radical playwrights to work in conservative settings cannot be
altogether neutral. It would seem that on occasion Ann Jellicoe's
approach to community plays has allowed the radical stokers
into the boiler-room by the back door while the conservatives are
still on the doorstep admiring the portico.

Chapter 7

Fragmentation in the 1990s?
The celebratory performance of John
Fox and Welfare State International

A new world order?

November 9, 1989, was a major watershed in post-war world
history. Around the globe millions watched their television
screens to see the Berlin Wall at last begin to come down. The
euphoria of Berliners freely dancing along that concrete outcrop
of the Cold War, breaking it up with hammers and crowbars, was
palpable. It was stunningly appropriate that such mundane tools
of demolition signalled the start of an all-pervasive transformation of the world order. The everyday objects took on new
ideological meanings, in good old Brechtian fashion. Maybe his
ghost was among the revellers, whooping it up on the wall. More
probably, though, it was hanging back, puffing on a ruminative
cigar, wondering what kind of protest the new political order
might demand.

The thaw in the Cold War was one result of the Soviet Union's
policy of *glasnost* and *perestroika*. On the international front,
two summit meetings between Presidents Gorbachov and Bush,
in December 1989 and May 1990, confirmed substantial agreements on the reduction of nuclear arsenals. In the Eastern bloc
the easing of old restrictions caused political destabilisation. As
the East Germans enjoyed open borders with the West, the
Balkan states of Albania, Latvia, Estonia and others demanded
independence from Moscow. This was another version of the
continuing political upheavals in Poland, Yugoslavia, Hungary,
Czechloslovakia, and later Romania. Communism was on the
retreat, as the Western media never tired of jubilantly pointing
out.

Despite the good news, in Britain ten years of Thatcherism

seemed to have created a chronically unstable socio-political order. In 1989 the very foundations of the social structure appeared to be cracking. The food chain proved to be desperately vulnerable; the environment was disgracefully polluted; the family seemed to be disintegrating. Across the country the ambulance service was thrown into crisis, forcing London to rely on a cut-to-the-bone emergency network operated by police and troops. Major doubts were raised about the legal system after the acquittal of the Guildford Four (who had been wrongly convicted of terrorism). The penal system was on the brink of chaos in the wake of a major riot that wrecked Strangeways Prison in Manchester. There were major closures in the shipbuilding, steel and coal industries, and commerce and industry were heavily hit by soaring inflation and interest rates. The general decline in the country's manufacturing base added to the rising levels of unemployment. The legacy of the 1980s appeared to be mainly an ailing 'free market' and a crumbling social infrastructure.

The membership of Thatcher's Cabinet was as volatile as the social climate. During 1989 and 1990 there was a series of resignations by senior ministers fed up with the inflexible rule of the Iron Lady. Not surprisingly, the government had begun to lose ground in the opinion polls, with the much-hated Poll Tax increasingly at the centre of popular dissatisfaction. In March 1990 there were demonstrations against the new tax, some of them violent, in many towns and cities. Over 300 people were injured during extensive rioting and looting in London's West End the day before the tax was introduced in England and Wales. At the other end of the country, and the social spectrum, the Lord Provost of Scotland had her bank account frozen for refusing to pay the tax. Many saw the tax as an attack on local democracy, because councils were forced to adopt budgets that forced a reduction of services. The near-ubiquitous resentment of the public proved to be the beginning of the end for Margaret Thatcher as Prime Minister: the tax she had so wholeheartedly championed turned out to be her worst enemy.

Such ironies seemed to be the order of the day at the start of the 1990s, despite the improvements in East–West relations. Hence, in Africa the release of Nelson Mandela signalled a new phase of rising influence for black people through the ANC; simultaneously millions in Ethiopia and elsewhere were on the verge of yet another catastrophic famine. In Central Europe the election of playwright Václav Havel as President of Czechoslovakia was an emblem of the new liberalisation of the communist states; yet in China the old-guard hardliners who had smashed the Tiananmen Square uprising continued to consolidate their power. All around the globe the Green movement was gaining ground, as the impact of unchecked industrial and technological growth promised devastating consequences; but the rapid spread of AIDS continued, with predictions of an epidemic of global proportions arising by the end of the new decade. The possibility of a peaceful world order seemed to increase beyond all hopes as more progress was made in arms control agreements between the super-powers; yet the Middle East was deeply unstable and the Gulf War was just over the horizon of history.

Such was the content of the daily news headlines on our television screens, the enormous scale of the global shifts ironically reduced to the size of a small box in the corner. Unfortunately, the miniaturisation brings no sense of increased empowerment. It reinforces the feeling that the ironies will never be ironed out. Despite the thaw in the Cold War the world is still running out of control. Are the 1990s going to be a decade of depressing destabilisation?

British culture in the early 1990s

Inevitably, the wider instabilities of the late 1980s and early 1990s were reproduced in the cultural sphere. Post-modernist pluralism was boosted by an increase in home-based cultural consumption as broadcasting deregulation encouraged the founding of many new local radio stations and independent video-production companies. Compact disc sales and video-tape hire had risen steadily in the late 1980s, as had attendances at cinemas, mostly by the under thirties (Feist/Hutchison 1990). The costs of electronic reproduction were falling, placing the means of production of the cultural industries (as they were increasingly called) within reach of grass-roots groups. A shift to more market-led orientations in cultural production generally fostered a riot of competing inter-textual codes: post-modernism had well and truly arrived. The traditional live arts seemed often to be forced into an elitist corner.

This was one outcome of continuing government pressure on

the grant-aid system. At the top, Rees-Mogg was replaced as Arts Council Chairman by Peter Palumbo, a multi-millionaire property developer who visited regional clients in his private helicopter. Palumbo supported government moves to 'streamline' the funding system through implementing the Wilding Report on the Regional Arts Associations. Wilding proposed the replacement of the RAAs by Regional Boards with much smaller governing bodies and (in some cases) wider geographical responsibilities. The Report also argued for the 'devolution' of funding responsibility for the majority of the Arts Council's directly funded clients to the Regional Boards, including most of the regional repertory companies and all of the alternative theatre groups. Those RAAs confronted with proposals to amalgamate – such as Northern Arts and Yorkshire Arts – fought back fiercely, if not always successfully. Many of the theatre companies resisted what they saw as 'demotion' from national to regional status, but only a few – including Welfare State International – won their case.

In the midst of these bureaucratic manoeuvrings British regional theatre ran into a severe funding crisis. The effects of the Poll Tax forced many local authorities to cut subventions to the arts, and those theatres which already had large accumulated deficits – most notably the Liverpool Playhouse – were forced onto the brink of illegal trading or bankruptcy. The seriousness of the situation led, in October 1990, to a Cambridge University conference on 'Theatre Under Threat?', which vigorously noted that the deterioration in levels of funding was affecting all categories of company, national, repertory and alternative. The sense of acute instability signalled by the conference was mirrored by government ministerial shuffles: in less than two years the job of Arts Minister changed hands three times – from Richard Luce, to David Mellor, to Timothy Renton.

Wilding's plans for devolution promised central Arts Council protection for the national theatres and a few 'centres of excellence' in the regions. But, as the Cambridge conference affirmed, 'the effects [of this policy] on touring and small scale community theatres had not been addressed' (Goodman 1991: 188). Whilst it was difficult to predict the detailed future for such companies, it was obvious that the general trends in the subsidy system would not work to their universal advantage. The 'movement' (or what was left of it) would be further fragmented even as the sector was strengthened by the growing number of funding schemes available to it.

The ironies inscribed in the shifting status of the sector are illustrated by two new sponsorship schemes which were set up in the early 1990s. Partly in response to criticism from the Independent Theatre Council that major sponsorship money invariably went to mainstream theatres, Barclays Bank announced its 'New Stages' project, and Sainsburys PLC quickly followed with a prospectus for 'Arts in Education'. Both these schemes were based on the competitive tender model, in imitation of earlier Arts Council programmes, such as the Business Incentive Scheme. 'New Stages' was designed to stimulate national avant garde studio-based touring (with an opening 'showcase' season at London's Royal Court Theatre); 'Arts in Education' was open to all comers, from the Royal Opera House to the smallest regional group.

The schemes were more significant for what they revealed about the changing patterns of cultural politics, than for the amounts of money involved. Such 'new money' came only at an ideological price: namely, the further encouragement of overt and intense competition between companies. Thus the fragmentation of the movement would be hastened in an environment that placed stable policies ever further out of reach, as companies were forced into more deals with an incoherent range of paymasters. Such rising competition in an increasingly complex 'market' was bound to reinforce two over-riding structural changes in the sector which had begun to emerge in the late 1980s. Firstly, companies which managed to survive as permanent entities would become, as it were, 'market leaders' attracting the resources needed to support the 'success' of their particular products. Secondly, any such company by definition would need to be politically and ideologically adroit if it aimed to mount an oppositional practice, as the risks of compromise and incorporation increased with competition.

The ideological paradoxes and contradictions which issued from this situation for one company – Welfare State International – are the main subject of this chapter. That company's 'success' through the 1980s and into the early 1990s, as it grappled with the tensions of the times, renders it simultaneously exceptional in its ability to survive and typical in the type of ideological issues it encountered as a result. Moreover, Welfare

State is especially interesting as it chose to pursue the core of its work during this period in an ideological 'hot spot': Barrow-in-Furness, in South Cumbria. The main business of this town – building nuclear submarines – meant that ideological changes on the international scene had a direct bearing on the future of the community and its identity. In addition, the community's reliance on this one defence-funded heavy industry meant that it was especially vulnerable to the changing socio-political and economic climate of Britain as a whole. The crises fostered by the Thatcherite culture of division, and the uncertainties produced by the emerging new world order, impacted on Barrow in both a condensed and a magnified manner. What Gorbachov and Bush said today mattered on the streets of Barrow tomorrow more immediately and complexly than for most other places in the land.

Welfare State moves to Barrow-in-Furness

In 1983, at a time when most alternative theatre companies were running for ideological cover, Welfare State International began a seven-year project in Barrow. John Fox, founder (with Sue Gill and others) and artistic director of Welfare State, described the project's aim as:

> developing a concept of vernacular art whereby we respond continually to local demand, producing plays, bands, dances, songs, ornaments and oratorios to order, so generating a social poetry of a high order within a very specific community context.

(Fox 1987: 3)

This was a new departure for Welfare State, which for fifteen years had been mounting mostly short-term creative initiatives in settings as diverse as British inner-city housing estates and Japanese international theatre festivals.

The company was one of the original 'class of '68'. For the first five years of its life it was aligned at the performance art end of the alternative theatre spectrum, though it also included 'namings' and other secular ceremonies among its activities. As the 1970s progressed it evolved into a mobile creative community, travelling gypsy-like from gig to gig with its own caravan village, blurring the distinctions between art and life. Accordingly, its early policies were couched in semi-visionary counter-cultural terms, claiming, for example, to make 'art as a necessary way of offsetting cultural and organic death' (Coult/Kershaw 1990: 258). By the mid-1970s it had taken up a residency with Mid-Pennine Arts in Burnley, staging events which combined the wayward visual aesthetics of its earlier work with a populist appeal to the local community. Notable among these was the first *Parliament in Flames* (1976), a 'community bonfire' for November 5th which featured the destruction of a massive mock-up of the Houses of Parliament.

No one else was producing carnivalesque agit prop on this scale. Moreover, the variety of cultural contexts in which the company staged its one-off hand-crafted performances encouraged imaginative verve and technical resourcefulness. Welfare State was (and is) unique, impossible to pin down in any of the existing categories. So in the space of a single year we find it featured as a political group alongside CAST, Red Ladder and 7:84, and as a performance art company grouped with the People Show, IOU, and Hesitate and Demonstrate (Itzin 1980b: 68–73; Craig 1980: 95–104). In an important sense, then, the company is a crucial example for the argument of this book, unafraid of taking often extreme risks in the search for strategies of performance that might be efficacious.

By the early 1980s Welfare State's work was predicated on an iconoclastic radical ideology, shaped by a deep opposition to the over-production and consumerism of the developed countries. At root the ideology rested on sympathy for the underdog, inspired by a primitive socialism – a collectivist, egalitarian utopianism that was not afraid to make grand, even visionary, claims for the healing power of creativity and the place of 'poetry' in a healthy culture. However, the anarchic edge to these ideas was honed by a pragmatism which produced, at the macro-level, an acute grasp of contemporary power structures, and, at the micro-level, an engagingly unpretentious commitment to local community activism (Fox 1988).

In the late 1970s and early 1980s Welfare State had tested this ideology through a series of large-scale epic models for radical performance in conservative contexts, which included shows such as *Tempest on Snake Island* (Toronto, 1981), *Tower of Babel* (Bracknell, 1982), and *The Raising of the Titanic* (London, 1983). These events were hugely successful and received considerable critical accolades. But John Fox has subsequently criticised them because:

> we were obliged to start from ART rather than from LIVING, to generate more product rather than process and work to rapid (and to an extent commercial) deadlines in strange lands. We could not allow ourselves to develop pieces organically over years or to respond to or follow up the longer term needs and rhythms of the host community, because essentially we were not part of any community.
>
> (Fox 1987: 1; White 1988: 203)

The desire to put down creative roots had led the company to settle in Ulverston, on the south coast of Cumbria, in 1979. By then it consisted of a core group of five employed full time, plus a network of fifty or so freelance artists who were brought in for particular projects. By 1983, having set up a successful annual festival and lantern procession in their new home town, it made sense to extend the local residency to Barrow, fifteen miles down the road.

Barrow the community

Approach Barrow-in-Furness from any direction and you will be struck by one thing: looming over the town, like a featureless cathedral to an anonymous god, the immense off-white hangar of the Devonshire Dock Hall. The town houses 70,000 people, and about 14,000 of them work for VSEL (Vickers Shipbuilding and Engineering Limited). This company owns the Hall, and inside it they are constructing Armageddon, in the shape of Britain's Trident-class nuclear submarines, able to deliver in one quick spurt more firepower than the whole of that used in the Second World War. The town is a remote place, and often seen by outsiders, such as the *Guardian's* northern arts correspondent Robin Thornber, as a cultural desert (Thornber 1987a).

Hence, in 1983 the town was totally dependent for its future prosperity on the making of nuclear submarines. And in the year following the Falklands war, with the sinking of the Belgrano fresh in the memory, it seemed certain that submarines would remain central to the global balance of power. Against this backdrop, any challenge that the radicalism of Welfare State offered to the local and global hegemony would inevitably seem puny, a futile gesture in the face of overwhelming odds, less ideologically efficacious than a hiccup.

This analysis, though, ignores crucial aspects in the nature of Barrow as a community. Whilst it is true that the presence of VSEL held the town almost totally in thrall to the most cherished economic and political values of the capitalist status quo, it does not follow that Barrow's cultural and social networks were completely subjugated by the same nexus. In fact, Barrow has long traditions of vigorous grass-roots culture, of working-class organisation, and of civic independence reaching back to its Victorian heyday. In the mid-nineteenth century the place was a boom town, flooded with offcomers attracted to work in the rapidly expanding local industries of steelmaking, mining, shipbuilding and shipping. One contemporary account encapsulates a common theme: the town was 'a combination in appearance of Birkenhead and a goldfinders city on the edge of one of the western prairies of America' (Trescatheric 1985: 13). Poverty and drunkenness were offset by trade unionism, a strong local co-operative movement, and religious non-conformism. In the late-Victorian period this produced a strong civic authority, determined to make Barrow into an outstanding example of the self-made town. The pride and independence of these roots can still be seen in its magnificent town hall, opened in Victoria's Jubilee Year, 1887.

Almost 100 years later many traces of this history also could be found in the town's wide range of community organisations, which included several drama, music and opera groups. The local political scene was equally lively: the borough council was Labour controlled, though the Member of Parliament was Conservative. However, the original industrial variety of the town had disappeared, so, whilst it had a moderately vigorous community life, in matters relating to employment the town was relatively, inevitably, docile. This was reflected in a common attitude to the shipyard and its lethal products – what was the point in arguing about an enforced necessity, an accident of history? Such ideological resignation, coupled with high levels of technological and engineering skill, pushed the place towards being – in John Fox's words – a 'perfect Thatcherite town'. But how was a company with such radical objectives going to be received in such a town? What was the best kind of creative introduction?

A celluloid nightmare

Welfare State's opening gambit in Barrow was the production of a full-length 'community feature film', based on a playscript commissioned from Adrian Mitchell, *The Tragedy of King Real*, which in its turn derived from Shakespeare's *King Lear*. The film was directed by John Fox and Paul Hayward (of Sheffield Polytechnic), and it was shot in a derelict warehouse and on location in Barrow. About fifty local, mostly unemployed, young people were involved in the production, and all the actors except King Real (who was played by Marcel Steiner) were Barrovian non-professionals. The world premiere of *King Real and the Hoodlums* (as the film was called) took place in the autumn of 1983, at Barrow's only cinema, the Astra, with all the silly razzmatazz of a feature film opening reproduced in satiric extravagance: glitzy limousines, red carpets, preening 'stars'.

The premiere showing of the film gave many Barrovians the chance to witness their daughters, sons, neighbours and friends ironically cavorting in the local landscape. And it was not a pretty sight, for they had transformed themselves into the 'Hoodlums', a kind of punk-medieval rabble in a wasted industrial junkyard, celebrating the crazy excesses of their loony monarch, King Real. And if that were not enough to send local sensibilities reeling, the film had a blatantly anti-nuclear story, which was bound to have an overtly subversive impact in Barrow. In fact, the 'politics' of *King Real . . .* were so radical for the context that Welfare State almost came unstuck at the very beginning of its residency in the town. The rewrite of Shakespeare seemed deliberately to invite the Barrovian cold-shoulder, even though, according to Welfare State, it was made in the best interests of the community.

The film opens with the rabble of Hoodlums marching in rowdy procession to King Real's throne, perched on top of a pyramid of bright pink wrecked cars, just by Walney Sound (where they bring in the nuclear submarines). Here Real attempts to distribute his great keys of power to his three daughters. But, true to the pattern of the original, the final key is refused by Cloudella (Cordelia), who together with the court musician, Poor Tom, is thrown out into the wasteland. Real joins the other two sisters, Raygal and Gonilla, in their nuclear bunker/submarine, but they refuse to feed him. He joins Cloudella in the wasteland, but even she rejects him. Back in the bunker he interrupts the two sisters as they prepare to spark off a nuclear war. So they put out his eyes and fire him out of the bunker through a torpedo tube before turning the keys of destruction. In a post-holocaust fire-raised industrial desert Real finds Cloudella again, but they die in each other's arms. In the bunker Gonilla and Raygal gorge themselves on an enormous confectionery globe before the roof finally collapses on top of them. The final scene is a flashback to the first, but instead of distributing the keys Real burns them on a blazing bonfire, and the Hoodlums march *away* from the pyramid of power, in celebratory procession back into the busy streets of Barrow.

Techniques of hope

Adrian Mitchell's adaptation of *King Lear* is a snappy, high-intensity modern parable. The mummers-play roots of the original are used to construct a kind of inverted fairy-tale, crazed and bitter, in which the silly King and the two ugly sisters get a disastrous come-uppance, and, ironically, so does the innocent princess. The unmistakable echoes of children's stories and entertainments are fundamental to the aesthetic of *King Real* .... The simplification of the plot and the rhetorical conventions of popular theatre forms, such as melodrama and pantomime, are designed make the text more accessible to a community audience, to families which might enjoy, say, a show at Christmas. At the same time the clear links with *King Lear* provide a game of teasing ironic parallels for audience members familiar with the original.

The poetry of *King Lear* undergoes a similar transmutation as Mitchell adopts five or so main idioms to explore the meanings of the nightmare territory, and to establish authenticating conventions which are rooted in common usage. His rewrite mingles simple rhyming verse, parodies of the language of authority, reggae-style raps, nursery songs, colloquial speech, to make a rich hotch-potch of verbal styles:

> There once was a King and he had three daughters
> And a nuclear shelter as snug as a tortoise.
> His daughters were the crunchiest from coast to coast
> They carried the aroma of hot buttered toast –
> *But* – he wondered which one of them loved him most.

So he announced a kind of freaky audition –
A Who Loves the King Most competition.

(Lowe 1985: 5)

The colloquialisms give the dialogue a sense of immediacy, and
the unlikely metaphors of the tortoise and the toast add a
childlike quality to the verse. They bring the concepts of the
shelter and great luxury into the sensory ambit of the youngest
spectators, while for older people they may produce the feel of a
curiously distorted universe. This is King Lear meets Edward
Lear, with a moderate kind of vengeance.

Equivalent techniques of a visual kind abound in the film. For
example, in the nuclear bunker the mad sisters order the
Archbishop of Stare to put out King Real's eyes. Real is forced
onto an operating table which points into a torpedo tube, Stare
dislodges his eyes with a complicated surgical contraption, then
as the eyes are drawn out with tweezers a line of tiny flags from
different nations strings back to his empty sockets. The effect is
reminiscent of parlour-illusionist tricks, and the grotesque
humour of the extraction works in a number of ways. Spectators
familiar with *King Lear* may note the irony of Real getting
Gloucester's punishment, especially as the violence of the original is replaced by neat surgery. The flags add further irony, for
although Real has given up his power his head is still full of
imperialist images. Similarly, after being rendered completely
powerless Real is shot out like a Polaris missile through the
torpedo tube. The multiple ironies open up this moment to a
range of readings by combining codes which normally are kept
separate and by the mixture of genres. Inter-textuality offers
insights into the operations of power.

It is the songs of *King Real . . .*, however, which provide the
ideological backbone of the film. Mitchell's words are set to
music by Pete Moser – Welfare State's musical director and
musician-in-residence in Barrow – and the settings are haunting
in their simplicity and range. The musical style perfectly matches
Mitchell's felicity in writing uncluttered and penetrating
dialogue. Consider, for example, Cloudella's song, which is sung
to Lear when he finds her with Poor Tom in the wasteland:

O no, I never loved you best of all
O no, I could not love you properly
For you controlled the ways

In which I spent my days
And you could order me to laugh or cry
And you could order me to live or die
Because I was your royal property
Because I was your royal property.

(Lowe 1985: 16)

This is a devastating thematic shift from the original play. The healing balm of Cordelia's love for Lear, with all its promise of a hope-filled future, is abandoned by Mitchell. In its place he substitutes a world governed by raw power relations, in which people are forced to become the commodities of each other's desires. It is the moral equivalent of nuclear apocalypse. Yet despite this devastating message, in the specific context of its performance the film is implicitly, and paradoxically, inscribed with hope. For it aims to stimulate resistance to being owned by others, as a sexual object, as a yes-person within a corrupting ideology, as a wage-slave – especially in the nuclear industry. In the context of Barrow such a message is deeply subversive. For if young Barrovians go anti-nuclear then perhaps VSEL might be starved of labour and Trident might end up with no one wanting to build it. The contextuality of the film offers Barrow a share in the Cold War thaw.

Rooting for sanity

Such an approach to the increasingly complex issues of global nuclear strategy opens up the film to accusations of naivety. The storyline simplifies chronically complicated power struggles into crude black-and-white issues. And to make matters worse the film falls awkwardly between a documentary record of a live Welfare State event and a full-scale filmic re-creation of Mitchell's nightmare vision, in the process detracting from its oppositional message. These accusations, though, tend to ignore the readings offered by the film's inter-textual and contextual construction.

Now clearly there are high levels of inter-textuality operating as the literary and mainstream-theatrical traditions of Shakespeare-as-great-author are filtered through the popular performance framework of Mitchell's script and through the cinematic overlay of the film. So, for example, the film's opening sequence uses fast-edit flash-forwards to future action (a technique borrowed from pop-videos), explicit illustrations of the artificiality of acting (a theatricalisation of performance drawn from popular theatre), and the cod-Shakespearean iambic verse of King Real's opening speech:

> There's a clock in my head. I hear it chime.
> Wintertime, wintertime, wintertime.
> And wintertime seems like a good hour
> To give up the three Great Keys of Power.
>
> (Lowe 1985: 6)

Such an intricate mixture of codes is far from naive. For it presumes an audience that is skilled in, and which can gain pleasure from, inter-textual reading: the spectator is credited with a cultural competence that enables her to construct a meaning out of seemingly disparate signs. Thus, though the story is simple, the means whereby it is explored are complex. In this sense *King Real . . .* is an 'open' text, which allows entry to readers approaching it from very different cultural directions.

It follows that *King Real . . .* is especially susceptible to contextuality. An audience from Barrow, for example, is likely to be especially alert to the harsh irony gained in setting the world-gone-mad of Shakespeare's Lear by Walney Sound. And the film's use of recognisable Barrovian settings and frequent allusions to submarines (though neither play nor film ever uses the word) are certain to animate the paradox that, in Barrow, daily survival depends on making the weapons of everlasting destruction. In this place, then, the text may be read in a particularly lively manner because the complexities of the issues it is dealing with are inscribed in its context. Thus, the film develops an exceptionally rich text–context dynamic because Welfare State unflinchingly engaged with the paradoxes embedded in the heart of such ideologically 'hot' territory.

This is the town where the outbreak of peace is bad news, and the film reflected this in its paradoxical strategies. Thus the recognisable Barrow landscape is turned into a post-holocaust wasteland that heightens the creativity of the town's youth; recycled junk from the shipyard demonstrates the necessity to stop producing junk; to stop the unthinkable we have to think the unthinkable. In working with the youth of Barrow so close to the nuclear nightmare Welfare State was rooting for sanity, right on the brink of the cliff-edge it was aiming to destroy. And the authenticating conventions of the film – the familiar landscape, the recognisable young people, the unmistakable local accents – partly validate the effort to disturb the community's embrace of the industry whose presence produces the paradoxes.

It is hardly surprising, then, that *King Real* . . . met with a fairly cool public response in Barrow. The march of the Hoodlums through the town centre had been mistaken by many for a CND demonstration – which was not al that far off the mark, given the film's ideological import – but the confusion undermined the potential wider impact of the project. Hence, it was efficacious mainly for the participants, providing them with a temporary creative outlet, and encouraging two to go on to study at art schools. Also it impressed the borough council, which, to its credit, saw the promise offered by more widespread cultural animation. To reach the wider community, Welfare State needed to scale up its creative imput. With a characteristic audacity, the company took on the civic authority on its own terms.

The exploding town hall

Four years after *King Real and the Hoodlums* was screened at the Astra, 15,000 Barrovians spent Sunday afternoon watching their town hall. Barrow Borough Council had invited Welfare State to effect a 'sculptural enhancement' of the building, to celebrate the centenary of its opening in Queen Victoria's Jubilee year. Robin Thornber described the event as 'not just an exceptional jollification but probably the biggest art work in Europe this year' (Thornber 1987b). Apart from its scale, *Town Hall Tattoo* was extraordinary for its integration of acceptable civic celebration, extravagantly anarchic imagery, and a subtle radicalism which poked gentle and good-humoured fun at the very values the event appeared to valorise. This was ironic agit prop on the grand scale, heavily disguised as a straightforward carnivalesque party.

The six-hour entertainment included: a Victorian market; a 45-minute town hall oratorio (composed and collaged from traditional songs by Pete Moser, sung by a large Centenary Choir of Barrow people, accompanied by the VSEL Works Band); a Queen Victoria lookalike competition; an official opening of the town hall by the Mayor; a grand parade of wildly decorated council vehicles, led by two astonishing Welfare State floats; a 10-

foot diameter three-tier exploding birthday cake; and the 'enhancement' of the building itself. This spectacular transformation involved hundreds of coloured 'smokes' burning on the roofs and parapets, the stringing of four miles of bunting in 4 minutes flat, a long series of exploding firecrackers and maroons followed by panicking bureaucrats abseiling down from the roof, and the flying of a giant pair of gaily fluttering Victorian bloomers from the tower-top flagpole 160 feet above the heads of the huge crowd of spectators. The witty effects, climaxing a long summer afternoon of fantasy, brought loud cheers from the assembled Barrovians and crisply confirmed Welfare State's claim to be Civic Magicians.

To get to this point of acceptance after the edgy start of *King Real* . . . the company had realigned its approach to the town. Careful behind-the-scenes negotiations with Barrow council gained support for a series of creative projects, collectively called 'Town Hall Bonanza', which included cabaret-style shows for the elderly, visual arts sessions in schools, a hand-made slide workshop for children with learning difficulties, a writing group (with Deborah Levy and Adrian Mitchell). Simultaneously, and crucially, Pete Moser was working with an enthusiastic clutch of existing music organisations to forge the Barrow Centenary Choir. Considered in isolation, much of this activity was little more than good-quality bread-and-butter community arts animation, deliberately calculated to appeal to the the local authority as a public relations exercise: Welfare State reaching the parts (and hearts?) that officialdom could not. Inevitably, the project became ideologically double-edged, as the company made accommodations to the authority in order to gain support for grass-roots activity. This is an uncomfortable tactic in most situations, but in Barrow it implied support (however reluctant and guarded) for VSEL, as the council derived income from the shipyard.

All aspects of the project were inflected ambivalently by the context. For example, the Centenary Choir drew on thirteen local choral and operatic societies – potentially a great populist base for giving voice to any doubts about the dominance of the shipyard and what it stands for. But the musical backing for the choir was provided by the VSEL band, in effect making such voicing extremely problematic, if not impossible. In such conditions, how could the celebration encompass protest, how could the company be confident that the cheers of the crowd at the climax of *Town Hall Tattoo* might represent more than just a hegemonic letting off of mildly satirical steam? What guarantee could there be that the veiled radicalism of the event was taking root in the local networks of the community?

The interaction of the rhetorical and authenticating conventions of *Town Hall Tattoo* may have provided the framework needed for oppositional efficacy. The rhetorical conventions were all drawn from non-theatrical sources: a market to begin with (*pace* Ann Jellicoe's community plays); an opening ceremony; an oratorio (but secular); a birthday party; a carnival parade; a daylight firework display coupled with quasi-military demonstration (the abseiling); the climatic flying of a 'flag'. Here was a mish-mash of forms connected only by their provision of conventions for mass public behaviour. It made an appropriate structure for jollification and it stimulated a carnival atmosphere, an anything-goes-and-might-conceivably-happen expectancy. This is a typical Welfare State tactic, and it was used to open out the spectator's horizon of expectation, to encourage a positive response to the curious combinations of authenticating codes that the company's shows often employ.

Sometimes these codes are subtly understated, so subtly in fact that they can easily be missed. For example, the logo for the lead-up to the *Tattoo*, prominently featured on thousands of booklets, leaflets and flyers, showed the town hall exploding with its main tower zooming up rocket-like, while two of the tower's side-pinnacles have broken away and are flying off in their own directions, for all the world like nuclear missiles. More overt critical use was made of another symbol of power, Queen Victoria. Her image and what she stands for were debunked several times. For example, the two main processional floats were satirically adapted from Barrow's coat of arms. The first represents a giant bee sitting on an arrow. The Lord Mayor of Fortune rides on the back of the bee, while the civic pest-control officer sits facing backwards beneath the bee's sting, which is pointing at the second float. This takes the form of a grossly bloated elephant, an awesome but ugly symbol of the power of Empire, on top of which rides Queen Victoria herself. She is, of course, facing the sting and the pest-control officer. The witty images could be read as just an innocuous jab at the heritage of monarchy, politically irrelevant to the present – except 1987 was election year and Prime Minister Thatcher had only recently announced her view that Britain should return to Victorian values.

Even more obviously, at the climax of the show two giant puppets of the Lord of Fortune and Queen Victoria chase each other – like a monstrous Punch and Judy – around the high parapets of the town hall tower. As the firecrackers ignite and the town hall appears to burst into flames the puppets disappear, and out of the smoke the giant pair of pink bloomers slowly rise up the flagpole. The broad northern music-hall humour is double-edged, blowing a faintly sexist raspberry at authority. But if the final image is ambivalent in its detailed meaning, in broad terms it is fairly unambiguous: it is anti-hierarchical in a carnivalesque way, poking fun at power and pretension whatever its nature. John Fox maintains that the context of the comic image ensures it will become part of Barrovian mythology, undermining the presumption of authority every time anyone who saw the show glances up towards the town hall tower.

But there was a further strand to the spectacle which inflected it with a more specific and authentically subversive significance. The oratorio ended with the singing of the Barrow anthem, written by John Fox to music by Pete Moser, and it was short enough to be printed on 25,000 tiny ticker-tape slips which fluttered down from the roof of the town hall:

> We sing to the stars, sing to the sea, sing to our neighbours heart.
> Hear the loving and the living. Rejoice!
> Hear the loving and the living. Rejoice!
> For the stranger is given a welcome, and hunger can't find the door
> When the winds of July blow warmer and the children outlaw war.

The general ideological import is little more than broadly humanitarian. But of course the context of Barrow endowed it with a subtler oppositional meaning. When it is sung by the massed voices of many Barrovians within the framework of a show that has so clearly, if jokingly, attacked the idea of a centralised and individualised power structure – well then, maybe its subversiveness is just a little catching? Maybe it could carry just a little efficacious power on its own account? Perhaps

by encouraging Barrow to deal more publicly – however indirectly – with the contradictions, paradoxes and ambivalences
which derive from its dependence on VSEL, Welfare State was
gently nudging the town towards a slightly more progressive
ideological identity?

But perhaps, too, the company was operating too close to the
heart of local power to take any really significant ideological
risks at this stage of its residency. Maybe carnivalesque escapism
had been the real order of the day. Yet one bit of serendipity
symbolically signalled the potential efficacy of the company's
presence in the town. At the climax of the show, as the town hall
exploded, all the council's vehicles and all the fishing boats on
Walney Sound hooted their horns and sirens. Ironically, the
cacophony triggered the emergency alarms inside the Devonshire
Dock Hall.

A dialectic develops

The civic success of the *Town Hall Tattoo* pursuaded Barrow
council to fund a further three years of Welfare State-initiated
participatory work in the town, collectively entitled 'A Tapestry
of Celebration'. This was made up of a huge variety of events and
projects, ranging from a large-scale fireshow to a primary school
opera, from a weekly alternative cabaret to a short mythological
film for Border Television, from extended writing and music
workshops to a large-scale 'community panto', and from the
formation of a stilt-walking troupe to a gently satirical ceremony
for turning on the decorative Christmas streetlights. The climax
of the project was the 'Feast of Furness', which took place in July
1990. The 'Feast' featured jazz and rock events by local bands,
Centenary Choir concerts, tea dances, a writers' group cabaret
night, a festival club with more music and cabaret, and exhibitions and street events involving, among many others, the VSEL
Works Band and the Barracudas, the extraordinary 200-strong
group of carnival musicians and masqueraders that had grown
out of Pete Moser's 1988 summer music project. Centrepiece of
the festival was *Shipyard Tales*, a season of eleven locally
generated shows. These were staged in Forum 28, the new Barrow
arts venue created by a major rebuild of the old civic hall. The
grand finale was provided by a Welfare State spectacle in the
grounds of Furness Abbey, *The Golden Submarine*.

Given the company's oppositional stance, it was probably inevitable that at times it would have a rough ideological ride in the town. For example, loud protests greeted the 1988 fireshow *Wildfire!*, featuring a 50-foot high old-style One Arm Bandit which (to local eyes) bore an obvious resemblance to the minimalist architecture of the Devonshire Dock Hall. As the machine transformed into a gigantic bonfire at the climax of the show there could be no mistaking the ideological import of the blaze. But the event was too aggressive towards the community. The local press found it crude, and there were complaints in the council chamber. Gigantic agit prop had got the better of celebratory protest. However, *Wildfire!* was soon followed, in January 1989, by a popular success. Robin Thornber claimed that the community pantomime *Robinson Crusoe Castaway* 'feels like a huge family party . . . an image of what the whole Welfare State project is about' (Thornber 1989). The party atmosphere resulted from high levels of community participation in the making of the show, in which Crusoe was a Barrovian fisherman shipwrecked on a fantasy island. He is eventually rescued by his mother and girlfriend, who arrive in a flying submarine discovered in the VSEL scrapyard. But even this oblique joke proved too much for a key council official, who accused Welfare State of a crusading attitude to the town.

Such disputes highlight the rich ideological dialectic of Welfare State's whole project in the town, and underline the sensitivity of the text–context dynamic in long-term residential community theatre of an oppositional kind. This is not simply a matter of *what* is performed; it also encompasses exactly *how* a company relates to the community, making every element of the cultural intervention part of the ideological negotiations. For example, there was an evolving tension between the civic requirements of the council and the subversive opportunities uncovered by working at the grass roots. This is a common problem in culturally democratic creative projects, but in Barrow it was further exacerbated by the topsy-turvy contradictions written into the needs of the town. In this context a desire for fantasy escapism is, to say the least, understandable. Equally, it may be essential to the future health of the community that the issues raised by the nuclear nest-egg are dealt with directly. Such considerations bear immediately upon an aesthetic which aims to be responsive and responsible. Translated into our main terms of reference, they problematise the balance, in particular shows, between carnivalesque escapism satisfying a desire for fantasy wish-fulfilment and satirical agit prop promoting socially engaged criticism. In what ways, then, was *Shipyard Tales* a successful shot at celebratory protest through carnivalesque agit prop?

Setting sail with *Shipyard Tales*

The tentacular nature of the participatory work of 'A Tapestry of Celebration' tended to diffuse the ideological focus of the 'Feast of Furness'. The outcome was culturally pluralistic, an anarchy of creative voices with no explicit cohesion of meaning (though all in much the same authentic accent). Implicitly, though, the pluralism signified, for Barrow, an unusual carnivalesqe release of pent-up energy and a public acknowledgement of the community's need for creative outlets. Moreover, parts of the programme clearly proposed new developments for the town as an ideological community. The most radical of these were provided by *Shipyard Tales*.

This 'cycle' of plays consisted of five shows devised and performed by the children of Barrow, four shows written or devised by Barrovian adults and young people, and two shows written and produced by Welfare State. It concluded with a typical Welfare State large-scale outdoor spectacle, *The Golden Submarine*. Almost all the 160 performers were local non-professionals; while Welfare State employed around 30 professionals – directors, designers, stage managers, and so on – to work on the shows (though over half of these had major commitments to other parts of the festival). Clearly, in terms of scale, the play-cycle was equivalent to one of Ann Jellicoe's community plays. The relatively high level of professional imput was a result of the number of shows, and, crucially, the nature of the venue.

Forum 28 was the name given to the civic hall following a major rebuilding scheme, which was partly inspired by the Welfare State project. Its auditorium has a traditional end-on apron stage that thrusts some 8 feet out from the wide (35 foot) proscenium, and a single bank of retractable tiered seating for around 300 people. For *Shipyard Tales* the featureless decor and bland, uninviting atmosphere of the theatre was offset partly by large banners made by the festival screen-printing workshop. But not even Welfare State could completely suppress the dour brick-

and-pine style of modern civic refurbishment at its most baldly practical. The end-on layout was used for all the shows but one (Robert Drake's *Cuckoo*), providing a singular challenge for many of the inexperienced performers. It was a great testament to the performers and production team that, on the whole, they managed to overcome the unhelpful space and to make lively theatre of a quality that was always creditable, often impressive, and perhaps more frequently brilliant than anyone had expected.

The project had been designed to encourage different groups in the community to create shows, across the generations and across social classes. In this sense, at least, they could be taken to be a fair collective representation of the variety of ideological interests in Barrow. The five children's shows were all revivals of previous projects in which socio-political issues were kept at a distance by allegory and parable, giving the children imaginative space to show with great immediacy that Barrow *could* have a more hopeful future. The two Welfare State shows – *Matey Boy* by Kevin Fegan and *Lord Dynamite* by John Fox and Kevin Fegan – offered moderately sophisticated analyses of Barrow as a community and weaponry as an aid to peace. Two of the four shows by adult Barrovians approached the town's problems more obliquely. Sarah Miller's *Getting Out* was an ironic look at production-line misery and its immediate antidote, gossip about going out, done as a mildly feminist and engagingly aggressive blues-musical; whereas *Cuckoo* was a street-show parable about a village which traps the cuckoo of Spring (a metaphor for Trident submarines), only to have it die and bequeath a perpetual Autumn. However, it was in the contrasts between the other two Barrovian shows – *Banger and Tyce* and *What'll the Lads do on Monday?* – that the voice of the community emerged most clearly in all its contradictory and paradoxical glory, showing how sometimes participatory theatre – and cultural democracy – can be a double-edged ideological weapon.

Banger and Tyce was written by a VSEL clerk, Paul Lake, and performed by three young Barrovians (two of whom were acting for the first time). Its main rhetorical conventions are those of sit-com naturalism. Three easily recognisable, near-stereotyped, characters – Banger, Tyce and Amanda – meet and argue during the course of a day in a Spanish hotel room. The dialogue is naturally lively, full of common idioms, references to known places and events, and appropriate scatological neologisms, and for the most part the acting stays stolidly behind the fourth wall. The action focuses on personal relationships in the present, showing shifts in allegiance as new information and attitudes emerge. The setting signifies the three walls of the hotel room mainly by the placing of furniture – two beds, a coffee table, an easy chair. Outside the hotel room, on the side of the stage, there is a stylised representation of the neighbouring building. The show starts untypically with three puppet-dogs on its roof barking an amusing medley, but otherwise there are few concessions to non-naturalistic rhetorical codes.

The two main characters have a particular authenticating significance for Barrow audiences because they work in the VSEL shipyard: Tyce as a welder and Banger as an industrial radiographer. They are friends sharing their annual package holiday, and their banter, verbal and physical, is skilfully constructed to represent (what we are expected to assume is) the typical give-and-take of Northern macho working-class friendship. In the first scene they discuss the drunken events of the previous evening's outing:

BANGER   I must have gotten very upset. I'd been trying to get off with Amanda all night. I was real hot for her. And then I saw her with a jerk-off like that.
TYCE   So, not surprisingly, he wanted to take some of your teeth home in his fist, the lad did.
BANGER   Sounds like a job for SuperTyce.
TYCE   You're a wazzock, Carl.

(Lake 1990: 5)

The rest of the play explores their attempts to 'get off' with Amanda, who is staying in the same hotel. Despite Banger's fluency and superior experience with women (he's got a regular girlfriend at home in Barrow), Amanda agrees to go to the evening's barbecue with the shyer Tyce. This provokes Banger to make increasingly frustrated attempts to win her back from Tyce.

In the penultimate scene, however, the steely banter between Amanda and Banger comes to a head and she announces that, after all, she has decided to go to the barbecue with her consort of the night before, because:

AMANDA   He's got more spunk in him than you'll ever have.

I've come for a good time, craphead – just like you!
So what's the problem? You've got to let yourself go
or you're brain dead. Some girls don t know how.
This one does. Sure I like sex. Love it. But I'm
choosy who with. And you ain't the one, brother.

BANGER   I might have got aids off you, anyway.

AMANDA   Come here. I've got something for you.

(*Banger moves closer. Amanda knees him in the
groin. Banger doubles over, groaning.*)

AMANDA   You won't be needing them tonight now. I bet you
haven't got a decent wank in you, anyway.

TYCE   Not anymore he hasn't.

(Lake 1990: 49–50)

So the play presents us with a vivid vision of Thatcher's children:
mostly selfish, self-interested, out for a good time, aggressive and
prepared for violence. In the context of the 'perfect Thatcher
town', and given that they were created by a native of the place, the
vision may seem particularly authentic. It is of some consequence,
then, what attitude the play takes to its creatures and their
differing beliefs.

Banger represents the loud-mouthed rebel: he makes claims to
socialism and support for all the 'right-on' causes of the 1980s,
such as 'sexual politics . . . the socio-economic structure . . . the
environment . . . unemployment . . . the poison of racism . . .
the futility of war' (Lake 1990: 29–30). However, he is
subsequently shown, especially in the 'sex war', to be craven,
unprincipled and totally fickle. Tyce is more of a private man.
Although he is physically strong he is emotionally sensitive:
emblematically, he is a boxer who can't stand the idea of
fighting. He is considerate, up to a point, which is the point at
which he might lose the girl. Given the sexual premise of the
play – that physical love is a battleground – we are clearly
expected to sympathise with him and, by implication, be
against Banger and for Amanda. She is a fan of Margaret
Thatcher and once thought of standing as a local Tory
councillor. She represents self-willed female independence, well
able to look after herself, and prepared to be ruthless to get what
she wants, particularly in the sexual stakes: a predatory,
emancipated woman. Her final exit is experienced as loss by
both men, resentfully by Banger and elegiacally by Tyce. The

audience clearly is expected to view it in the same way. As an ideological construct of 1990, *Banger and Tyce* can be read most convincingly as an admiring celebration of Thatcherism.

If there was a chink anywhere in this pattern of reactionary reinforcement, it stemmed ironically from the same source that produced it. The broad playing of the two men at times made their characters' friendship appear highly unlikely. Local reviewers, for example, suggested that the audience may 'wonder why these two prats ever became friends in the first place' (*Barrow Advertiser* 2/8/1990). But the fault was not large enough to bring the whole structure tumbling down. Just before the interval Banger picks up his guitar, breaks out of the fourth wall convention, and sings directly to the audience (to the tune of 'La-Bamba'):

> Am-Amanda
> See my bamba
> Nothing grander
> Excuse my candour
> But I want to pop it in your handa
> Am-Am-Am-Am-Am-Amanda.

(Lake 1990: 35)

It was a wonderful carnivalesque moment, and the Barrovian audience, for the most part, went wild. Here was outrageous male sexual fantasy displayed in an entirely engaging moment of immediate actor–audience contact of the kind that can be achieved only in participatory community theatre. Given its ultimate ideological import, even Margaret Thatcher might have found it hard to condemn.

By way of acute contrast *What'll the Lads do on Monday?* celebrated the 'outbreak of peace' promised by the Cold War thaw. This show was devised by a cast of eighteen local people, with the guidance of writer Albert Hunt and director Rachel Ashton. Contextuality was fundamental to its ideological impact, even in the title. Barrovians would know it was borrowed from a recent comment by the town's Conservative Member of Parliament, Cecil Franks, which ran: 'If Labour gets in on Friday, what'll the lads do on Monday?' It was the only play in *Shipyard Tales* which so obviously used the gathering phase of performance to prepare the audience for an explicitly 'political' show dealing with the issues raised by VSEL's dominance of the town. It is of some significance to my argument, therefore, that the show attracted the same size of audiences as the others in the cycle. The title perhaps stimulated interest *because* it promised to deal with matters of fundamental importance to the town's future, to its ideological identity.

Certainly *What'll the Lads do on Monday?* more than sustained its promise of a political night out. But it took care to be a good night out as well, using many of the rhetorical conventions of popular and people's theatre to create a gentle but forceful form of ironic agit prop that drew on documentary material, facts, and stories relating to the shipyard and the Cold War. Structurally, it abandoned narrative and plot in favour of collage and montage, and patterned its scenes primarily through three inter-related strands of parallel action. The first adopted the conventions of the stand-up comic duo, especially the urbane dottiness of Morecambe and Wise. The second used the old music hall format of a comic domestic scene, but modified by being performed only by women. The third took its shape from film or television court-room drama, and consisted of a mock trial which only one character – an undertaker/MP – seemed to take seriously. This description, though, makes the show seem neater than it was: there were also several dance numbers, and ten songs ranging from solo to large chorus turns, and from Mozart to Sweet Honey in the Rock! This was a performance rich in inter-textuality.

The first scene is a classic double act performed by two international comedians, who grope across the stage blindfold until they find each other. Then they uncover their eyes:

GORBACHOV	Mr President!
BUSH	Oh, come on Gorby, you can still call me George. There's nobody here, not even any interpreters.
GORBACHOV	No interpreters? How can we understand each other, George?
BUSH	It's a little device dreamed up by a design team in Devonshire Dock Hall in Barrow. They've got the most advanced engineering in the world there, Gorby. This device enables you to speak in Russian and me to

	hear you in English. Go on, say hello in Russian.
GORBACHOV	Hello, George.
BUSH	That's it!

(Hunt 1990: 1)

Their summit meeting is in a submarine (the show abounds with such ironies), and in the true spirit of *glasnost* Gorby talks Bush into tearing up a 250 billion dollar cheque on world television, thus completely cutting the US defence budget, wiping out the world debt, and becoming a greater superstar than Bob Geldof. This is the witty start to the first strand of the show, which gives us an insider's view of Vickers, for we soon learn that Gorby and Bush are really two workers in the shipyard, Tony and Les. They spend their enforced idleness, while waiting for an inspector, playing VSEL golf (ash trays for holes), conning the manager, and chatting about the effects of the 'peace dividend' on the submarine trade.

The same topic, but from a concerned outsider's point of view, runs through the second, all-female strand of the show. Here we are presented with the women of Barrow, first at a 'naughty knickers' sales party, then hanging out the washing. This last is an extraordinary scene in which 'gossip' about poor pay-packets in the town modulates with complete naturalness into an analysis of how international money markets and defence budgets cause suffering for the children of Zaire. It is also the scene which first raises the issue of alternatives to Trident:

DAWN	Well if people don't want Subs, we'll just have to build something else.
JULIE	Well, what do people want?
JANETTE	The yard's big enough, surely they could think of something else to build . . . they've all got brains
DAWN	and muscles . . .
JULIE	you should see some of the arses on them fitters!
JANETTE	Look!! It would take ages to turn it all round to something else. That doen't help us now.
DAWN	Well maybe we have to start small . . .

> *(Has a pair of knickers in her hands.)*
JULIE/JANETTE Dawn!!!!

(Hunt 1990: 24–5)

In the final women's scene, Janette, who was selling naughty knickers earlier, turns to selling new ideas for products which the yard could make, such as low-energy pre-fab housing and rail buses. In performance this scene was too close in format to an illustrated lecture (complete with slides), and remained unconvincing. However, the other scenes in this strand success-fully caught the collective voice of Barrow's dependent women. Moreover, the counterpoint with the voices of the working men, the double perspective on the same issues from both inside and outside the yard, was especially effective in suggesting we were listening to the authentic voice of the community exploring the great ideological issues of the times.

The show's greatest strengths were in its animation of the deep paradoxes faced by a community where the outbreak of peace is bad news, and in its display of the resourcefulness of its people. The strong sense of a community in crisis was infectiously created by such moments as the lament for the great liners built in the shipyard between the wars:

There were liners I remember
Which sailed past my garden
Fine launches from the slipway
Their bow waves go before them

Sailing so proud down Walney Channel
Sailing so proud past Walney

There were liners I remember
Which sailed down the channel
With decks as white as wedding cakes
With smoke in their funnels

But those days are gone
No launches anymore
How can we call that progress to share that no more

(Moser/Fox 1990: 2)

Sung in a quaveringly frail voice by 78-year-old Lena Newton, this was one of the most powerful moments in the whole of

Shipyard Tales, partly because Lena had seen what she sang about, but mostly because nostalgia was kept completely at bay as the choir, *then the audience* – representing all the living generations in the town – took up the song in support of her. The rhetorical conventions of community singing ensured that the sound of solidarity across the generations was both clear and resonant. The resonance derived from the loss of a Barrow once prosperous from the production of peaceful pleasures. And in the context of a show which celebrated the community's creative skills – in the shipyard and on the stage – the song was inscribed with authentic hopes for a similar future.

But no one in Barrow knows what else might be made successfully in the Devonshire Dock Hall. By fastidiously refusing to fudge the issue of what, exactly, the lads (and the lasses) might do on Monday, the show animated the stupendous ironies facing the town. As Albert Hunt's title song had it:

What'll the lads do on Monday
Now that the Cold War has gone
What'll the lads do on Monday
And all other days from now on

There'll be no more pay in the packets
The orders are all down the drain
So what'll the lads do on Monday
Now that the world has gone sane

(Hunt 1990: 25)

The paradoxical context rendered the show's agitation of such issues more thought-provoking than emotion-rousing. The chief source for this was the relationship between performers and audience, which was direct and friendly, tough-toned but good-humoured, implying that it was natural for Barrovians to want to air their predicament in public together. Thus the only propaganda peddled by the show was that the town is creative enough to win through to a peace-based prosperity of gainful employment. Hence, its good humour was founded on hope chiselled out of a cliff-edge desperation, an ironic celebration of the community's ability to look despair in the eye without flinching.

This quality unquestionably arose out of the cast's intimate knowledge of the social and industrial context producing the paradoxes. Many of them had relatives who worked for VSEL. Indeed, as Gorby and Bush met again in the final scene it was salutary to reflect that the two performers themselves actually worked in the shipyard that, ultimately, was the subject of their comic encounter:

TONY   Gorby! What are you doing?
LES   I'm putting my blindfold back on, Mr President. I'm looking to my defences.
TONY   O.K. If that's the way you want it. I'll put my blindfold on too. You're not putting anything over on me.
       (*They have their blindfolds on*)
LES   Well, at least we know where we are.
       (*They fumble around*)
                                                    (Hunt 1990: 34)

The audiences clearly found this hilarious. It seems fairly certain that Margaret Thatcher, somehow, would not have been amused.

Framing the dialectic

The close juxtaposition of *Banger and Tyce* and *What'll the Lads do* . . . provides a unique opportunity to explore the problematics of performance as an ideological transaction in participatory community theatre. Their ideologies were diametrically opposed, yet they were framed by the project to appeal to the same audience. *Banger and Tyce* reinforced hegemony by presenting the sexual politics of private relationships as if they were part of an inevitable pattern of conflict between genders. The community was background to the action of the play, represented as a necessary set of evils to be met with survivalist humour and the energy recharges of package holidays abroad. Despite their temporary escape in the present, the characters, and the community of Barrow, are assumed to be trapped by history. The power structures which ensnare the town are a permanent fixture, so the cooling of the Cold War can *only* be bad news. *What'll the Lads do* . . . aimed to uncover hegemony through a dramatisation of public issues forced on the local culture through its intimate engagement with international politics. The community is in the foreground, with contradictory responses to the situation in which it finds itself. History thus becomes problematic, for the present is shot through with the dilemmas it has bequeathed. However, collectivism, egalitarianism, local democracy, peaceful co-existence are advocated as effective antidotes to the Cold War, so its thaw *could* be good news. Thus, two shows recommended totally contradictory strategies; but were they likely simply to confirm existing ideological divisions in the community, or was there any chance that, as a result of their conjunction, a new synthesis would emerge?

Any answer will be complicated by the fact that the contradictions and paradoxes within *Shipyard Tales* were reproduced in the whole project's relationship to the wider community and the borough council. The shows were staged in Forum 28 because it would have been politically tactless for Welfare State *not* to use the venue, as the company had been instrumental in creating the climate which led to the refurbishment of the civic hall. But as a magnet for attracting a large popular audience it would seem that Forum 28 was something of a handicap. Overall, the audiences for *Shipyard Tales* were not as big as the town could reasonably be expected to provide, despite the high-profile local advertising, the relatively low ticket prices, and its attraction as a community-based event.

The strategy also animated a further problematical dialectic, and its tensions impacted on the aesthetics of the whole event. On the one hand, the rhetorical conventions of *Shipyard Tales* were derived from repertory theatre, with the gathering phase including ticket-booking, queuing, pre-show refreshments, the performing phase using end-on staging in a darkened auditorium, the dispersal phase producing a noisy crowd at the bar, and so on. On the other hand, the authenticating conventions, as we have seen, were mostly rooted firmly in the unique culture of the local community, presenting the ideas and opinions of the different classes, genders, generations in the town. The first promoted a centrist and possibly elitist approach to cultural production; the second was more pluralistic and democratic.

The mis-match reflected the dual demands of the borough council and the community, and the different needs of civic and grass-roots politics. In terms of cultural theory we may say that the Forum 28 aspect of the project was caught on the horns of a dilemma, between the democratisation of culture and cultural democracy. Inevitably, to some extent that would undermine a potential synthesis of the dialectic set in motion by the shows. A lingering suspicion remains that a more dispersed set of venues, spread throughout Barrow, with the shows circulating between them, would have produced a larger and more popular response. That in turn would have improved the chances of a synthesis of the dialectic in the wider networks of the community. Ironically, the earliest advertising for *Shipyard Tales* suggested its staging might follow the pattern used by medieval mystery cycles.

Sinking the submarine

For many years Welfare State had been searching for resolutions to such dilemmas through the staging of large-scale outdoor spectacles, such as the *Town Hall Tattoo*. The approach has the advantage of creating rhetorical conventions that make events accessible to very large popular audiences. Usually, though, it suffers from two major disadvantages. Firstly, spectacle may well produce a kind of surrogate celebration through quasi-carnivalesque excesses of imagery and action that amaze and overwhelm spectators. However, as a form of protest and socio-critical agitation it is saddled with the necessity to use simple codes which resist anything but the broadest ironies, the most straightforward satire. Secondly, as a vehicle for community participation, spectacle is deeply problematical, because it depends upon hierarchical organisational structures which must be operated with a near-militaristic efficiency. Within such structures participation can all too easily be little more than a tokenist nod towards self-determination and empowerment. In the circumstances of Barrow, therefore, participatory spectacle would risk reproducing aspects of the very ideology that was at the heart of the community's most crucial problems of identity. As we have seen, *Town Hall Tattoo* may only just have avoided this trap with the help of contextual serendipity.

Given this, it was typical of Welfare State's aesthetic and cultural audacity that *Shipyard Tales* concluded with *The Golden Submarine*, which was billed as:

> the finale to the Feast of Furness . . . the climactic event of *Shipyard Tales* . . . featuring the themes, characters, bands and participants from the other stories . . . an unmissable comic party for an audience of 10000 in Furness Abbey Amphitheatre.

This was a wonderful setting for the finale, a gently curving concave hillside overlooking a large flat expanse of grass backed by trees, with the evocative ruins of the Abbey within sight. Although some four miles from the town centre and relatively inaccessible, the singular location and the participation of hundreds of Barrovians promised an exceptional climax to the project.

By 9.00 pm the amphitheatre held around 5000 spectators, many huddled under umbrellas against the spasmodic rain, facing a giant mock-up of the Devonshire Dock Hall some 80 feet long by 30 feet high. The show opens with a large procession towards the 'Hall', led by the Barracudas and featuring the inhabitants of the Land of Barra – wild engineers and inventors of fantastic machines, which they push, drag and ride along like carnival floats. The Barras are taken over by the monstrous Shellbent, a 30-foot high cross between a striped-suited businessman and a George Grosz politician. Shellbent tries to herd the Barras into the giant shadow-factory of the 'Hall', where they will be consumed by the Golden Cuckoo, a monster image of ruthless domination which devours all progressive ideas and inventions. When the people of Barra resist, led by Madonna, a cleaner from the shadow-factory, Shellbent calls on his henchmen, the Pillars of Society. These are represented by more grotesque giant puppets on top of a high-tech siege-tower, complete with a dockside crane from which swings a massive ship-launching champagne bottle. They try to release the Golden Cuckoo by smashing the bottle against the 'Hall', and in a moment of spectacular magic the enormous shed is 'launched', sliding away to one side to reveal the giant Cuckoo on its nest of skeletons and electrical detritus. However, Madonna and the Barras fight back, as she rides into battle against Shellbent on a witty war-wagon in the shape of an enormous vacuum cleaner. Shellbent and his cronies are vanquished, the Cuckoo is put to the torch, and the shadow-factory transforms into a great lantern displaying animated 'blueprints' of inventions for a more hopeful future. As the Barracudas lead a celebratory procession of victorious workers, the sky lights up with exploding pyro-technics, and the crowd – as always – gasps at their brief-burning rainbow beauty.

The extraordinary effects of the show once more vindicated Welfare State's claim to be Guardians of the Unpredictable, at least so far as spectacular imagery is concerned. However, the impressive staging was offset by the storyline, which had all the simple predictability of agit prop at its crudest. Judged as straightforward political satire this was fairly hard-hitting – the grotequeness of the villains was appropriately repulsive, the references to VSEL and the establishment were brashly bitter. But the very transparency of the ideological 'message' made it easy to reject by unsympathetic observers, and easy to absorb by the powers that be – in similar fashion to the stereotypes of *The Cheviot* .... As the *Barrow Evening Mail* put it:

> I would be surprised if everyone . . . agreed with the left of centre political sentiments of the show . . . But you can't please everyone and I'm sure the shipyard is more than big enough to shrug off this sort of theatrical 'attack'.
>
> (Hill 1990)

Hence *The Golden Submarine* could be read as offering the status quo a fine opportunity to exercise repressive tolerance – a reading which was reinforced by the list of credits announced as the last fireworks faded. Gratitude was extended to Barrow Borough Council, to the Arts Council, and, among the many others, to Vickers Shipbuilding and Engineering Limited.

This reading, though, down-plays the levels of inter-textuality and contextuality in Welfare State's whole Barrow project. Local interpretations of *The Golden Submarine* were certain to be influenced by its allusions and references to other performances created by the residency. For example, the submarine-as-cuckoo metaphor had appeared in Robert Drake's *Cuckoo*, a show that had been well received in the town. Moreover, the musical and choral backing to the story was provided by the Centenary Choir, with songs and accompaniments that were especially evocative of many of the previous shows and processional events, and including the anthem sung at the *Town Hall Tattoo*. The web of supportive meanings established by the technique, visually and aurally, was certain to add thematic complexity to the story for Barrovians, increasing its authenticity. The necessarily simple agit prop 'message' of the spectacle was inflected by the multi-vocal nature of the whole project. Similarly, the up-front presence of the Barracudas and the Centenary Choir, and the knowledge that other local residents had been involved in the construction of the show, were likely to give the rhetorical conventions an added charge. The spectacle was not simply laid on by Welfare State professionals; rather it had in large part grown out of the creative participation of the community.

Hence, the admittedly crude explicit message of the show was complicated by the implicit ideology of the event, which partly fostered opposition to the Barrovian status quo and the maintenance of the dominant world order. If Barrow's people had no choice and little voice in their dependence on Vickers, then the participatory processes of the 'Tapestry of Celebration' inverted that subordination. The same people who were socially and economically disempowered by the military–industrial complex were creatively and symbolically empowered by cultural democracy. As the ideological identity of Barrow was explicitly challenged through the show's most blatant crisis - if the Dock Hall *was* pushed out to sea how would the town survive? - an answer was implied in the very means of issuing the challenge. Far from being a crude escapist event, *The Golden Submarine* was a grand example of carnivalesque agit prop, participatory celebratory protest, perhaps at its most powerfully subversive.

Cultural democracy in the making

Over 2000 Barrovians actively took part in Welfare State's seven-year project, as performers, writers, musicians, singers, makers, designers, and so on. Though this is a relatively small proportion of the town's population - some 2% - the relatively isolated and self-contained nature of the community ensured that many more were affected by its activities. As with our previous examples, but on a much larger and more extended scale, the networks of the community had to adjust to its impact at the grass roots. The size of such adjustments individually may be very small, but the collective effect is likely to be much more significant than the sum of its parts. Cultural intervention on this scale in such a context lays strong foundations for an efficacious outcome to individual performances. At an institutional level this was most clearly evidenced in Barrow Borough Council's massively increased funding of arts and cultural projects (from nil to almost £500,000 per annum). At the grass-roots level there was the creation of new and permanent groupings - the writers' group, the Centenary Choir, the Barracudas - together with an obvious growth of confidence in the community's creative abilities.

Thus Welfare State introduced a new cultural and ideological discourse to Barrow. Prior to the company's arrival, high-profile critical representations of the shipyard were always imported into the town from outside, mainly through CND demonstrations. Welfare State's singular contribution was to invent and develop an aesthetic language through which the community could itself express its attitudes to the malignant/beneficent presence. Initially that language was relatively unambiguous: in *King Real* . . . the means of cultural production were still largely shaped by the company's oppositional stance. But as the company became more integrated into the community, and control of production was more equally shared between non-professional and professional participants, then ambiguity, contradiction and paradox emerged as major 'grammatical' constructs in the language. This is hardly surprising, given the ambivalent attitude of the community to the shipyard.

More importantly, the language enabled that ambivalence to be shown as having its roots in the contradictions of the dominant order. For example, the *raison d'être* of nuclear deterrence, and thus of the shipyard, is to protect Western 'democracy' and 'freedom of choice'. Yet the dominance of VSEL in the town certainly reduced freedom of choice for Barrovians, potentially raising issues about the validity of Western democracy. Thus the contextuality of the performances animated connections between contradictions in the local community and in the global political order. Problems in the ideological identity of the town could be traced back, as it were, to their source in the national and international status quo. But did this then imply continuing incorporation into the contradictory circus, for both Barrow and Welfare State, or had the project offered a route to a more positive, and subversive, destination?

Perhaps an answer is most easily identified in the contextuality of the performances, in their special relationship to the community. The people of Barrow were publicly animating the dilemmas, contradictions and paradoxes in their situation for themselves, enabled by Welfare State. They were giving voice to the fraught identity of the community and to the ideological tensions forced onto it by the global nuclear arms race. The most explicit resolution to the dilemmas was posed by *What'll the*

Lads do . . . in suggesting the crucial tactic of 'turning the yard round' (though most of the other shows had complementary themes). However, all the performances, even including *Banger and Tyce,* proposed an implicit solution by showing that Barrovians had the talent and the will to make their own cultural identity, which in its positive creativity offered a profound alternative to the angst produced by VSEL. The context made this particular use of theatre as a voice for the community deeply paradoxical – the expression of fraught identity implies its own resolution – but it also turned the whole event into a subtle example of theatre as a weapon. Maybe, then, a synthesis did emerge out of the dialectic. And perhaps a healthier, less contradictory, ideological identity began to form through the example set for community development by the people of Barrow-in-Furness and Welfare State together.

Conclusions
On the brink of performance efficacy

> The *poetics of the oppressed* is essentially the poetics of liberation: the spectator no longer delegates power to the characters either to think or act in his [*sic*] place. The spectator frees himself; he thinks and acts for himself! Theater is action!
> . . . Perhaps the theater is not revolutionary in itself; but have no doubts, it is a rehearsal for revolution!
>
> (Boal 1979: 155)

The conditions of performance efficacy

All the practitioners studied in detail in this book ultimately had hopes for theatre as bold as Boal's, though they were usually expressed in totally different terms. I hope I have shown that those hopes were not ill-founded; that a strong case can be made for the potential efficacy of their theatre – both in itself and as part of the wider cultural history – through an investigation of the conditions they chose and created for performance. A brief summary of those conditions will show how their innovations in the text–context dynamic of performance constructed forms of cultural experiment which were complementary. The account will in the main ignore some differences of detail in order to suggest an underlying coherence uniting their practices.

All these projects were part of a major structural change in British theatre, and the effort to break free of the traditional constraints on production and distribution led to an impressive variety of policy, programming and aesthetics. For example, imaginative constitutional and organisational innovations were an essential foundation for cultural experiment. Whether operating as independent individuals (Arden/D'Arcy), as a mobile collective (7:84), as a kind of holding company (Colway Theatre Trust), or as a confederation of affiliated artists (Welfare State International), each group tailored its constitution to enhance its chances of addressing the needs, and meeting the demands, of the community. In similar fashion, approaches to administration and management were designed to increase the responsiveness and the accessibility of the company to the community. These structural strategies were part and parcel of each group's determination to forge a new relationship with its audiences and their communities.

The range of relationships between company and community can be expressed, in simplified general terms, as a diagram incorporating four main operational approaches:

Making theatre *for*  Taking theatre *to*

Making theatre *with*   Mounting theatre *in*

John McGrath and 7:84 obviously occupied the top line; *Muggins is a Martyr* can be placed on the 'for' to 'in' diagonal; the majority of shows studied are firmly on the bottom line; while only the Barrow Barracudas carnival group fit the 'with' to 'to' diagonal (reflecting the problems of touring with non-professionals). These differences derive from the localism of the groups, as they geared their projects to the particular circumstances of their audiences. The pragmatic means for establishing localism differed – living in the community, constantly visiting over a long period, stressing links with the regional culture, and so on – but the underlying aim was always to demonstrate a commitment to the culture of the locality.

Such committed localism is always in danger of appearing presumptuous or patronising, especially when professed by outsiders. The main quality counteracting this was an 'ethic of openness', a willingness to keep no secrets, to make clear to the community what the project was hoping to achieve. The crucial mechanism for openness was the participation of non-professionals variously in all aspects of production and distribution, from management of the company or project (through boards and advisory groups) through the whole gamut of creative roles needed to get the show performed. Participation was justified overtly in a number of ways, including ensuring that documentary information used in shows was accurate, that dialogue had an authentically inflected accent, that professionalism was demystified, that the 'community' was fully involved in the project, and so on. But its fundamental purpose was to ensure an identification with the community, to reassure the community that the company had *its* interests, *its* needs, demands and desires, centrally at heart.

Where projects are undertaken with communities of interest then the creation of such company–community identity may be relatively unproblematic, as the community's needs are more likely to be shared among the variety of its members (though of course there are always grounds for internal dispute!). But in projects with communities of location, where sub-groups often have conflicting interests, then the identification of needs and desires can easily work against efforts to achieve identification with the whole community. Such projects throw the fundamental problems of culturally interventionist performance into high relief. They show that the negotiations between company and community can be exceedingly complex. They also invariably highlight the ideological functions of performance, because, at root, the identity sought between company and community is an ideological one, an acknowledged recognition that certain values can be shared by both groupings. At its most thorough-going, ideological identification will result in the incorporation of the company into the networks of the community. In any event, though, the upshot of identification is often celebration, a reinforcement of achieved commonalities, what John McGrath calls 'solidarity and collective determination' (McGrath 1981a: xxvii).

So far, so straightforward: if we were investigating practices which simply aimed to celebrate existing community identities the case might be comfortably closed right there. But these shows/projects were not just culturally interventionist – they were also, to a greater or lesser degree, ideologically oppositional, politically and/or socially and/or culturally radical. Not only that: they were staged in communities which were, relatively, conservative. What, then, were the chief methods used to balance identification and opposition? What were the fundamental devices of performance which aimed to ensure that ideological incorporation and resistance were mutually productive?

A dialectical aesthetic

The two key concepts for understanding how a dialectical aesthetic was created by these shows and projects are contextuality and inter-textuality. These concepts in turn need to be understood in relation to the rhetorical and authenticating conventions of performance. What now follows is a kind of whistle-stop tour of generalisations arising out of my earlier detailed arguments. I will deal with the main concepts in reverse order.

The authenticating conventions of these shows were always drawn, in one way or another, from the community which was their context. Whether this was a matter of local dialect, or of local allusions, or of local issues, these performative signs always implicitly indicated an interest in, and often a respect for, the socio-political world which they represented, over and above their explicit significations. We might say such authenticating conventions always celebrate their source by raising its public importance through performance. Moreover, the authenticating signs of these shows almost always dealt with hidden or obscure histories, relationships, issues and problems which were important to the culture from which they were drawn. This focus served two main functions. Firstly, the public valorisation of previously ignored local material was a major performative route towards incorporation of the company into the ideology of the community, a kind of peak to the validation offered by participation. Secondly, and most crucially, this material usually enabled the companies to introduce oppositional ideologies into the discourse of performance, for the material, having been suppressed by the dominant socio-political order (and by the community as part of that order), was implicitly critical of that order. As we have seen, by skilful use of these signs the companies also could introduce more explicitly subversive ideological perspectives to the community, as part of an agitation for change. In these ways authenticating conventions/signs could simultaneously signify incorporation *and* resistance, thus becoming a major building block in the dialectical aesthetic.

The rhetorical conventions of the performances similarly served a number of complementary functions. At the most obvious level, by usually avoiding the conventions of mainstream theatre they aimed to make performance more accessible, to attract a public which might not otherwise enjoy live theatre.

This obviously applies to the gathering and dispersal phases of performance, where the accessibility of the venue was enhanced by its location and nature, and where the usual formalities of theatre-going were replaced by more familiar, though in the context often unusual, conventions. It also applies to the performance itself. Whether in the form of a nativity play, a ceilidh, a market-framed promenade, a feature film, or an outdoor spectacle, the shows usually derived their chief rhetorical conventions from a combination of popular performance traditions and a variety of non-theatrical social gatherings. This technique served a number of functions, but two are most central to my argument. Firstly, such conventions crucially altered the dominant stage–auditorium relationships of establishment theatre, so that performer–audience interaction became more direct and flexible, less mediated by codes that restrained responses within a relatively narrow range of possibilities (or close horizon of expectation). This was a foundation for actor–audience solidarity (especially when performers were non-professional), and another major route for the incorporation of the company into the community. But, secondly, we have seen that these rhetorical conventions often provided a launch-pad for excess, for forms of discourse which can be disruptive and dangerous, for the carnivalesque, and the companies used this to encourage communities to encounter alternative and radical ideologies. Thus rhetorical conventions/signs might also serve diametrically opposite purposes: to promote the security of community cohesiveness *and* to introduce acceptable forms of disruptive anarchy within which subversive signs could circulate. This is the second main building block in the dialectical aesthetic.

Now clearly inter-textuality is crucial to both these performative dimensions. In the rhetorical realm inter-textuality enabled audiences to recognise that the performances were inviting behaviour and responses which were determined as much by the identity of their community as by the pragmatic circumstances of the particular event. This was the main point of mixing non-theatrical social conventions with conventions drawn from, say, popular theatre traditions. The social conventions enabled the audience to contribute more easily as a community, while the theatrical conventions allowed the company to open the door to subversive responses (though our examples were never as clear-cut as this description suggests).

Similarly, inter-textuality was fundamental to the impact of authenticating codes, in two main ways. Firstly, it ensured that audiences recognised that the performance was speaking to them in their 'local dialect', so to speak, and that it therefore would have a particular significance for them and their community. Secondly, it provided a framework of reference within which the most important symbols of community identity might be located, in order to be celebrated and criticised.

The interaction of rhetorical and authenticating conventions, experienced and read through a localised inter-textuality, is at the heart of the dialectical processes of community-based performance. This is because it may allow the production of an ideological crisis for the audience/community, without leading to schism between company and community. Hence, the Christmas festival is entangled with dubious political events, the ceilidh invokes the oppressions of the forgotten dead, the market–promenade leads to a dark and shameful secret, and the magic of spectacle challenges a town to turn from the abyss. In each case the current ideological identity of the community is celebrated and potentially placed in crisis, the carnival (however muted) is inflected by agitation for change. Thus it is the dialectical aesthetic of celebratory protest, of carnivalesque agit prop, which enables a company to express and explore the fine balance between ideological incorporation and resistance in conservative community contexts.

However, this type of inter-textuality is dependent on con-textuality. Somehow the company must gain the trust of the community, establish identification with the audience, in order to acquire a right to challenge the identity of the community in its own terms. I suggest that this can be best achieved by context-specific performance practices, which actively take contextuality into account in the construction of performative codes and conventions. Moreover, contextuality is utterly fundamental to the potential efficacy of the dialectical aesthetic of celebratory protest, because it makes the ideological transaction of performance acutely relevant to the community for which it is designed. Contextuality lends terrific resources to oppositional codes in performance, allowing them to provoke crises which may reach to the ideological roots of the community, offering a positive challenge to the community's identity. In this sense, contextuality is the source of performance efficacy.

The problems of contextuality

We must acknowledge, though, that the very localism which might give performance this kind of power is an acutely mixed blessing. For while contextuality may greatly increase the chances of an efficacious outcome at the micro-level of individual performance, it offers serious disadvantages to the achievement of a more general efficacy. There are two main ways of describing the shortcomings of a deliberately localised contextuality: either it reduces the appeal of performance to relatively small numbers of spectators; or it prevents performance from successfully travelling beyond its original source. In either case, though, if a company wishes to have an impact on a wider front, then there are three basic strategies which it can adopt.

Firstly, performance can construct a text that does not demand membership of the originating community for the decoding of its full significance. This was the strategy adopted by John Arden and Margaretta D'Arcy in *The Business of Good Government* and *Ars Longa, Vita Brevis*, where the non-specific rhetorical conventions of allegory and parable were inflected by local authenticity through accent and turns of speech. Clearly the text is open to this process of inflection in other contexts, but the price of such transferability is a generalisation of ideological codes which may then have no deep effect in the new context. A related technique was used in *The Cheviot, the Stag and the Black, Black Oil*, when explicit parallels were drawn between the regional tale told by the Scottish documentary material and the operations of international capitalism in other lands. The approach aims to ensure that new audiences will read the show in much the same way as Highland villagers might, but the localism of the documentary material still runs the risk of seeming irrelevant in those other contexts. In this case the specificity of the ideological codes may render them opaque to other audiences. It is worth remembering, though, that the video of the show was internationally well received, so the objection may not be as serious as it seems.

Secondly, whilst individual shows may not be usefully transferred, the methods for making them can be adopted as a model in new contexts. Aspects of Arden and D'Arcy's approach to community dramas became commonplace in the 1970s community arts movement. John McGrath and 7:84 helped to promulgate a collectivist ethic that influenced a good deal of regional and national touring in the 1970s. Ann Jellicoe and the Colway Theatre Trust's techniques for community play-making were widely imitated in the 1980s. While Welfare State's penchant for creating celebratory performances specially designed for each context also spread to other groups in the late 1970s and throughout the 1980s. There was no guarantee, of course, that the ideological purposes of the original models would feature in the reproductions. As we have seen, even creative projects for cultural democracy can be used to promulgate ideologies based on hierarchies and elitism. (In fact, Ann Jellicoe has been accused – probably unfairly – of encouraging such uses of community plays through writers' workshops and summer schools.) The effort to ensure that the passing-on of techniques is inflected by appropriate ideologies has led Welfare State recently to run an extensive training and education programme. But ultimately the ideological use of any model is just as likely to reflect the general ethos of the theatre movement/sector in any particular period, as the particular policies of the groups which invented it. This is a consideration which bears centrally on the general efficacy of alternative theatre as a whole.

Thirdly, and perhaps most crucially, the specific location of a practice is especially significant to its wider influence. The ideological identity of a community may reflect to a greater or lesser degree the chief socio-political concerns of a particular historical period. It follows that at different times different communities may become what I have called ideological hot-spots: places in which the great ideological issues of the times are deeply inscribed in the networks of the community. Community-based performance projects in such places thus may be dealing with ideological questions which have an immediately obvious relevance to communities elsewhere and the culture as a whole. In these cases contextuality can even facilitate transferability, as the focus on a particular locality can help to crystallise the issues and questions in a form which is still accessible to other communities, even in foreign cultures. This partly explains the international success of 7:84's *Cheviot* . . . video, and the growing influence that Welfare State has had on other groups. The 'difficult' community context raises the stakes in the struggle to achieve efficacy, and such projects – if successful – may even take on an iconic quality, setting a powerful example to be followed elsewhere. Creative work at these particular grass roots may even acquire a little glamour.

Trends in alternative theatre

The evolving trends within alternative theatre were in part the result of such influences between groups. However, its internal structure was also deeply affected by the wider socio-political constituents of the times. This makes the general outlines of its history relatively easy to detect. It is a progress which moves from initial experimentation (1960s), to proliferation and consolidation (1970s), to retrenchment, reorientation and finally fragmentation (1980s/1990s). Alternative theatre was a kind of cultural litmus paper, modifying its atomic structure as it interacted with the changing historical environment.

Hence, we might explain the movement's initial primary tendency towards an exclusive experimentation as a response to the breakdown of the post-war consensus in Britain, particularly as mirrored in the new 'gaps' between generations. Similarly, its proliferation and consolidation into a widening range of overlapping practices in the 1970s can be read as a search for roots beneath the deep socio-political uncertainties generated by the conflicts and crises of that troubled decade. Again, its growing sophistication, specialisation and fragmentation in the 1980s were reactions to Thatcherism's placing of monetarist and market-led policies at the top of the economic agenda. It is not difficult to see such patterns, and it is even encouraging to think that at least the movement avoided structural ossification as it grew towards industrial maturity. But, of course, the analysis is fundamentally debilitating.

In this interpretation, the movement/sector is cast as an object, always, as it were, at the beck and call of the dominant order. Individual components in its constitution only appear as a *result of* changes in that order. For example, community theatre emerges as a force in the 1970s because national economic, social and political uncertainties prompted a widespread desire for self-determination and autonomy. Or the soft ideology groups of the 1980s appeared in all their ambiguous finery because of the repressive ideological threat of rising neo-conservatism. This type of historical analysis is one source for the marginalisation of alternative theatre on the national cultural topography.

Yet the changing internal structure of the the movement can just as easily be seen as a strategy for mounting much more active and innovative interventions into the socio-political history. The sheer growth in the number of trends and strands of practice can signify a tentacular effort to infiltrate and influence the dominant order, by attacking it on many fronts. Thus the impressive flourishing of women's and feminist theatre in the late 1970s and early 1980s played to an ever-widening range of venue-types, and to the unconverted as much as to the already committed. Similarly, the emergence of reminiscence theatre, theatre for disability, prison theatre, and others geared to the needs of 'minority' groups signified a drive to reach out to every possible social grouping with performances that were at least implicitly oppositional. In this version, the expansionist growth of the movement is cause for celebration, as it provides strong evidence of alternative theatre's active contribution to the general history.

But this analysis, too, is problematic. For the centrifugal growth undoubtedly led to the ideological fragmentation of the *movement*, and this then was the foundation for the emergence of the *sector* in the 1980s. The approach in fact *reduces* the likely general efficacy of alternative theatre as an oppositional ideological movement by stressing its growing overall incoherence. This is what I called, perhaps too tentatively, the paradox of cultural expansionism. How can we rescue alternative theatre from such problems? What description would acknowledge both its responsiveness and its innovative contribution to the history of post-war society, and thus justify a claim for its potential general efficacy?

A general efficacy

We must recognise that probably the issue of the alternative theatre movement's potential general ideological efficacy in Britain, and elsewhere, will always be open to debate. Viewed from one perspective its history is definitely a cause for pessimism. Ideologically, it is a story of incorporation, as companies increasingly became dependent on state agencies, and as those agencies gradually took greater control of the movement's operations in order to dampen its oppositional thrust. Industrially, it is a double-edged success story, as the creation of a new sector of British theatre with its own infrastructure enabled an increasing number of conservative companies to survive, forcing out more radical groups in an age of reactionary repressions. Socially and politically, the movement has left hardly any marks at all: it is just a small footnote in the big text of history.

However, that version of alternative theatre history ignores the dialectical relationships it secured with the major cultural institutions of the land and with the successive counter-cultural formations of the past two decades. For example, successful negotiations with the funding agencies throughout the 1970s did indeed lay the foundations for ideological incorporation in the 1980s, but they also enabled the creation of a national network, via organisations such as the Association of Community Theatres and the Independent Theatre Council, which lent effective support to the movement's oppositional ambitions. Then, as subjugation to the main state funding agencies forced the movement to transmute into a market-led industrial sector in the 1980s, many companies developed a new alignment with the radical policies and agencies of cultural democracy, particularly in the metropolitan boroughs, and quintessentially with the Greater London Council. However, dialectics seemed to fly out of the window in the late 1980s, as neo-conservatism finally dismantled the main sources of support for widespread, ideologically oppositional art. Moreover, the post-modernist drift of British culture generally encouraged further ideological fragmentation in a theatrical sector that, to all intents and purposes, had totally supplanted the alternative movement which, ironically, had been its source. This version of the history would give alternative theatre rather more than a footnote, but its tone would almost certainly be elegiac.

A much more encouraging historical picture can be drawn, however, if we view alternative theatre from the perspective of cultural history. True, we will probably still be talking about fragmentation and decline in the post-modernist mid-1980s to early 1990s. But by locating the movement in the context of the successive counter-cultures we can make a strong claim for its potential general efficacy in the earlier period, in three main ways. Firstly, the movement played the role of a classic avant garde formation within the counter-cultures, testing and suggesting developments of their oppositional ideologies through the concrete medium of performance projects. In this sense, although it was numerically small, its ideological impact was greater than its size might suggest, as often it was on the leading edge in manufacturing the specific focus that the widespread oppositional action should adopt. Secondly, alternative theatre provided important features on the public faces of the counter-cultures in their negotiations with the dominant cultural formations. Often alternative theatre practices, albeit sometimes in entirely disparate and unco-ordinated ways, were an important part of a continous expansion of different methods for mediating cultural change. The community-based performances studied earlier are an example of this function at the grass roots; but the role was played out also through alternative theatre's effects on mainstream theatre, on the mass media and in the educational system, raising the profile of the counter-cultures still further. Thirdly, by creating 'models for cultural action' within the counter-cultures, which then spread through their networks to influence cultural practices in other spheres, alternative theatre made significant contributions to the changing patterns of cultural production generally. Thus, mid-1970s experiments in participatory community theatre in part provided models for the community activist movement which in the 1980s influenced many local authorities to adopt culturally democratic policies. The process was much more complex than this linear outline suggests, of course, but nonetheless alternative theatre practices frequently were the seeds of, or at least an initiating element for, such growth.

These somewhat circuitous routes, when used together, led alternative theatre towards a potential general ideological efficacy in the cultural and socio-political history of the 1970s and 1980s. The movement thus significantly contributed to the emergence of feminism and gay rights, the strengthening of community activism, the championing of minority causes of many kinds, and other emancipatory and liberationist movements of the period. Moreover, it was an important element in the widespread 1980s resistance to the cultural repressiveness of Thatcherism and the confusions of post-modernism. It could achieve this kind of impact because underlying all its remarkable variety there was often an abiding commitment to egalitarianism and participatory democracy. Given this, alternative theatre surely deserves a few paragraphs, at least, in any decent social history of Britain. More importantly, the movement set an example that is still worth following, especially in these mean hard times.

And now?

Recently, commentators on alternative and community theatre have been pessimistic about the future for oppositional performance. Thus, Eugène van Erven, at the end of his international survey, argues:

> If the present developments are any indication, the radical theatre will, undoubtedly, continue to make more and more compromises . . . Furthermore, disillusion and frustration constitute a real danger for those who work in radical popular theatre. The long-term political results of their work are hard to measure and seem to be negated – on the surface at least – by the increasing depoliticisation of public life.
>
> (van Erven 1989: 187)

Unfortunately, such views are emerging as a common theme even in sympathetic histories and critical commentaries.

I think that a more hopeful prognosis arises if alternative theatre is viewed in terms of cultural intervention, community action and performance efficacy. From this perspective, as we have seen, the history of the movement shows an intriguing dialectical countenance. While there are certainly signs of accommodation to, and incorporation into, the status quo, there is also plenty of evidence which demonstrates successful popular resistance and subversion through the uncovering of the hegemony of the status quo. And if this has happened in the past, why not in the future?

Oppositional theatre practices always have been particularly responsive to their socio-political environment, as we have seen. Now there are signs that the limits to economic and industrial growth may have been reached, possibly already passed, in the ecological damage evident at local and global levels. Perhaps a new counter-cultural force is emerging in the network of organisations focusing on 'green' issues. In what must count as the first serious analysis of the theatre of the Greens, Joel Schechter writes:

> The Greens openly oppose both violence and the hierarchical and elitist leadership of government. They have risen in prominence primarily due to broad-based public support for their anti-nuclear pro-environmental activities . . . If the Greens expand their performance area still further by winning

> more votes, and hold larger protests in the future, the result
> could well be a cross between a carnival and a general strike
> ... a political festival opposing 'business as usual'.
>
> (Schechter 1985: 210–11)

Maybe a new counter-culture, but with an even broader and more
popular support than those of the last two decades, is beginning
to emerge. And maybe, as Raymond Williams has argued, a new
ideological force can be generated by an imaginative synthesis of
the Red and the Green (Williams 1989: 167–72). If so, it could
make good use of the techniques of celebratory protest and
carnivalesque agit prop invented by alternative theatre. It might
even discover new ways to increase the potential efficacy of
oppositional performance. Then theatre could again join in a
new global effort to resist a hegemony that seems set, despite the
Cold War thaw, to eliminate us all. That could be rewarding, for
everyone.

Glossary

Authenticating conventions: the conventions or signs through which the spectator establishes a relationship between the 'fictions' of performance and the nature of the 'real world' of his/her socio-political experience (especially its values/norms, etc.).

Contextuality: the propensity of a performance text to achieve different meanings according to the context in which it occurs. The 'ideological relativity' of a text results from contextuality.

Ideological transaction, performance as: the ways in which spectators are actively engaged in the construction of meaning as a performance proceeds; the continuous negotiation between performers and audience, company and community to establish the significance of the signs and conventions through which they interact.

Inter-textuality: the ways in which the codes (conventions/signs) of a performance text gain meaning for an audience through its relationships with other texts.

Performance: all the events in and around the staging of a show, including everything done in preparation (the 'gathering phase') and in the aftermath (the 'dispersal phase') of the production itself.

Performance consciousness: the frame of mind (or *ludic* role) created by performance conventions which enables the spectator to accept that the events of the production are both 'real' and 'not real', and to 'play around with' the norms, customs, regulations, laws, which govern society.

Performance crisis: the effect produced by a breaking or rupturing of the rules/laws/norms which govern the uses of conventions/signs (authenticating and rhetorical) in performance.

Performance efficacy: the potential that the immediate effects of performance may have to influence the community and culture of the audience, and the historical evolution of wider social and political realities.

Rhetorical conventions: the conventions or signs which enable the spectator to recognise and react to a performance as a particular type of theatre event; they establish distinctions between different genres, styles and kinds of theatre/performance.

Bibliography

Althusser, Louis (1971) *Lenin and Philosophy, and Other Essays*, London: Monthly Review Press.

Ansorge, Peter (1975) *Disrupting the Spectacle: Five Years of Experimental and Fringe Theatre in Britain*, London: Pitman.

Arden, John (1963) *The Business of Good Government*, London: Methuen.

—— (1964) *Ars Longa, Vita Brevis*, in *Encore*, March–April, Vol. 11, No. 2.

—— (1977) *To Present the Pretence: Essays on the Theatre and its Public*, London: Eyre Methuen.

Arts Council of Great Britain (1970) *The Theatre Today in England and Wales* (The Report of the Arts Council Theatre Enquiry, 1970), London: Arts Council of Great Britain.

—— (1977) *Value For Money: Thirty Second Annual Report and Accounts*, London: Arts Council of Great Britain.

—— (1984) *The Glory of the Garden*, London: Arts Council of Great Britain.

Bakhtin, Mikhail (1968) *Rabelais and His World*, Cambridge: MIT Press.

Barba, Eugenio (1979) *The Floating Islands*, ed. Ferdinando Taviani, Holstebro: Thomsens Bogtrykkeri.

Barker, Clive (1978) 'From Fringe to Alternative Theatre', *Zeitscrift für Anglistick und Amerikanistick*, Vol. XXVI, No. 1.

Barker, Howard (1981a) 'Energy – and the Small Discovery of Dignity', *Theatre Quarterly*, Vol. X, No. 40.

—— (1981b) 'The Poor Man's Friend', unpublished MSS.

—— (1984) 'An interview with Tony Dunn', *Gambit*, Vol. 11, No. 41.

Baxandall, Lee (1972) 'Spectacles and Scenarios: A Dramaturgy of Radical Activity', in Lee Baxandall (ed.), *Radical Perspectives in the Arts*, Harmondsworth: Penguin.

Bédarida, François (1979) *A Social History of England: 1851–1975*, London: Methuen.

Bennett, Susan (1990) *Theatre Audiences: A Theory of Production and Reception*, London: Routledge.

Bennett, Tony *et al.* (eds) (1981) *Culture, Ideology and Social Process*, Milton Keynes: Open University Press.

—— (1986) *Popular Culture and Social Relations*, Milton Keynes: Open University Press.

Blau, Herbert (1990) *The Audience*, Baltimore: John Hopkins.

Boal, Augusto (1979) *Theater of the Oppressed*, London: Pluto Press.

Bradby, David and John McCormick (1978) *People's Theatre*, London: Croom Helm.

Brake, Michael (1985) *Comparative Youth Culture: the Sociology of Youth Culture and Youth Subcultures in America, Britain and Canada*, London: Routledge & Kegan Paul.

Brandreth, Giles (1986) *Great Theatrical Disasters*, London: Grafton Books.

Bratton, J. S. (ed.) (1986) *Music Hall: Performance and Style*, Oxford: Oxford University Press.

Brenton, Howard (1981) 'Petrol Bombs Through the Proscenium Arch', in Simon Trussler (ed.), *New Theatre Voices of the Seventies*, London: Eyre Methuen.

Browne, Henzie and Martin E. Browne (1945) *The Pilgrim Story*, London: Frederick Muller.

Bull, John (1984) *New British Political Dramatists*, London: Macmillan.

Burns, Elizabeth (1972) *Theatricality: a study of convention in the theatre and in social life*, London: Longman.

Collins, Jim (1989) *Uncommon Cultures: Popular Culture and Post-Modernism*, London: Routledge.

CAST (Cartoon Archetypal Slogan Theatre) (1979) *Confessions of a Socialist*, London: Pluto Press.

Chambers, Colin (1980) *Other Spaces: New Theatre and the RSC*, London: Methuen.

—— (1989) *The Story of Unity Theatre*, London: Lawrence & Wishart.

Chambers, Colin and Mike Prior (1987) *Playwrights' Progress: Patterns of Postwar British Drama*, Oxford: Amber Lane.

Chapman, Claire (ed.) and Pam Schweitzer (comp.) (1975) *Theatre in Education Directory*, London: Theatre Quarterly Publications.

Cohen, Anthony P. (1985) *The Symbolic Construction of Community*, Chichester: Ellis Horwood.

Collins, Jim (1989) *Uncommon Cultures: Popular Culture and Post-Modernism*, London: Routledge.

Coppetiers, Frank (1975) 'Arnold Wesker's Centre Fortytwo: a Cultural Revolution Betrayed', *Theatre Quarterly*, Vol. V, No. 18.

Cork, Sir Kenneth (1986) *Theatre Is For All: Report of the Enquiry into Professional Theatre in England*, London: Arts Council of Great Britain.

Coult, Tony and Baz Kershaw (eds) (1990) *Engineers of the Imagination: the Welfare State Handbook*, (rev. edn), London: Methuen.

Craig, Sandy (ed.) (1980) *Dreams and Deconstructions: Alternative Theatre in Britain*, Ambergate: Amber Lane.

Croyden, Margaret (1974) *Lunatics, Lovers and Poets: the Contemporary*

Experimental Theatre, New York: Delta.

Davies, Andrew (1987) *Other Theatres: The Development of Alternative and Experimental Theatre in Britain*, London: Macmillan.

Deller, Pamela (1989) *Plays without Theatres: Recollections of the Compass Players Travelling Theatre 1944–1952*, Beverley: Highgate Pubs.

Eagleton, Terry (1981) *Walter Benjamin: Towards a Revolutionary Criticism*, London: Verso.

—— (1991) *Ideology: An Introduction*, London: Verso.

Edgar, David (1985) 'All aboard the "A" train and join the carnival', *The Guardian*, Monday, June 10.

—— (1988) *The Second Time As Farce: Reflections on the Drama of Mean Times*, London: Lawrence & Wishart.

Elder, Eleanor (1939) *The Travelling Players: the Story of the Arts League of Service*, London: Frederick Muller.

Elsom, John (1979) *Post-War British Theatre*, (rev. edn), London: Routledge & Kegan Paul.

Esslin, Martin (1987) *The Field of Drama*, London: Methuen.

Faulds, Andrew (ed.) (1976) *The Democratic Renewal of the Performing Arts*, Strasbourg: Council of Europe.

Feist, Andrew and Robert Hutchison (eds) (1990) *Cultural Trends in the Eighties*, London: Policy Studies Institute.

Fiske, John (1989) *Understanding Popular Culture*, Boston: Unwin Hyman.

Foster, Hal (ed.) (1985) *Postmodern Culture*, London: Pluto.

Fox, John (1987) 'Background Paper – How, Why and When Welfare State is working in Barrow-in-Furness', Ulverston: Welfare State International.

—— (1988) 'Between Wordsworth and Windscale' (an interview with Baz Kershaw), *Performance Magazine*, No. 54.

Goldberg, Rose Lee (1988) *Performance Art: From Futurism to the Present*, (rev. edn), London: Thames & Hudson.

Gooch, Steve (1984) *All Together Now: an Alternative View of Theatre and Community*, London: Methuen.

Goodman, Lizbeth (1991) 'Conference in Cambridge: Theatre under Threat', *New Theatre Quarterly*, Vol. VII, No. 26.

Goorney, Howard and Ewan MacColl (eds) (1986) *Agit-Prop to Theatre Workshop: Political Playscripts 1930–50*, Manchester: Manchester University Press.

Gramsci, Antonio (1971) *Selections from the Prison Notebooks*, London: Lawrence & Wishart.

Gray, Frances (1982) *John Arden*, London: Macmillan.

Greater London Council (1986) *Campaign for a Popular Culture*, London: Greater London Council.

Hammond, Jonathan (1973) 'A Potted History of the Fringe', *Theatre Quarterly*, Vol. III, No. 12.

Hay, Peter (ed.) (1987) *Theatrical Anecdotes*, Oxford: Oxford University Press.

Hayman, Ronald (1969) *John Arden*, London: Heinemann Educational.

—— (1979) *British Theatre since 1955*, London: Opus.

Haynes, Jim (1984) *Thanks for Coming*, London: Faber.

Hebdige, Dick (1979) *Subculture: the Meaning of Style*, London: Methuen.

Hewison, Robert (1986) *Too Much: Art and Society in the Sixties – 1960–75*, London: Methuen.

—— (1988) *The Heritage Industry*, London: Methuen.

Hill, Chris (1990) 'Hellfire!' *Barrow Evening Mail*, Monday, July 30.

Hilton, Julian (1979) 'The Other Oxfordshire Theatre: the Nature of Community Art and Action', *Theatre Quarterly*, Vol. IX, No. 33.

—— (1987) *Performance*, London: Macmillan.

Howard, Tony (1980) 'Theatre of Urban Renewal; the Uncomfortable Case of Covent Garden,' *Theatre Quarterly*, Vol. X, No. 38.

Hulton, Peter (ed.) (1985) *Theatre and Communities: A Council of Europe Workshop*, Dartington: Dartington Theatre Papers, Series 5, No. 16.

Hunt, Albert (1974) *Arden: a Study of His Plays*, London: Eyre Methuen.

—— (1975) *Rural Community Theatre: Problems and Practice*, Brussels: Council of Europe, CCC/DC (75) 52.

—— (1990) 'What'll the Lads do on Monday?', unpublished MSS.

Hunt, Hugh *et al.* (1978) *The Revels History of Drama in English 1880 to the Present Day*, Vol. VII, ed. T. W. Craik, London: Methuen.

Itzin, Catherine (ed.) (1976) *Alternative Theatre Handbook*, London: Theatre Quarterly Publications.

—— (ed.) (1979, 1980a, 1986) *British Alternative Theatre Directory*, Eastbourne: John Offord.

—— (1980b) *Stages in the Revolution: Political Theatre in Britain Since 1968*, London: Eyre Methuen.

Jellicoe, Ann (1987) *Community Plays: How to Put Them on*, London: Methuen.

Jencks, Charles (1986) *What is Post-Modernism?* London: Academy.

Johnson, Richard (1982) *Disability, Theatre and Education*, London: Souvenir.

Jor, Finn (1976) *The Demystification of Culture: Creativity and Animation*, Strasbourg: Council of Europe.

Kelly, Mary (1939) *Village Theatre*, London: Thomas Nelson.

Kelly, Owen (1984) *Community, Art and the State: Storming the Citadels*, London: Comedia.

Kershaw, Baz (1978) 'Theatre Art and Community Action: the Achievement of Medium Fair', *Theatre Quarterly*, Vol. VIII, No. 30.

—— (1983a) 'Beyond City Limits', *Platform*, Issue 5.

—— (1983b) 'Theatre Through Community', *Theatre Ireland*, No. 3.

Kidd, Ross (1982) *The popular performing arts, non-formal education and social change in the Third World: a bibliography and review essay*, The Hague: NUFFIC/CESO.

Knight, Malcolm (1980) 'Theatre and the Regime: state support for the Arts without state control', *Platform*, Issue 2.

Koestler, Arthur (1975) *The Act of Creation*, London: Picador.

Lancaster, Roger (1977) *Moving On* (A Report for the Arts Council of Great Britain on Small and Middle-Scale Drama Touring in England), London: Arts Council of Great Britain.

Lake, Paul (1990) 'Banger and Tyce', unpublished MSS.

Langley, Gordon and Baz Kershaw (eds) (1982) *Reminiscence Theatre*, Dartington: Dartington Theatre Papers, Series 4, No. 6.

Lowe, Stephen (ed.) (1985) *Peace Plays*, London: Methuen.

Lowery, Robert G. (1984) *A Whirlwind in Dublin: 'The Plough and the Stars' Riots*, London: Greenwood.

McGillivray, David (ed.) (1988–91) *British Alternative Theatre Directory*, London: Conway McGillivray.

McGrath, John (1975) 'Better a Bad Night in Bootle', *Theatre Quarterly*, Vol. V, No. 15.

—— (1979) 'The Theory and Practice of Political Theatre', *Theatre Quarterly*, Vol. IX, No. 35.

—— (1981a) *The Cheviot, the Stag and the Black, Black Oil*, London: Methuen.

—— (1981b) *A Good Night Out – Popular Theatre: Audience, Class and Form*, London: Methuen.

—— (1985) 'Popular Theatre and the Changing Perspectives of the Eighties', *New Theatre Quarterly*, Vol. I, No. 4.

—— (1987) 'Theatre for the People: an interview with John McGrath of the 7:84 Theatre Company' (Eugène van Erven), *Minnesota Review* February.

—— (1990) *The Bone Won't Break: on Theatre and Hope in Hard Times*, London: Methuen.

Mannheim, Karl (1952) *Essays in the Sociology of Knowledge*, London: Routledge & Kegan Paul.

Marowitz, Charles *et al.* (eds) (1965) *The Encore Reader*, London: Methuen.

Marwick, Arthur (1982) *British Society since 1945*, Harmondsworth: Penguin.

Melly, George (1971) *Revolt into Style: The Pop Arts*, New York: Anchor Books.

Moser, Pete and John Fox (1990) 'The Barrow Songbook', unpublished MSS.

Mulgan, Geoff and Ken Warpole (1986) *Saturday Night or Sunday Morning? From Arts to Industry – New Forms of Cultural Policy*, London: Comedia.

Myerscough, John (ed.) (1986) *Facts About the Arts II*, London: Policy Studies Institute.

Neville, Richard (1971) *Playpower*, London: Paladin.

North West Arts (1984) *Haughty Culture*, Manchester: North West Arts.

Nuttall, Jeff (1969) *Bomb Culture*, London: Paladin.

—— (1979) *Performance Art: Memoirs*, Vol. 1, London: John Calder.

Owusu, Kwesi (1986) *The Struggle for Black Arts in Britain*, London: Comedia.

Pick, John (ed.) (1980) *The State and the Arts*, Eastbourne: John Offord.

—— (1988) *The Arts in a State*, Bristol: Bristol Classic Press.

—— (1989) *Managing the Arts? The British Experience*, London: Rhinegold Publishing.

Pinder, Carol (1985) 'The Decline of Community Theatre?' *The Journal of Arts Policy and Management*, Vol. 2, No. 2.

Rees-Mogg, William (1985) *The Political Economy of Art*, London: Arts Council of Great Britain.

Roszak, Theodore (1969) *The Making of a Counter Culture*, New York: Anchor Books.

Rowell, George and Antony Jackson (1984) *The Repertory Movement: A History of Regional Theatre in Britain*, Cambridge: Cambridge University Press.

Samuel, Raphael *et al.* (1985) *Theatres of the Left 1880–1935: Workers' Theatre Movements in Britain and America*, London: Routledge & Kegan Paul.

Schechner, Richard (1988) *Performance Theory*, London: Routledge.

Schechter, Joel (1985) *Durov's Pig: Clowns, Politics and Theatre*, New York: Theatre Communications Group.

Shaw, Roy (1987) *The Arts and the People*, London: Jonathan Cape.

Simpson, J. A. (1976) *Towards Cultural Democracy*, Strasbourg: Council of Europe.

Sked, Alan and Chris Cook (1984) *Post-War Britain: a Political History* (2nd edn), Harmondsworth: Pelican.

South West Arts (1980) *Touring Theatre and Dance: South West* (Conference report), Exeter: South West Arts.

Stamm, R. (1982) 'On the Carnivalesque', *Wedge 1*.

Stallybrass, P. and A. White (1986) *The Politics and Poetics of Transgression*, Ithaca: Cornell University Press.

Stourac, Richard and Kathleen McCreery (1986) *Theatre as a Weapon: Workers' Theatre in the Soviet Union, Germany and Britain, 1917–1934*, London: Routledge & Kegan Paul.

Sturrock, John (ed.) (1979) *Structuralism and Since: From Levi Strauss to Derrida*, Oxford: Oxford University Press.

Styan, J. L. (1981) *Modern Drama in Theory and Practice: Symbolism, Surrealism and the Absurd*, Vol. 2, Cambridge: Cambridge University Press.

Sutcliffe, Tom (1975) 'Fringe Benefits; *Time Out*, and the Fringe Arts', *Time Out*, October.

Tax, Meredith (1972) 'Introductory: Culture is not Neutral, Whom Does it Serve', in Lee Baxandall (ed.), *Radical Perspectives in the Arts*, Harmondsworth: Penguin.

Taylor, John Russell (1978) *Anger and After* (rev. edn), London: Eyre Methuen.

Thompson, John B. (1990) *Ideology and Modern Culture*, Cambridge: Polity Press.

Thompson, Kenneth (1986) *Beliefs and Ideology*, Chichester: Ellis Horwood.

Thornber, Robin (1987a) 'Cultural desert blooms', *The Guardian*, Saturday, July 11.

—— (1987b) 'Town Hall Tattoo', *The Guardian*, Monday, July 13.

—— (1989) 'Silly Burghers', *The Guardian*, Monday, January 9.

Time Out (1971) 'Guide to Underground Theatre', *Theatre Quarterly*, Vol. I, No. 1.

Trescatheric, Bryn (1985) *How Barrow Was Built*, Barrow-in-Furness: Hougenai Press.

Trussler, Simon (1969) 'Political Progress of a Paralysed Liberal: The Community Dramas of John Arden', *The Drama Review*, Vol. 13, No. 4 (T44).

Trussler, Simon *et al.* (eds) (1967) *Theatre at Work*, London: Methuen.

Turner, Victor (1982) *From Ritual to Theatre*, New York: Performing Arts Journal Pubs.

—— (1986) *The Anthropology of Performance*, New York: Performing Arts Journal Pubs.

van Erven, Eugène (1989) *Radical People's Theatre*, Bloomington: Indiana University Press.

Wager, Walter (ed.) (1968) *The Playwrights Speak*, New York: Dell Publishing.

Wandor, Micheline (1986) *Carry on Understudies: Theatre and Sexual Politics*, London: Routledge & Kegan Paul.

Wesker, Arnold (1970) *Fears of Fragmentation*, London: Jonathan Cape.

White, Mike (1988) 'Resources for a Journey of Hope: the Work of Welfare State International', *New Theatre Quarterly*, Vol. IV, No. 15.

Williams, Raymond (1965) *The Long Revolution*, Harmondsworth: Pelican.

—— (1976) *Keywords: A Vocabulary of Culture and Society*, London: Fontana.

—— (1981) *Culture*, London: Fontana.

—— (1989) *What I came to Say*, London: Hutchinson Radius.

Woodruff, Graham (1989) 'Community, Class and Control: a View of Community Plays', *New Theatre Quarterly*, Vol. V, No. 20.

Index

Abbey Theatre 2, 27–8
access/accessibility, of
  performance 72, 79, 85, 88, 113,
  114, 120, 121, 122, 143, 156,
  184, 185, 192–3, 216
Action Space 100
Adorno, Theodore 149
aesthetics of protest 8
affluent society 112
African National Congress (ANC)
  207
agit prop 8, 68, 69, 72, 77, 78–84,
  85, 86, 110, 130, 160, 164, 220,
  225, 226, 231, 239; *see also*
  carnival agit prop; carnivalesque
  agit prop
AgitProp information services
  127
AgitProp Street Players 102
AIDS 208
Albania 206
Aldermaston marches 111
Aldwych Theatre 136
allegory 114, 116, 122, 126, 227,
  249
alternative cabaret 224
alternative theatre 4–11, 15, 17–18,
  36, 41–59, 67–9, 82–92, 100–5,
  137, 138–42, 145–8, 166–7, 175–
  181, 204–5, 251–4; aims of 10–
  11; categories of 9–10, 48, 52–9,
  139–40, 177–9; class of audience
  for 145–8; and conservative
  contexts 8, 18, 110, 150, 183,

201, 204, 205, 212, 245; critical
intervention 6–8; decentralising
trend in 102, 144, 148, 181;
emergence of 100–5; in the
1970s 138–42; in the 1980s 175–
81; in the late 1970s 166–7;
issues in history of 84–6, 90–2;
marginalisation of 10, 55, 65,
251; myth of '68 90–2; outline
history of 8, 87–90; as
paranational movement 10, 44;
scale of 8, 42, 46–52, 104, 137,
139–40, 175–6; as sector of
British theatre 7, 8, 42, 47–8, 58,
181, 210, 250, 252; seeds of 67–
9; and specialisation 89, 140,
180, 182–3, 251; spectrum of
practice in 68, 82–4, 101, 104,
140; terminology of 8, 52–66;
texts about 45; trends in 9, 69,
84–6, 100–7, 176–81, 251–2
unionisation of 141; *see also*
community theatre; counter-
cultures; experimental theatre;
fringe theatre; underground
theatre
Althusser, Louis 19, 149, 159
Ansorge, Peter 45, 54, 57, 70, 77,
  90; Disrupting the Spectacle 45,
  57
anti-racist movement 134
Archbishop of Canterbury 99
Arden, John 9, 92, 98, 106, 107–

11, 112–22, 124–31, 186, 243,
249; *Ars Longa, Vita Brevis* 110,
120–2, 249; *The Business of
Good Government* 109, 113–17,
144, 249; *The Happy Haven*
107; *Harold Muggins Is a
Martyr* 110, 124–31, 244; *The
Royal Pardon* 122; *Serjeant
Musgrave's Dance* 108; *see also*
community dramas; D'Arcy,
Margaretta
Aristotelian catharsis 21
Armageddon 213
Arrabal, Fernando 119
Artaud, Antonin 81, 82, 103
art-for-art's sake 71
arts centre movement 106
arts centres 48, 52, 146, 177, 179
Arts Council of Great Britain
(ACGB) 46–7, 50, 51, 70, 98,
104–5, 136 –7, 141, 145, 170–3,
177, 183–4, 209, 210, 239;
Business Incentive Scheme 210;
The Glory of the Garden 171,
173; *see also* funding; Regional
Arts Associations
Arts Laboratory, Drury Lane 70,
100–1, 127, 140
arts labs 101
Arts League of Friends 90
Ashford, John 56
Ashton, Rachel 230
Association of Business
Sponsorship for the Arts
(ABSA) 171
Association of Community
Theatres, the (TACT) 141, 253
Astra cinema (Barrow-in-Furness)
215, 220
audience/s 3, 5, 6, 7, 16, 17, 24,
28–9, 34, 44, 58, 64–5, 80, 82,
88, 115, 130, 140, 143, 145–8,
166, 175–6, 180, 183, 190, 192–3,
194, 195, 197, 198, 202, 221,
230, 234, 236, 257
authenticating conventions/signs
26–7, 32, 33, 69, 79, 83–4, 102,
104, 154, 246, 248, 257; of
agit prop 79–80; of *Ars Longa,*

Vita Brevis 120, 122; of *Banger
and Tyce* 228–30; of *The
Business of Good Government*
114, 115, 116, 117; of CAST
(Cartoon Archetypal Slogan
Theatre) 77–8; changing uses in
alternative theatre 87–9; of *The
Cheviot, the Stag and the Black,
Black Oil* 157, 160–1, 163; of
community plays 193–4, 195,
201; of *Harold Muggins Is a
Martyr* 126, 129, 130; of *King
Real and the Hoodlums* 216,
220; of popular forms 154; of
Shipyard Tales 236–7; of *Town
Hall Tattoo* 222–4; of *What'll
the Lads Do On Monday?* 232–
4; *see also* rhetorical
conventions/signs
avant garde 6, 7, 42, 53, 86, 87,
107, 113, 210, 253

Bakhtin, Mikhail 71–2, 74, 204
Balkan states 206
Barba, Eugenio 64, 193
Barbican, the (London) 173
Barclays Bank (New Stages) 210
Barker, Clive 55
Barker, Howard 187, 189–90, 195–
202; *The Poor Man's Friend*
189–90, 195–202, 205; *see also*
community plays; Jellicoe, Ann
Barnsley 118
Barracudas (Barrow-in-Furness)
224, 238, 239, 240, 244
Barrow Advertiser 230
Barrow Borough Council 220, 239,
240
Barrow Centenary Choir 221, 224,
239, 240
Barrow Evening Mail 239
Barrow-in-Furness 211–42
barter 64, 193
Baudrillard, Jean 19
Baxandall, Lee 96
BBC 148; *Arena* 175
Beaford Festival 122
Bédarida, François 98–9, 112
Beeching, Dr R. 118, 121

Belgrade 123
Belgrade Theatre (Coventry) 98
Belgrano 213
Belt and Braces Theatre Company 166, 175
Bennett, Susan 24
Bennett, Tony 3, 37, 74
Berkhoff, Stephen 101
Berlin 123; Wall 206
Bett, John 166
Better Books 70
Bill Stickers Street Theatre 101
Birchall, Bruce 102, 145
Birkenhead 214
Birmingham 188
black consciousness 38, 139
black theatre 57, 58, 59, 138, 139, 179
Black Theatre of Brixton 138
Blackburn 188
Blackpool 74
Blau, Herbert 24
Blue Blouse 77
Blue Streak 111
blues musical 227
Boal, Augusto 183, 243
Boyle, Mark 101
Bradby, David 45, 66, 79–80
Bradford 125, 188
Bradford College of Art Group 101, 127
Brake, Michael 38, 96
Brandreth, Giles 2
Bratton, J. S. 154
Bread and Puppet Theatre 10, 103
Brecht, Bertolt 5, 18, 55, 77, 81, 114, 115, 119, 174, 198, 204; Threepenny Opera 174
Brechtian 107, 114, 198, 206
Brent Knoll 109, 113–17
Brenton, Howard 15, 44, 187
Bridgewater 113
Bridport 175, 187–8, 189–90, 195–201
Bristol University 113
British Empire 190, 195, 196
British National Oil Corporation 164
British social/cultural history 95–

9, 111–12, 122–4, 132–8, 150–2, 168–75, 183–5, 188–9, 206–11, 213–14; 'community' and 'culture' in the 1970s 134–8; conflict and contradiction in the 1960s 95–7; crisis and confrontation in the 1970s 132–4; cultural democracy vs democratisation of culture 183–5; cultural provision in the 1980s 170–5; divided nation of the 1980s 168–70; in the early 1960s 111–12; in the early 1990s 208–11; in the late 1960s 122–4; nationalisation of culture 97–9; new world order (1990s) 206–8; Scotland in the early 1970s 150–2; socio–political context (1980s) 188–9; see also culture
Brixton (South London) 188
Broadside Mobile Workers' Theatre 166, 173
Broadway 174; musicals 22
Brook, Peter 103, 120, 122
Browne, Henzie 90
Bruce, Lenny 70, 78
Bruvvers Theatre Company 147, 166
Bull, John 45, 68, 86
Burnley, Claire 75, 76
Burns, Elizabeth 25–6
Bush, President 206, 211, 231–2, 235

cabaret 180, 183, 221, 224
Caillois, Roger 73
Callaghan, James 49, 133, 134
Cambridge University 209
Camden Town 67, 76
campaign companies 139, 180, 183, 204
Campaign for Nuclear Disarmament (CND) 30, 75–6, 99, 111, 132, 220, 241
Campaign for Real Ale 134
Campbell, Beatrix 170
capitalism 99, 123, 126, 189, 249
capitalist 11, 40, 97, 110, 126, 134, 160, 191, 202, 214

caricature 79, 160
Carnaval (Rio) 73–4
carnival 68, 69, 71–5, 84, 107, 118,
164, 166, 192, 204, 222, 224,
238, 244, 248, 256; see also
carnivalesque
carnival agit prop 82–4, 140
carnival floats 238
carnivalesque 8, 40, 68, 69, 71, 78,
81, 101, 109, 117, 119, 163, 190,
191, 201, 204, 220, 223, 224,
226, 230, 237, 247; see also
carnival
carnivalesque agit prop 68, 212,
226, 240, 248, 256
cartoon theatre 82
CAST (Cartoon Archetypal
Slogan Theatre) 67–8, 75–8, 82,
83, 86, 100, 101, 110, 124–31,
166, 173, 212; *John D. Muggins
is Dead* 77; *Muggins Awakening*
77; *Muggins Is a Martyr* 110,
124–31, 244; *The Trials of
Horatio Muggins* 77; see also
Muldoon, Roland
Catford 175
ceilidh 137, 153, 155, 247, 248
celebratory performance (of
Welfare State International)
220–42; cultural democracy in
the making 240–2; a dialectic
develops 224–6; the exploding
town hall 220–4; framing the
dialectic 235–7; setting sail with
Shipyard Tales 226–35; sinking
the submarine 237–40; see also
Fox, John; Welfare State
International
celebratory protest 21, 40, 68, 74,
82, 130, 180, 225, 226, 240, 248,
256; see also agit prop; carnival
Celtic 138
Centre 42 90, 105–6, 107, 118, 144,
148
centres of excellence 171, 209
Chaikin, Joe 101
Chambers, Colin 45, 127, 137
Chaplin, Charlie 119
Chapman, Claire 49, 50

Chaucer 108
Cheeseman, Peter 105
China 208
classical tragedy 24
Clause 28 169
Cohen, Antony P. 30, 32; *The
Symbolic Construction of
Community* 30
Cohen, Stan 96
Cold War 38, 97, 111, 206, 208,
218, 230, 231, 234, 235, 236
collage 114, 231
collectives/collectivism 64, 73, 97,
102, 134, 145, 154, 156–7, 163,
212, 236, 237, 250
Collins, Jim 19–20
Colway Theatre Trust 9, 187, 190,
244, 250, 256; see also Jellicoe,
Ann
Combination, the (Brighton/
Deptford) 100
Come Together Festival 70
commedia dell'arte 108, 121, 141
commercial theatre 22
commune movement 39
Communicado 178
communism 207
communitas 28, 60, 64, 117
communities of interest 30–1, 65,
139, 164, 172, 245
communities of location 30–1, 65,
101, 139, 164, 245
community 17, 29–35, 59–60, 97,
106, 134–6, 167, 168, 190–1, 201;
of Barrow in-Furness 211, 213–
42, 224, 233, 237, 240; of Brent
Knoll 109, 113, 114; of Bridport
189–90; of Camden Town 125;
and 'culture' 134–6; decline in
1980s 168; development of 10,
61, 62; in Highlands 152, 162; as
ideological 'hot spot' 211, 219,
250–1; ideological identity of
30–1, 163, 190, 191, 201, 202,
211, 224, 226, 231, 240, 241–2,
247, 248, 250; of Kilbroney 31–
2; of Kirkbymoorside 118; and
performance 29–31, 59–61; and
performance efficacy 31–5; and

society 29–30; as term in 1970s
134–5; *see also* communities of
interest; communities of location
community activism 212, 254
community activist movement 39,
131, 134
community art/s 63, 102, 107, 110,
135, 183, 221, 249
community artist 63, 183
Community Charge 169; *see also*
Poll Tax
community dramas (of Arden/
D'Arcy) 107–11, 113–22, 124–31,
144, 249; carnival in
Kirkbymoorside 117–22;
disunity at Unity 124–7; the first
107–11; paradoxical nudity 127–
31; politics in church 113–17;
see also Arden, John; D'Arcy,
Margaretta
community feature film 215–20
community medicine 135
community pantomime 225
community performer 63, 182
community play movement 183,
184
community plays (of Jellicoe) 174,
175, 182, 184, 185–8, 189–205,
222, 226, 250; conventions of
191–5; cries of opposition 198–
201; event and the play in the
event 201–5; ideological tensions
189–95; politics of 185–8;
resignation and resistance in
The Poor Man's Friend 195–8;
see also Barker, Howard;
Jellicoe, Ann
community politics 38, 62
community theatre 3–6, 17–18, 23–
4, 42, 57, 59–66, 105–11, 113–31,
138–40, 142–5, 148–50, 152–66,
181–3, 185–8, 189–205, 209,
243–51; of Arden/D'Arcy 107–
11, 113; characteristics of 143–5;
and *communitas* 60; and
community development 61–2,
189–205, 209, 242, 243–51;
contextuality of 249–51;
dialectical aesthetics of 246–8;

and directness 64, 103, 122, 152–
3, 159–60, 205, 230, 234, 247;
early community theatre 99,
101–2, 105–6; *for* communities
63, 117–20, 124–31, 148–50,
152–67, 220–4, 244; of Fox/
Welfare State International 220–
42; as genre 5, 135; hypothetical
example of 32–3; the idea of 59–
66; and identity with
community/audience 60–2, 62,
116–17, 153–4, 156–7, 161, 163,
180, 190–1, 193, 201, 204, 224,
241, 244–5; in the 1970s 138–40,
141, 142–5, 166–7, 251; in the
1980s 175–6, 181–3, 179; of
Jellicoe 175–6, 185–8, 189–205;
of McGrath 148–50, 153–67;
and popular forms 153–4; rural
community theatre 3–4, 60; scale
of 49, 139–40, 176–7; and
specialisation 182–3; as a voice
of community 11, 61, 62, 65–6,
145, 165, 203, 227, 241, 242; as
a weapon 65–6, 227, 242; *with*
communities 63, 76, 113–17,
120–2, 185–8, 188–205, 224–42,
244; *see also* community,
ideological identity of; cultural
experiment; cultural innovation;
efficacy; empowerment;
localism; participation; self-
determination
compact disc 208
Compass Players 90
concert parties 153
conservative/conservatism 144,
145, 182, 183, 196, 205
Conservative Party 111, 123, 133,
168, 189, 214, 230
Comtemporary Theatre 101
contextuality, of performance 33–
4, 35, 66, 71–5, 145, 164–7, 182,
203, 205, 218–20, 230, 239, 241,
246, 248, 249–51, 257; and
carnival 71–5; problems of 249–
51
Cook, Chris 112, 151, 168
Coppetiers, Frank 106

Cork, Sir Kenneth (the Cork Report) 50, 51, 52, 137, 171, 173
Cosmic Circus 101
Coult, Tony 57, 212
Council for the Encouragement of Music and the Arts (CEMA) 184
Council of Europe 135
counter-cultures 36–40, 80, 91, 98–9, 129, 130, 134, 170, 203; and alternative theatre 6–7, 10, 11, 21, 37–8, 45, 53, 54, 59, 64, 68–9, 72, 75–6, 77, 78, 80, 83–4, 86, 88–9, 99, 101, 102, 127, 138, 142, 147, 164, 180, 252–4; and Arden/D'Arcy 92, 106, 126–7, 131; and carnival 72–3, 75; and CAST 75–6, 78, 126–7, 131; and expressivity/expressiveness 101, 126, 130, 131, 138, 147, 187; and generational membership 37–8, 39, 76; institutions of 38–9; and Jellicoe 186–7, 203; and McGrath 148–50, 155, 164; and 1968 187, 253–4; and Welfare State International 211–12; see also black consciousness; community activist; feminism; feminist movement; gay liberation movement; participatory democracy; women's liberation movement
court-room drama 231
Covent Garden Community Theatre 62
critical reification 34
culture 6, 17, 35–40, 134–6; see also British social/cultural history; counter-cultures; sub-cultures; youth sub-culture
cultural activist/activism 112, 124, 150, 153, 165, 166
cultural animation 220
cultural critics 37, 38, 45, 135
cultural democracy 10, 145, 169, 183–5, 225, 227, 236, 240–2, 253, 254; see also democratisation of culture
cultural experiment/

experimentation 7, 16, 56, 105–6, 142–3, 148–50, 172, 182, 243
cultural imperialism 106, 118, 137
cultural industries 73, 172, 208
cultural innovation 101, 106, 142, 172
cultural intervention 6, 86, 99, 142, 225, 240, 245, 255
cultural pluralism 80, 138, 166, 226
cultural politics 173, 210
cultural production 19, 39, 97, 131, 136, 172, 174, 175, 183, 185, 186, 208, 236, 254; theatre as 5, 10, 16, 108, 148, 150, 166, 167, 176, 241
cultural revolution 39, 106, 148–9

Dadaist 70
D'Arcy, Margaretta 9, 92, 98, 106, 107–11, 112–22, 124–31, 144, 186, 243, 249; see also Arden, John
Darling, Julia 67
Dartington College 59
Davies, Andrew 43, 45, 56, 65, 110, 129; Other Theatres 110
Deller, Pamela 90
Democratic Convention (Chicago) 122
democratisation of culture 10, 183–5, 236; see also cultural democracy
demystification of culture 135
Deptford 144
Derby 188
Derrida, Jacques 19
Devonshire Dock Hall (Barrow) 213, 224, 225, 231, 234, 238, 240
dialectical aesthetics 246–8
Dickens, Charles 108
Dionysus 119
Doc Martens 170
Dogg's Troupe 101
Doppio Teatro 10
Dorchester 202; Quarter Assizes 196
Drake, Robert 227, 239; Cuckoo 227, 239

Drambuie 159
Dublin 2, 27, 120
Duke of Sutherland 159, 163
Durkheim, Emile 19
Durov, Leonidowitz Vladimir 1–2
Dvinsky, Emanual 2

Eagleton, Terry 19, 73
East Germans 206
Eastern Angle Theatre Company
 177
economic importance of the arts
 23, 174
Edgar, David 44, 68, 71–2, 78–9,
 80, 85–6, 145–6, 150, 153–4, 187,
 202, 203, 204; *Entertaining
 Strangers* 202; *Nicholas
 Nickleby* 174
Edinburgh Festival 177
educational drama 103
efficacious 3, 84, 104, 115, 125,
 130, 152, 162, 164, 165, 212,
 214, 220, 223, 240; *see also*
 efficacy
efficacy: and alternative theatre 16,
 141, 142, 249, 252–4; and
 celebratory performance 224;
 community and 31–5; of
 community dramas 115, 117,
 122, 126; of community plays
 191, 201, 202–4; and community
 theatre 59, 144, 148; conditions
 of 243–5; definition of 1–3;
 general 20, 252–4; and
 performance 1–3, 5, 16, 21–9,
 31–5, 59, 115, 117, 122, 126,
 141, 142, 144, 148, 152, 155,
 164–7, 191, 201, 202–4, 222, 224,
 243–5, 248, 249, 252–4, 255, 256,
 257; and popular political
 theatre 152, 155, 164–7; *see also*
 efficacious; performance, as
 ideological transaction
egalitarianism 18, 39, 145, 157,
 164, 191, 196, 236, 254
el Teatro Campesino 10
Elder, Eleanor 90
Eldridge Pope 202

elitist/elitism 79, 91, 136, 148, 172,
 173, 178, 208, 236, 250
Elsom, John 42, 45, 56, 70
Emergency Exit Arts 178
EMMA Theatre Company 138,
 166, 181
Empire Pool, Wembley 186
empower/empowerment of
 audience/community 34, 60, 61,
 62, 66, 74, 104, 141, 145, 167,
 180, 193, 208, 237, 240; *see also*
 performance, as ideological
 transaction
Encore 107
entertainment 2, 5, 22, 23, 78, 107,
 117, 153, 155, 166, 178, 216
environmental theatre 139, 183
Esslin, Martin 34–5
Estonia 206
Ethiopia 207
'ethnic' theatre 57; *see also* black
 theatre
Evening Herald, Dublin 27
Everyman Theatre, Liverpool 148
experimental theatre 52–3
Exploding Galaxy 101

Falklands War 163, 213
Falls Road (Belfast) 33
fanzines 133
Faulds, Andrew 135
Feast of Furness 224, 226
Fegan, Kevin 227; *Lord Dynamite*
 227; *Matey Boy* 227
Feist, Andrew 173, 177, 208
feminism 38–9, 121, 180, 181, 252
feminist 20, 30, 227; movement
 131, 203; theatre 45, 57, 58, 142,
 166, 180, 181, 252; *see also*
 women's theatre
Festival of Fools 101
festivals 103, 106, 110, 117, 118,
 119, 172, 226, 248, 256
Fields, W. C. 119
fireworks 239
Fiske, John 34, 72
flower-power 87
Fo, Dario 153, 178

Foco Novo Theatre Company 138, 147, 166, 179
folk-lore 33, 153
folk-memory 162, 163
Footsbarn Theatre Company 138
Fortunati 178
Forum 28 (Barrow-in-Furness) 224, 226, 236
Foster, Hal 28
Foucault, Michel 18, 81
Fox, John 9, 101, 125, 127, 211, 212, 213, 214, 215, 223, 227, 233; *see also* Welfare State International
Franks, Cecil, MP 230
Freehold Theatre Company 101
French Resistance 53
French Revolution 196
fringe theatre 15, 42, 43, 44, 48, 52, 53, 70
funding, of arts 47, 137, 172, 240; *see also* Arts Council; Regional Arts Associations
funding agencies/bodies 46, 97–8, 104–5, 136–7, 140, 141, 145, 170–5, 181, 253; *see also* Arts Council; Regional Arts Associations
funding system 9, 50, 147, 177, 179, 181, 209; *see also* Arts Council, Regional Arts Associations
funfairs 103
Furness Abbey (Barrow-in-Furness) 224, 226, 237

Gaelic 157
gay arts festival 172
gay liberation movement 134, 139
gay rights/politics 38–9, 254
Gay Sweatshop Theatre Company 138
gay theatre 57, 58, 59, 138, 139, 179
GCHQ (Cheltenham) 169
Geldof, Bob 233
General Will Theatre Company 138, 166
generation gap 96, 251

Germany 79, 80
Gill, Sue 211
Girl Guides 120, 122, 186
glasnost 206, 232
Glaswegian 164
Glorious Twelfth 32–3
Goldberg, Rose Lee 57
Gooch, Steve 43, 45, 56, 64–5, 90; *All Together Now* 64–5
Goodbody, Buzz 137
Goodman, Lizbeth 209
Goodman, Lord 106
Goodman, Paul 39
Goon Show 77
Goorney, Howard 79
Gorbachov, President 206, 211, 231–2, 235
Graeae Theatre Company 179
Grampians 151
Gramsci, Antonio 19, 149, 153, 175
Gray, Frances 107, 110, 115, 121
Great George's Project 100
Great Train Robbery 97
Greater London 172
Greater London Council (GLC) 62, 169, 170, 172–3, 184, 253
Greece 122
'Green' issues 183, 255
Green movement 208
Greenham Common 75, 169
Greens, the 255–6
Grosz, George 238
Grotowski Jerzy 101, 138
Grunwick 133
Guardian, the 213
Guildford 123
Guildford Four 207
Gulf War 208
Guy Fawkes 175

Hair 130
Hammond, Jonathan 49, 54
Handsworth (Birmingham) 185
happenings 69
Hardy, Thomas 108, 195
Hare, David 101, 187
Havel, Vaclav 208
Hay, Peter 2

Hayman, Ronald 45, 108
Haynes, Jim 100
Hayward, Paul 215
Hayward Gallery 173
Hebdige, Dick 95, 132–3
hegemonic 20, 135, 180, 184, 202, 222
hegemony 19–21, 37, 39, 41, 73, 99, 149, 179, 199, 213, 235, 255, 256; *see also* hegemonic
heritage industry 174, 183
Hesitate and Demonstrate 177, 212
Hewison, Robert 15, 16, 44, 45, 53, 55, 69, 147, 174
hidden/alternative histories 157, 164, 194, 195, 246
'high' arts 34, 98, 119, 135, 184
Highland clearances 152, 155–6, 162–3
Highlands 152, 155–6, 158, 162–3, 165, 249
Hill, Chris 239
Hilton, Julian 24–5, 61
Hinchco, Tamara 129
hippy sub-culture 87
Hoggart, Richard 135, 170–1
Holub, Robert C. 24
horizon of expectation 24, 26, 102, 222, 247
Hornsea College of Art 123
House of Commons 112
Houses of Parliament 212
Howard, Tony 62
Hull Truck Theatre Company 139
Hulton, Peter 60
Hungary 206
Hunt, Albert 60–1, 101, 108, 110, 115, 120, 125, 128, 230–5; *What'll the Lads do on Monday?* 227, 230–5, 241
Hunt, Hugh 54–5
Hutchison, Robert 173, 177, 208

ideological relativity 33, 145, 257
ideological resistance/ incorporation 8, 142, 175, 204–5, 210, 221, 246, 252–4; *see also* contextuality

ideology 16–17, 18–21, 83–4, 162–4; aristocratic 160; bourgeois 149, 153; bourgeois feminism 180; of communities 29–31, 32; of counter-culture 39–40; egalitarian 18, 84, 102, 123, 130, 135, 160, 186, 205, 212; emancipatory 18, 39, 40, 205, 254; humanitarian 223; of individualism 35; liberal humanism 196; libertarian 119, 134, 150, 164, 254; radical feminism 180; socialist feminism 180; *see also* capitalist; hegemony; Marxist; performance, as ideological transaction; socialist; utopian
Impact Theatre Co-operative 177
improvisational theatre 139
Independent Theatre Council (ITC) 141, 177, 210, 253
Inter-Action 57, 101, 102
Intenational Outlaw University (IOU) 212
International Times 53
Interplay 102, 138
inter-textuality 33–4, 35–6, 203, 208, 217, 218–19, 231, 239, 246, 247–8, 257; *see also* text–context dynamic
Irish nationalism 27
Irish Republican Army (IRA) 33, 133, 169
irony 80–2, 200–1
Irving, Henry 55
Islay 163
Itzin, Catherine 43, 45, 48, 49, 50, 55, 76, 77, 78, 106, 119, 125, 126, 128, 138, 212; *Alternative Theatre Handbook* 55; *British Alternative Theatre Directory* 48, 50

Jackson, Antony 98, 105
Jagger, Mick 99
Jameson, Fredric 20
Jarrow Marches 169
Jarry, Alfred 119
Jauss, Hans 24

Jellicoe, Ann 9, 57, 119, 175–6, 183, 185–8, 189–205, 222, 226, 250; *The Knack* 186; *The Reckoning* 186; *The Sport of My Mad Mother* 186; *see also* community plays
Jencks, Charles 19–20
John Bull Puncture Repair Kit 83, 85
John o' Groats 138
Johnson, Richard 57
Joint Stock Theatre Company 138, 166, 179, 192
Jor, Finn 135
Joyce, James 108

Keeler, Christine 112
Kelly, Mary 90
Kelly, Owen 183–5
Kennedy, President 111
Kershaw, Baz 4, 57, 61, 185, 192, 212
Khan, Naseem 62–3
Kick Theatre Company 175
Kidd, Ross 10
Kilbroney, Northern Ireland 31–2
Killarow, Highlands 163
Kilmennay, Highlands 163
King, Martin Luther 112
Kings Cross 127
King's Head Theatre 187
Kirkbymoorside 107, 110, 117–22, 186
Knight, Malcolm 147
Koestler, Arthur 80–1
Kray twins 126

Labour Party 49, 111, 123, 126, 127, 133, 134, 164, 170, 214
Lake, Paul 227–30; *Banger and Tyce* 227–30, 242
Lambert, J. W. 108
Lancaster, Roger 49
Land's End 138
Langley, Gordon 57
Larsen, Sangestad 32
late-capitalism 39, 149, 153
Latvia 206
Lear, Edward 217
Leavisite 108

Lecoq, Jacques 178
Leeds 188
Leicester 188
lesbian arts festival 172
Levy, Deborah 221
Liberals (Liberal Party) 111, 123
Littlewood, Joan 90, 109, 127
Live Theatre 166
Liverpool 100; Playhouse 209
Living Theatre 103
Livings, Henry 119
localised democracy 138, 205, 236
localism 109, 126, 144, 148, 154, 181, 244, 249
Lochinver 159, 162
London School of Economics (LSE) 123
London Theatre Group 101
Long, Mark 67
Lord Chamberlain 97, 109, 127
Lord Provost of Scotland 207
Lowe, Stephen 217, 218, 219
Lowery, Robert G. 2, 27
Luce, Richard 209
Lumiere and Son 138
Lyceum Theatre 55
Lyme Regis 185–6

MacClennan, Dolina 157
MacColl, Ewan 79, 101
McCormack, John 45, 66, 79–80
McCreery, Kathleen 79
McGillivray, David 49
McGrath John 10, 11, 23, 44, 71, 138, 146, 148–50, 152–67, 187, 244, 245, 249; *Blood Red Roses* 165; *The Cheviot, the Stag and the Black, Black Oil* 150, 152–67, 239, 249, 250; *see also* popular political theatre
Machiavelli 119
Macmillan, Harold 111, 112, 116
Madonna 34
mainstream theatre 9, 44, 47, 55, 60, 64, 65–6, 88–9, 98, 104, 108, 110, 127, 139, 147, 148, 153, 177, 181, 191; *see also* national theatres; repertory theatre

mainstream theatre critics/
  historians 10, 54–5, 102, 110
Manchester 207
Mandela, Nelson 207
Mannheim, Karl 37–8
Manpower Services Commission
  (MSC) 189
Marcuse, Herbert 39
Marowitz, Charles 78, 108, 120,
  186
Marsden, Bill 101
Marwick, Arthur 97, 124, 134
Marx, Karl 19
Marxism 75, 149, 164, 186
Marxist 19, 44, 56, 75, 78, 89, 112,
  126, 138, 140, 149, 150, 161;
  carnivalesque 75
mass media 34, 73, 77, 80, 85, 96,
  99, 102, 110, 127, 148, 153, 155,
  206, 254
Maze prison 168
medieval mystery cycles 237
Medium Fair Theatre Company 3,
  61, 138, 166, 181, 185–6
Meeting Ground Theatre
  Company 178
Mellor, David 209
Melly, George 53
melodrama 108, 216
Merseyside 172
Mexico City 123
Mid-Pennine Arts Association 212
Mikron Theatre Company 119
Milan 123
Miller, Sarah 227; *Getting Out* 227
Mitchell, Adrian 215, 216, 217,
  218, 221; *The Tragedy of King
  Real* 215
mixed economy 97
modernist 53
Mods 95–6, 132
Molina, Alfred 175
monetarism 46, 168
monetarist 251
Monmouth Rebellion 185
Monstrous Regiment Theatre
  Company 146, 166
montage 58, 231
Moors Murders 97

moral panic 96, 133
Morecambe and Wise 231
MORI (opinion poll) 189
Moscow 206
Moser, Pete 217, 220, 221, 223,
  224, 233
Mozart 231
Muldoon, Roland 68, 75–8, 124–5,
  128–9
Mulgan, Geoff 173
Mummerandada 178
mummers play 114, 216
musuem theatre 182
music hall 4, 67, 77, 103, 108, 154,
  223, 231
music theatre 139, 178
Muswell Hill 124
Myerscough, John 50, 51, 52
myth of '68

Naden, David 130
National Association of Arts
  Centres 52
National Front 134
National Theatre 50, 105, 136–7,
  173–5; *see also* national theatres
national theatres 47, 50–2, 105,
  136–7, 171, 173–5, 184, 209; *see
  also* National Theatre; Royal
  Shakespeare Company
nationalisation of culture 97–9
nativity play 106, 110, 113–17, 247
naturalism 180, 227
neo-conservatism 137, 142, 147,
  172, 180, 181, 205, 251, 253
neo-Conservative 46
neo-expressionist 178, 183
neo-Marxist 19
neo-naturalistic 138
Nerval, Gerard 81
Neville, Richard 53
new circus 178, 182
New Left 75, 91, 99, 111, 129
Newcastle-upon-Tyne 204
Newton, Lena 233
Nietzsche, Frederick 81
nihilism 133
Nixon, Richard 122
North Sea Oil 156

North West Arts 171; *Haughty Culture* 171
North West Spanner Theatre Company 83, 147, 166
Northend Troupe 101
Northern Arts 209
Northern Ireland 48, 122
Northumberland 144
Notting Hill 67; Carnival 133
nuclear apocalypse 38, 216, 219
nuclear arms/weapons 99, 111, 206, 222, 241
nuclear disarmament 111; *see also* Campaign for Nuclear Disarmament
nuclear submarines 111, 211, 213, 215; *see also* Polaris; Trident
Nuttall, Jeff 67, 69, 70, 95; *Bomb Culture* 70

pageant 24, 166
Palumbo, Peter 209
pantomime 24, 103, 108, 154, 156, 216, 225
parable 116, 126, 216, 227, 249
Paradise Now 128
Paris 122, 149
Parker, Charles 106; *The Maker and the Tool* 106
parlour illusionist 217
participation 134, 143, 172, 185, 190, 193, 238, 244–5, 246; of audience 103–4, 115, 156; of community 103, 118, 225, 237, 240; *see also* empowerment; participatory projects
participatory community theatre 254
participatory democracy 39–40, 102, 104, 134, 142, 145, 164, 254
participatory projects 140, 178, 182, 183, 185, 191, 224, 226, 227, 230, 235
patriarchy 20, 38, 129, 131, 142
peace dividend 234
Pentabus Travelling Theatre Company 138, 166
People Show 67–71, 72, 75, 78, 82, 83, 84, 85, 100, 129, 212

People's March for Jobs 169
people's theatre 47, 68, 231
percent for art 172
perestroika 206
performance 1–3, 6–10, 15–17, 18–29, 29–31, 31–5, 35–40, 243–5, 246–9, 249–51; community and 29–35; conditions of efficacy 243–5; and context 5–6; and crisis 27–8, 117, 203, 248, 257; culture and 35–40; dialectical aesthetic of 246–9; dispersal phase of 26, 102, 236, 247, 257; efficacy 1–3; and efficacy 21–9; gathering phase of 24–5, 26, 32, 102, 121, 130, 193, 230, 236, 242–7, 257; as ideological transaction/negotiation 16, 18, 23, 33, 59, 63–4, 66, 84, 127, 128, 145, 146, 152, 154, 162, 183, 203, 225, 235, 245, 248, 257; ideology and 18–21; oppositional 6–10; problems of contextuality of 249–51; *see also* authenticating conventions; horizon of expectation; rhetorical conventions
performance art 48, 57, 68, 69–71, 72, 82, 86, 211, 212
performance consciousness 24–5
performance theory 22–4, 57
permissive society 97
permissiveness 130–1
Perspectives Theatre Company 138, 166
physical theatre 56, 58, 139
Pick, John 23, 98, 104
pigeon fanciers 30
Pilgrim Players 90
Pinder, Carol 65
Pip Simmons Theatre Company 75, 101
Poland 206
Polaris 111, 217
political theatre 6, 43, 80, 125, 148, 149, 152, 179; groups 56, 58, 59, 62, 74, 76, 101–2, 106, 138, 139, 142, 145–6, 165, 166, 183, 212

politics of the personal 142
Poll Tax 169, 207, 209
Pope, Christopher 202
popular performance traditions
 108, 247
popular political theatre (of
 McGrath) 148–50, 152–67;
 aesthetic strategies 152–5;
 McGrath sets up 7:84 148–50;
 reading of *The Cheviot*... 157–
 62; staging *The Cheviot*... 155–7;
 text, context and ideology 162–7
popular theatre: forms/traditions
 47, 68, 77, 85, 153, 216, 219,
 231, *see also* cabaret, concert
 parties, music hall, Punch and
 Judy, spectacle, variety theatre;
 groups 139, 141, 142
pop videos 219
Portable Theatre Company 101,
 166
post-modernism 103, 208
post-modernist 19–20, 33, 35, 103,
 141, 178, 180, 208, 253
post-modernity 20
post-structuralist 19, 35, 141
Priestley Report 173
Prior, Mike 45
prison theatre 252
Profumo, John 112
promenade staging 185, 192–3,
 197, 198–9, 247, 248
Protestantism 32
proto-semiotic 25
PSST! (Please Stop Screaming
 Theatre!) 102
psychodrama 103
Punch and Judy 223
punk 132–3, 215

Queen Victoria 159, 214, 220, 222

Rachman, Peter 112
R.A.T. Theatre 138
Rayner Report 173
reception theory 24
Recreation Ground 187
Red Ladder Theatre Company 75,
 83, 102, 166, 212
Red Shift Theatre Company 177

Rees-Mogg, William 170, 171–2,
 209
Regional Arts Associations
 (RAAs) 47, 51, 141, 171, 209
Regional Boards 209
reminiscence theatre 57, 58, 182,
 252
Renaissance 74
Renton, Timothy 209
repertory movement 98, 105
repertory theatre 49–52, 137, 148,
 171, 175, 184, 209, 236
repressive tolerance 239
*Revels History of Drama in
 English* 54–5
rhetorical conventions/signs 25–6,
 28, 32, 33, 69, 79, 83–4, 102,
 104, 154, 246–7, 248, 258; of
 agit prop 79; of allegory/parable
 249; of *Ars Longa, Vita Brevis*
 121, 122; of *Banger and Tyce*
 227–8; of *Business of Good
 Government* 114, 115, 116, 117;
 of CAST 77; 160–1, 163;
 changing uses in alternative
 theatre 87–9; of *The Cheviot,
 the Stag and the Black, Black
 Oil* 156–7, 160–1, 163; of
 community plays 191–3, 195,
 201; of community singing 234;
 of *The Golden Submarine* 239–
 40; of *King Real and the
 Hoodlums* 216; of popular
 forms 154; of promenade
 staging 198–9; of *Shipyard Tales*
 236–7; of spectacle 237; of *Town
 Hall Tattoo* 222–4; of *What'll
 the Lads Do On Monday?* 231–
 2 *see also* authenticating
 conventions
riots 133, 188–9, 195, 203, 207
riots, in theatre 2, 21, 27–8, 32, 35
rites of intensification 61
rites of passage 61
Rittner, Luke 171
ritual 22–3, 61, 99, 103; Broadway
 theatre as 22–3
Rock Against Racism 75, 133
Rockers 95–6, 132

Romania 206
Romantics 7
Roszak, Theodore 39–40, 72
Rowell, George 98, 105
Roy Hart Theatre 101
Royal Court Theatre 70, 108, 127, 148, 186, 187, 210
Royal Opera House 210
Royal Shakespeare Company (RSC) 50, 103, 105, 110, 120, 122, 136–7, 173–5, 187; see also national theatres
Rushdie, Salman 271

7:84 Theatre Company (England) 179
7:84 Theatre Company (Scotland) 9, 138, 148–50, 152–67, 175, 212, 244, 249, 250; see also McGrath, John
Sainsburys PLC (Arts in Education) 210
samba school (Rio) 74
samizdat 56
Samuel, Raphael 79
San Francisco Mime Troupe 10
Scarborough 118
Scarlet Harlets 179
satire 67, 68, 72–3, 77–8, 81, 130, 157–61, 237, 239
satiric irony/ironic satire 81–2, 160
scale: of alternative theatre 46–52; of community plays 202, 226; of Welfare State shows 226; see also statistics
Schechner, Richard 22–3, 25
Schechter, Joel 2, 81, 255–6
Schweyk 77
Scope of Community Theatre and Dance, The (Conference) 63
Scottish Arts Council 166
Scottish nationalism 151, 160–2, 164
Scottish Nationalist Party (SNP) 151, 161, 164
Scottish Oil 151, 152, 160, 164
Second World War 53, 213
self-determination, of audiences/

communities 11, 61, 66, 138, 142, 164, 167, 201, 237, 251
semiotic 25, 30
Sensual Laboratory 101
Shadow Syndicate, The 178
Shakespeare 78, 108, 215, 216, 217; King Lear 215, 216, 217
Shared Experience 138
Shaw, Roy 170–1, 183–5
Sheffield Polytechnic 215
Sillitoe, Alan 96; Saturday Night and Sunday Morning 96
Simpson, J. A. 135; Towards Cultural Democracy 135
Sistren Theatre 10
sit-com naturalism 227
site-specific companies 179, 183, 204
Sked, Alan 112, 151, 168
skiffle 133
Skybolt 111
socialism 187, 212, 229
socialist 44, 65, 67, 75, 90, 97, 123, 126, 139, 148, 156, 160, 163, 187, 194
socialist theatre 44, 146
society of the spectacle 81, 96, 170
soft-ideology groups 178–9, 180, 204, 251
South Bank 136, 173
South West Arts 63
Southall (London) 188
Southampton 144
special needs companies 179, 183, 210
spectacle 72–3, 103, 166, 180, 204, 221, 223, 224, 226, 237, 239, 240, 247, 248
sponsorship 171, 172, 177, 210
Stalinist 187
Stallybrass, P. 73
Stamm, R. 73
statistics, of alternative theatre 43, 46–52, 176; see also scale
status quo 7, 8, 20–1, 40, 41, 45, 48, 50, 69, 82, 83, 87, 99, 147, 153, 194, 201, 202, 214, 239, 241, 255; opposition to 99, 109,

134, 145, 149, 180, 191, 195, 204, 240; *see also* hegemony
Steiner, Marcel 215
Stoke documentaries 105
Stourac, Richard 79
Stowe, Harriet Beecher 159
Stratford-upon-Avon 136
Strangeways Prison 207
structuralist 19
Sturrock, John 19, 81
Styan, J. L. 42
sub-culture 37, 87–8, 95–6, 99, 132–3; *see also* beats; flower-power; hippies; mods; moral panic; punk; rockers
Sunday Times 189
'sus' laws 188
Sutcliffe, Tom 57
Sweet Honey and the Rock 231

Tara Arts 138
Taunton 113
Taylor, John Russell 108, 110
Tax, Meredith 41
Temba Theatre Company 138
Territorial Army 122
terminology, of alternative theatre 8, 52–66; 'alternative' 55–6; 'experimental' 52–3; 'fringe' 54–5, 136; generic categories 52–6; middle–scale 46–7, 176; small-scale 46–7, 176, 181; sub-categories 46, 56–66; 'underground' 53–4, 127
Tet Offensive 122
text–context dynamic 83, 117, 121–2, 146, 156, 162–4, 219, 221, 225, 243; *see also* inter-textuality
Thatcher, Margaret 6, 49, 134, 168–70, 207, 223, 229, 230, 235
Thatcherism 168, 169, 181, 188, 204, 206, 230, 251, 252
Thatcherite 211, 214
Theatre Babel 178
Theatre of Black Women 179
Theatre and Community (Conference) 59
Theatre of Cruelty 103, 120
theatre for disability 57, 58, 252

theatre-in-education 48, 57, 58, 101, 106, 171, 180
theatre managers 22
Theatre Passe Murraile 10
Theatre Quarterly 61
Theatre Workshop 75, 127
Theatre Writer's Union 141, 176
Thomas, Tom 79
Thompson, John B. 19
Thompson, Kenneth T. 18
Thornber, Robin 213, 220, 225
Tiananmen Square 208
Times, The 170
Time Out 49, 54, 56
Tokyo 123
TOOT (The Other Oxford Theatre) 61
Tories 111, 173, 188
Tory 112, 168–9, 170, 183, 185, 229; Party 49
Toxteth (Liverpool) 188
trade unions/movement 105, 123, 133, 141, 169, 214
Trades Union Congress 105–6
Tramshed Theatre 166
Trescatheric, Bryn 214
Trident, 213, 218, 227, 232
Triple Action Theatre 101
Trussler, Simon 107, 109, 110, 115, 119, 120, 122, 125, 126–7, 128
Turner, Victor 24, 28, 60, 64, 73–4, 117
Tynan, Kenneth 123
Tyne and Wear 172

Ulster 32
Ulverston 213
underground press 53–4
underground theatre 53–4, 56, 75
Unity Theatre (London) 75–7, 90, 110, 124, 125, 128–9, 131, 144
utopian egalitarianism 196, 216
utopian radicalism 72
utopianist idealism 39

van Erven, Eugène 10, 45, 78, 90–1, 149, 150, 255
variety theatre 67, 77
venues, for alternative/community

theatre 23, 46, 48, 50, 58, 68, 76, 85, 88, 90, 100, 102, 103, 104, 144, 147, 150, 154, 156, 177, 179, 226, 236, 247, 252; Arts Laboratory 100–1; studios 85, 101, 141, 146, 176; *see also* access; arts centres; arts labs
vernacular art 211
Vickers Shipbuilding and Engineering Ltd (VSEL) 213, 214, 218, 220, 221, 224, 225, 227, 228, 231, 232, 235, 239, 240, 241, 242
Victoria, Queen *see* Queen Victoria
Victoria Theatre (Stoke-on-Trent) 105
Victorian 67, 96, 125, 159, 214, 221, 223; Victorianism 112
Vietcong 122
Vietnam 39, 91, 122, 123
visual theatre 57, 58, 139

Wager, Walter 118
wakes celebrations 74
Walney Sound (Barrow-in-Furness) 215, 219, 224, 233
Wandor, Micheline 45
Wandsworth (London) 144
Warehouse (RSC studio) 136
Warner, Deborah 175
Warpole, Ken 173
Watson, Ian 119
Watts, Alan 39
Wedge 73, 145, 146, 147
Welfare State International, 9, 57, 75, 83, 85, 100, 101, 125, 175, 176, 192, 203–4, 209, 210–13, 215–42, 250; *Banger and Tyce* 227–30, 242; 'Feast of Furness' 224, 226; *The Golden Submarine* 224, 237–40; *King Real and the Hoodlums* 215–20, 221, 241; *Parliament in Flames* 175, 212; *Raising the Titanic* 212; *Robinson Crusoe Castaway* 225; *Shipyard Tales* 224, 226–42; 'Tapestry of Celebration' 224–6, 240; *Tempest on Snake*

Island 212; *Tower of Babel* 212; 'Town Hall Bonanza' 221; *Town Hall Tattoo* 220–4, 237, 239; *What'll the Lads do on Monday?* 227, 230–5, 241; *Wildfire!* 225; *see also* Fox, John
Westbrook, Mike 101
Weston-super-Mare 113
Wesker, Arnold 78, 90, 98, 105, 106, 107, 109, 112, 150
West End 49, 50, 51–2, 136, 191
Wherehouse La Mama 101
Wherehouse Theatre 101
White, A. 73
White, Mike 213
Wildcat Theatre 166
Wilding Report 209
Wilhelm II 7
Williams, Raymond 4–5, 6, 8, 29, 36, 41, 91, 135, 149, 175, 256
Wilson, Harold 106, 112, 123, 126, 134
Winter of Discontent 133
Wolverhampton 188
women's liberation movement 134, 139, 200, 203
women's theatre 57, 58, 59, 139, 142, 179–80, 252; *see also* feminist theatre
Women's Theatre Company 138
Women's Theatre Group 138
Wood, David 134
Woodruff, Graham 191
Workers' Theatre Movement 75–6, 79, 90, 129
writers' theatre 56, 57–8

Yeats, W. B. 28
York 118
York Arts Centre 100
Yorkshire Arts 209
Yorkshire Post 119
youth sub-culture 53
Yugoslavia 206

Z–Cars 148
Zaire 232